GOLD-DUST AND ASHES

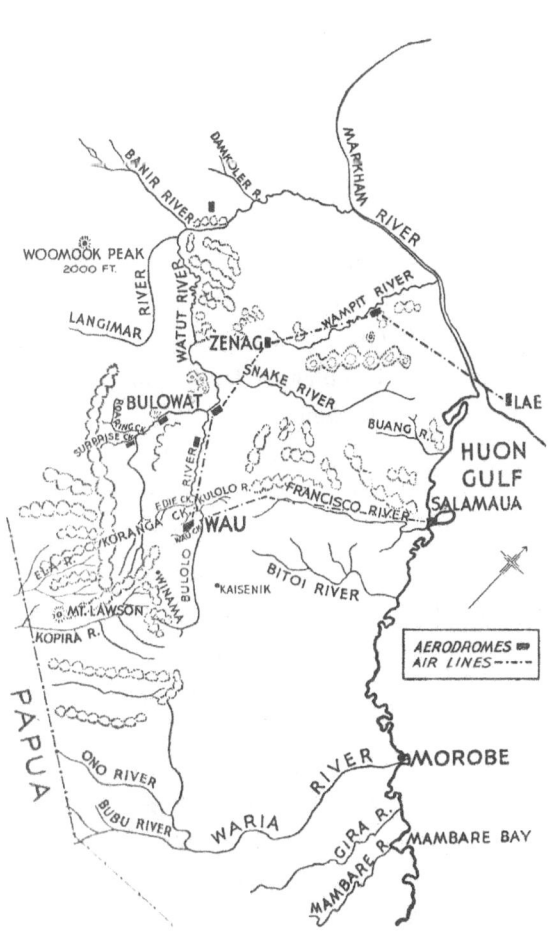

ETT IMPRINT has the following ION IDRIESS books in print in 2024:

Prospecting for Gold (1931)
Lasseter's Last Ride (1931)
Flynn of the Inland (1932)
The Desert Column (1932)
Men of the Jungle (1932)
Drums of Mer (1933)
Gold-Dust and Ashes (1933)
The Yellow Joss (1934)
Man Tracks (1935)
Over the Range (1937)
Forty Fathoms Deep (1937)
Madman's Island (1938)
Headhunters of the Coral Sea (1940)
Lightning Ridge (1940)
Nemarluk (1941)
Shoot to Kill (1942)
Sniping (1942)
Guerrilla Tactics (1942)
Trapping the Jap (1942)
Lurking Death (1942)
The Scout (1943)
Horrie the Wog Dog (1945)
In Crocodile Land (1946)
The Opium Smugglers (1948)
The Wild White Man of Badu (1950)
Outlaws of the Leopolds (1952)
The Red Chief (1953)
The Silver City (1956)
Coral Sea Calling (1957)
Back O' Cairns (1958)
The Wild North (1960)
Tracks of Destiny (1961)
Gouger of the Bulletin (2013)
Ion Idriess: The Last Interview (2020)
Ion Idriess Letters (2023)
Walkabout (2024)

GOLD-DUST AND ASHES

The Romantic Story of the
New Guinea Goldfields

Ion Idriess

ETT IMPRINT
Exile Bay

This 29th edition published as an Imprint Classic, Exile Bay 2025.

This book is copyright. Apart from any fair dealing for the purposes of private study, research, criticism or review, as permitted under the Copyright Act, no part may be reproduced by any process without written permission. Inquiries should be addressed to the publishers.

ETT IMPRINT
PO Box R1906
Royal Exchange NSW 1225 Australia

First published by Angus & Robertson Publishers 1933. Reprinted 1933 (four), 1934 (two), 1935 (two), 1936, 1937, 1938, 1939 (two), 1941, 1942, 1943, 1944, 1945, 1947, 1948, 1949, 1950, 1951, 1953, 1959, 1964.
First published by ETT Imprint in 2020.
First electronic edition published by ETT Imprint in 2024.

© Idriess Enterprises Pty Ltd, 2020.

The Publisher acknowledges the courtesy of Leonie Christopherson in allowing us to reproduce the original photographs of Frank Pryke seen on the cover of this book, and on pp 46, 89, 101, 102, 121 and 140.
ISBN 978-1-923205-83-3 (pbk)
ISBN 978-1-922384-79-9 (ebk)

Cover: The Junction of Merri and Edie Creeks, 1927, by Frank Pryke.

CONTENTS

GOLD	8
MANY FIGHTERS	14
SEEKING A NATION'S GOLD	21
SHARK-EYE PARK	30
CECIL JOHN LEVIEN	34
THE GOLDEN CALF	38
WHILE THE VILLAGE BURNS	42
SHARK-EYE SEEKS A MATE	48
THE BUBU PATROL	51
THE AMBUSH	57
THE FINDING OF SHARK-EYE PARK	66
BATTLING THROUGH TO A NEW LIFE	71
WHILE THE CARRIER SLEEPS	78
THE MIDGET AND THE STAR	85
THE FINDING OF EDIE CREEK	90
THE FAREWELL OF SHARK-EYE PARK	94
THE BOM-BOMS COME	100
FIFTY POUNDS OF MEAT	108
THE EYE THAT SAW ALL THINGS	112
ELDORADO	117
THE RACE STARTS	122
THE CAGING OF YABBI THE LULUAI	127
THE PUNITIVE EXPEDITION	133
THE CYCLONE	141
THE MOUNTAIN FLIGHT	147
THE OPPOSITION ARRIVES	154
FACING DISASTER	164
THE DEAD MAN "SHOUTS"	170
SIDE SHOWS AND GOLDEN LININGS	174
THE FLYING MEN	181
TRIUMPHS OF THE AIR	190
GOLD-DUST AND ASHES	197
GLOSSARY	202

C. J. LEVIEN'S PIONEER CAMP, KORANGA CREEK

AUTHOR'S NOTE

This book is an authentic record of some of the struggles and adventures, the failures and successes of men who risked their all in a luring quest in a fascinating country. None of the incidents used are fictional and all the names are of actual persons who played their part in them. My heartfelt thanks are due to them for the trouble they have taken to supply me with much of the rich material the reader will find in the following pages. Without that help the book could not have been written.

I am particularly indebted to those ex-officials of the Mandated Territory, and to others who can speak authoritatively, for checking certain incidents described: to old-timers George Arnold, Frank Pryke, Joe Sloane, and other survivors of romantic Papuan days, for material used in the early chapters of the book; and to various companies for valuable data.

To Dr Albert Hahl, ex-Governor of German New Guinea, and to several of his staff, I am indebted for the courtesy and readiness with which they responded to my requests for information they are specially qualified to give.

My one regret is that I have not been able to use all the interesting material placed at my disposal. Generous correspondents have sent me enough to fill several volumes.

One, only, is allowed me by my publishers. I am glad, therefore, to be able here to make this explanation and to record my thanks to many friends.

The task of putting my material into chronological order, arranging incidents in their proper setting, and verifying data, has been great.

For permission to make use of photographs, reproduced in this book, my thanks are due to Mrs C. J. Levien, Brigadier-General E. A. Wisdom, Captain G. E. Williams, and Messrs C. V. T. Wells, L. V. Waterhouse, H. L. Downing, A. Gibson. W. Digby, W. Morrison, H. Phillips, R. W Robson, F. Pryke, and V. Newberry.

CHAPTER I

GOLD

Gold! Yellow gold—heavy gold! He stared at it with burning eyes, this man on the mountain tops. His are unusual eyes that, when startled, instantly cloud over in a wary waiting. Throughout New Guinea he is known as "Shark-eye Park," or "Shark-eye Bill," rarely as William Park. He is a jungle-man, master too of the forest and of the wild men who dwell in both. Breathing deeply, he stared at the gold, a soundless laugh erasing the harshness from his face. In civilized surroundings that face would have smiled good humouredly, but here it portrayed the battler, the seeker. He was of middle age, of more than medium height, with spare frame that suggested a panther-like strength. When he walked, his steps were noiseless as he moved among the trees.

Around him now the pines and red cedars of the Upper Bulolo towered above a maze of jungle. Near by on the Wau plateau the sun shone upon acres of kunai grass that, walled by jungle, made a green amphitheatre which might have been a giants' sports ground. The sun shone across the deep gorges on to other grasses upon other mountain peaks hedged by jungle and sombre with scrub. Towering mistily above these peaks was grim Kaindi, swathed in rolling clouds. Truly, nature here reigned supreme: a land that was as it might have been in the Beginning, after it had first been made habitable for man. It was deathly quiet. Presently, up over everything crept a furtive sighing—the wind-blown breath from the great Bulolo Gorge far below. Upon a tree on the jungle edge flashed a thing of beauty, displaying a cascade of scarlet and gold. In tremulous colours agitated by its dance a bird of paradise pirouetted, then suddenly called in a strange, harsh tone.

This man was alone, yet not alone. Savage men dwelt on the unseen peaks around; village after village between him and the coast—a journey of eight days. Grim villages some, their stockaded portals stained with violence.

The white man's hands trembled as he gripped the dish. He had just washed the gold from Koranga Creek above where it splashed into the Bulolo.

Although his face smiled now, his mesmeric eyes held the attention of the head-hunting tribesmen squatting around. Two Lambura men, also crouching there, with lowering brow and thick lips, were from a cannibal tribe. To these savage nature-men he was a *bom-bom* (white man) and *long-long* (mad) in the joy that he found in those yellow sands of the creek. They wondered in silent mistrust of his pleasure, for he was no white fool. He had but to glare and they felt their minds numbed, while their limbs moved to do his bidding, leaving them to ponder afterwards. He was an "unexplainable" to them, this grim personality whose *tambaran* (devil) could cow their own sorcerers; meet their wiliest planning with a tambaran yet more cunning; who could live among them as a right; even compel them to work. They did not fear the man. They feared his tambaran, the "devil power" that enabled him to do as he wished, go where he willed, in this their own land as even they could not. That he found his strange pleasure under the shadow of giant Kaindi was suspiciously natural, for it had been cursed in the days of long ago. These slopes had long since been taboo to them and theirs. Why did yellow stones spat out from the bowels of Kaindi, though worthless to them, appear to be of magic value to the bom-bom? Gloweringly they watched, apprehensive that the spirit of the mountain and the tambaran of the bom-bom were conspiring against them.

Park scraped the gold from the dish into a small canvas bag. With the little three-pound prospecting pick he dug again into the creek. From the hole he dug he washed a confirming dish of dirt. The gold glittered there in ounces. He stared, trembling, with a delighted smile.

The tribesmen squatted motionless. This man held some queer mental power over all these people. In the gloom of a native house he could stare at a hostile man until the fellow hung his head or got up and uneasily slouched away. Without speaking, he could alter the course of their thoughts; change their contemplated actions. His ally was an iron command over his own will. He could enter a stockaded village and observe with those cold eyes of his, even should the warriors come dancing in yelling triumph, holding aloft a freshly severed head. He could give the impression that he was silently admiring the head; it was a good head, a warrior's head, a token to be proud of if only properly cured. But when covertly they glanced at *his* head, they were afraid.

He understood and could intimately transmit his understanding of their mentality, their mysticism, their ceremonial life, their complete life. He could live among them in village after village, with tribe after tribe—and survive.

He stared in ecstasy at the gold. A goldfield! He had found it—and alone! That knowledge and the gleaming stuff thrilled his heart. He wanted to throw the dish into the air, to yell his delight. After many years he had realized the prospector's dream. Untold wealth lying underfoot! A fortune for himself; fortunes for others! This yellow metal could transform him from an unknown wanderer into a financial giant, in a moment; make him a god among men if he wished. Gold might be lying here in tons, within the creeks, among the roots of the trees, under the river terraces. The law of the jungle here was ended. In a second of time this land had commenced a new era in its history.

He looked at the natives, a thought dawning behind those eyes that could see and say so much. The kanakas glowered back. What would that yellow metal mean to them and the tens of thousands like them?

A distant *kundu* boomed, hollow and sinister. It seemed to toll "One—white—man"—"One—white—man—". The drum's tones rolled over the Bulolo Gorge, over those sighing valleys, and were caught up by dimmer drums on farther peaks: "One—white—man"—"One—white—man—".

Park read the message; and staring at the cocked ears of the tribesmen he read, too, their expressive faces. War-drums!

He put away the gold, brushing the last grains from the dish with his finger. His face was again stern, almost expressionless, as he worked deftly, but without seeming haste, though wildly excited. He stood up, one hand to his side, one grasping the gold he had won that day, and gazed at the glimpses of sky among the pines. The blood rushed to his heart and brain and he laughed aloud.

For he had found gold! Gold! Gold! He drew a delirious breath, then with his eyes fairly dancing under feelings that they would never fathom, he nodded to the tribesmen. Grunting, they picked up their long bows and, stepping softly as cats, stole back into the jungle, while the white man stood listening to the beat of the kundu drum.

We will leave Park for a time—he can well look after himself—while we take a broad view of matters and visualize the influence his discovery may have on the world. Strange that a lone prospector should make history, but a fact nevertheless.

New Guinea rises sheer out of the Pacific like some vast thing crouching to spring. It is a fiercely beautiful but a dangerous land: once seen and breathed it may lure you back again and again. Anchor in a quiet bay mirrored by cliffs whose foliaged heights are crowned by the clouds and you are aware of a vague sweetness—the smell of old New Guinea.

It is no illusion: many of us know it in various ways. A city man who figures in this story instantly detects it every time he opens a parcel from New Guinea. Alas, the last time, it came with the belongings of his dead friend.

New Guinea! Nature's last stronghold, luring the white man and the civilization she dreads! New Guinea! Land of sudden death, delirious happiness, tragic despair! Land of vivid colour in herself and in the deeds of her people! In the old days she attracted the Spaniards and Portuguese in quest of an "isle of gold." The Dutch came, too, with those hardy sea-dogs, the English, beating up wind for a bite at the bone, while the tricolour raced with them all. The Spaniards and Portuguese faded out during a highly romantic squabble between Holland and England over the "Spice Islands." The Dutch, after a hundred years of war with the natives, gained Java and the East Indies, which interest Australians now because of the population of fifty millions within a few days' sail—a few hours by plane—of our shores. Holland later, by a treaty with a native prince of the Moluccas (the Rajah of Onin), virtually bought Dutch New Guinea for "a packet of tea." Later still adventurous sea-rovers of numerous nationalities found the Pacific and South Pacific a sea-rover's paradise. American whalers in tall-masted ships sought oil and isles in the sun. Missionaries came, displaying a heroism and self-sacrifice that often served their country well. There were patriots among the sea-rovers who took national possession of great island systems, only to be bitterly disappointed when their respective governments failed to ratify the possession. Empire builders were not always taken seriously in those days, to the loss of the short-sighted nations. France took her share in New Caledonia and French Oceania and won a firm foothold in the New Hebrides side by side with John Bull. Uncle Sam, growing up and wanting to tell the world about it, crossed the Pacific and annexed Hawaii, the Philippines, Guam, and eastern Samoa.

SIGNED BY THE WARDEN AS THE FIRST MINER'S RIGHT ISSUED IN THE MANDATED TERRITORY GOLDFIELDS DISTRICT

(Top) Cecil John Levien, 1930. (Below) Exploring New Guinea 1911, as photographed by W. Whitten.

New Guinea was not partitioned until almost the last; her mountain barriers turned the adventurers to spoils easier of access. They chased whales all over the waters; raided the sea-bed for pearl-shell and bêche-de-mer; traded for copra and tortoise-shell; landed on smaller islands to cut the sandalwood beloved by the Chinese; and eventually settled far and wide on the smaller isles and started coconut plantations. In those coral seas and South Pacific isles, energetic characters made little private kingdoms and ruled sometimes kindly, sometimes with a fist of iron. That story is brightened with love and romance, and darkened with blood and tragedy.

Britain stepped in at last (after a far-seeing Queensland statesman had forced her hand) and took possession of the south-eastern portion of New Guinea. It is now known as Papua, and is politically a part of the Australian Commonwealth. So Time brings Australia into the picture.

The total area of Papua, with its adjacent island systems is 90,540 square miles. Adjoining it is Dutch New Guinea, 151,789 square miles, almost one-half of the main island. An area of 91,000 square miles was left unoccupied; and this has turned out to be the richest portion of New Guinea. It is now our Mandated Territory. Again Time tossed the dice in favour of Australia. The "last shall be first" as it were; for Australia as a nation was not dreamed of when the Powers were busy seeking good things in the South Pacific.

America testily refuses to recognize Australia's mandate. She refused because a lone prospector among the cannibals of the Territory had found gold. However, she was good enough to recognize Japan's mandate of the Carolines and the Marshalls.

More than thirty years before the beat of that kundu drum which shook Park's nerves, Germany entered the South Pacific and was just in time to take possession of that remaining area of New Guinea, to be called until the Great War "German New Guinea."

But a slip of a girl forestalled Germany by years. Captaining a handful of braves, with guns in her belt, she sailed in a small boat and took possession of the future Bismarck Archipelago. Later, as Queen Emma, she took the salute of the German fleet; was feasted by emperors; and became one of the world's wealthiest women—only to die tragically at the height of her great romance.

But space does not allow wandering in these fascinating bypaths—and I hear the beat of a kundu drum!

CHAPTER II

MANY FIGHTERS

From adjoining Papua, such well-known prospectors as old Matt Crowe, Jim Preston, Arthur Darling, the Pryke brothers, George Arnold, the Kruger brothers, Bob Newcombe, Belford, Billy Ivory, Joe O'Brien, and Gus Nelsson, turned longing eyes towards the forbidden land.

"It's no good," growled one in Samarai. "The Germans would never let us in; and even if they did the kanakas would eat us."

"Sounds like the 'Doo Drop Inn,'" said Arthur Darling with a laugh.

"More like sour grapes," commented Jim Pryke.

"It's no goot," declared old Gus Nelsson. "You can't tell me about te plutty golt-mines anyways, I'se lost tousands an' tousands of plutty quids in 'em."

But old Gus's name was written indelibly on Woodlark Island. When he struck it rich there later, didn't he make those "thousands" fly!

The more adventurous of these Papuan prospectors reckoned there was gold in German territory and warily set out to find it. One party loaded sixty carriers from Tamata (a Papuan gold post) and laboriously cut their way right into the rugged heads of the Waria. But there the war-drums boomed and the ridge crests were suddenly fringed with befeathered warriors. The prospectors closed around the terrified carriers lest they stampede. In a sharp skirmish the whites were repulsed and forced back into Papuan territory, only to be attacked again by the Ikori warriors and driven right down-river where, in direst straits and to their amazed delight, they saw a cruiser. She was German, with Dr Albert Hahl (the Governor) aboard.

That was in October 1897. The warship's object was the exact location of the Mitre Rock, regarded then as the frontier point between British and German New Guinea. Dr Hahl gave the castaways protection, food, and equipment and offered them a passage to Kokopo. But now, with food-stuffs and more ammunition, they declined, expecting the arrival of a schooner from Samarai. The cruiser sailed, leaving three prospectors and twelve surviving carriers waving good-bye from the beach. They were again attacked and with only two carriers left were driven to sea on a raft, eventually drifting across the Huon Gulf like a coffin-ship. The Finschhafen mission people rescued them and Dr Hahl sent them to Sydney in the cruiser after all.

Old Matt Crowe and Arthur Darling had better luck. They crossed from the Yodda valley and penetrated deep into the Waria head. Old Matt was one of Papua's famous prospectors. An assertive, truculent old fellow, contemptuous of the natives, but respectful of their numbers and cunning. His "push straight ahead" style, his abrupt "up and at 'em boys!" carried him round many a tight corner; while his gigantic frame was a tower of strength. The savage stands in awe of brute strength.

"I like the kanakas to be enemies," growled Crowe always. "When they're enemies you know how to treat 'em; when they're friendly you never know when you'll stop an arrow in the back."

Arthur Darling was an energetic type also, though his appearance belied his extraordinary adventures. A small man of hardly eight stone weight, no one would have dreamed of his tenacity of purpose, his sometimes single-handed fights against frightful odds. Fair-complexioned and invariably smiling, he was quick in action and initiative, with an unconquerable eagerness to "push on!" His fatal accuracy with the rifle was a byword throughout Papua.

To meet Crowe and Darling emerging from a jungle path was to see a string of savage carriers pass by on noiseless feet watched over by a grim and heavily armed giant of 6 ft 6 in., and a small and slim figure, eager of face, with a bandolier of military cartridges slung across his shoulder, and a military rifle as long as himself in his hand.

Once when "Big" O'Brien imagined himself to be suffering under a slight from Darling, he wrote, threatening to thrash him. Darling wrote back:

"Can't fight. Won't run. Bring your rifle."

O'Brien didn't.

Crowe and Darling located the first patch of payable gold on one of the head-waters of the Waria. But it wasn't big enough for them. They returned to Papua, recruited fresh carriers, and returned to ascend the Markham and push farther into the mountains seeking bigger stuff. The mountains whispered it was there.

Meanwhile Frank Pryke brought his crowd in from the head-waters of the Ikori. They were the first party to systematically work a patch of payable gold on the Waria. The Germans didn't dream they were there.

Several German authorities had for some time a genuine fear that a premature disclosure of treasure-trove would bring "hordes of wild Australians, descendants of Bendigo and Ballarat days" to invade their colony and perhaps cause international complications. "We might even lose New Guinea over it," said one of their officials.

Frank Pryke is probably the best-known Papuan prospector of to-day, with a number of fields to his credit. A big, level-headed man—one who always looks before he leaps, and who always treats the savage as a man like himself-he has helped to place much of Papua "on the map." He has lived through it all to win a moderate fortune with no more than two arrows through his body.

Thus several parties won gold in forbidden territory. They found it wise, however, to keep the results to themselves.

Germany's geologists, supported by strongly armed native police, slowly penetrated from the coast, finding it a frightful job. In 1898 the New Guinea Company dispatched an expedition up the Ramu, but the tiny steamer was wrecked and the expedition had to fight its way back overland to Madang. The same company in 1901 equipped another expedition under Schlentzig, a mining engineer; but the hostility of the natives and sickness drove them back. In 1907 Dr Hahl marched from Astrolabe Bay through the Minjen valley to the Middle Ramu; thence endeavouring to penetrate the great range beyond the watershed and to the Markham. News reached him yet again that Australian gold-miners in large numbers were working in German territory. In 1908 he went up the Waria as far as Pio Waria and surprised miners at Jatuna and even higher up. But Dr Hahl was always courteous to the Australian prospectors with whom he came in contact. They told him that they could get gold but that it was patchy, very quickly worked out, and could not be classed as a goldfield. They were certain there was a goldfield somewhere about. The difficulty was the warlike natives higher in the mountains.

Bergrat Stolle, mining engineer and geologist, proved portions of the Upper Waria and Ono to be auriferous. But here again the natives prevented further investigations by the German expeditions.

Germany had one outstanding prospector, Herr Dammkoehler, a fine old bearded fellow who had spent years on the Western Australian goldfields. In 1908 he, with his mate Ohldorp, located gold somewhere in the vicinity of the present goldfields. The kanakas, however, suddenly attacked them, killing Dammkoehler. In the confusion, while the carriers were being killed, the desperately wounded Ohldorp escaped. He kept the locality a secret and on recovery set out again with a stronger expedition. In a storm at the mouth of the Markham the schooner went down with all hands.

Although Germany lost her best prospector, she had first-class geologists working. Now, a mining geologist is a scientifically trained man, generally under a staff appointment, who examines an area of country and declares it to be probably mineral-bearing or not. A prospector wanders over the country as best he can and locates gold wherever it may be—if his luck is in!

If these two, prospector and geologist, would work systematically and sympathetically together, Australia might find more goldfields.

In 1909 the German governor decided to erect a strong government post on the coast at Morobe. In this year, too, the Boundary Commission got to work, British and German survey parties working side by side, to fix definitely the boundary between British and German New Guinea.

Meanwhile, Germany was on the tiptoe of expectancy, awaiting news of a great gold find in her far-distant South Sea colony. But just where was the gold? German New Guinea officialdom turned to the Australian prospector, and sent a special invitation to such men as Shark-eye Park, Matt Crowe, and Arthur Darling. These men accepted the invitation in a spirit of great adventure. It is not often that a nation invites a handful of "hard-doers" to undertake for it a work of magnitude.

That, however, is an historical fact; and if the men engaged had been anything but prospectors the world would have known all about it.

Germany had pressed for the definite fixation of the boundary. Its course was surveyed with the liveliest anticipations, for it was uncertain whose territory the Waria gold-bearing country was in. It was surveyed as being twenty miles within German territory.

Inland, near Mount Strong, Captain Detzner of the German Imperial Army, was working on the Boundary Commission. The Lamanai tribesmen declared war on the whites and they, with other Bubu warriors, attacked Detzner, on one occasion burning and looting his main camp. He burned a mountain village, in return for which the mountaineers made raids on his supply carriers, killing some and a few black soldiers. The Lamanai kept on fighting, stealing down from their mountain heights to buy a fight in the good old kanaka way.

But the boundary was surveyed at last.

The prospector-adventurers felt very uneasy over the activities on the boundary, but the apprehensions of several were relieved—to a degree anyway.

While bringing stores by cutter from Papua into the mouth of the Waria, Frank Pryke stared uneasily at a German armed yacht, the *Seestern* (soon to disappear with all hands). The cutter was hailed:

"Are you Mr Pryke?"

"Yes, bringing up stores."

"No need to report. Go in and anchor."

Later, the prospectors were greeted by Dr Hahl: "The impression is wrong," he said, "that we want to hunt the Australian prospectors. We have good geologists, but we know that Australian prospectors are the best in the world to open up new country. And we want this country opened up."

But the prospectors were hunted by lesser officials. They worked always under the fear that, if they did open up a payable field in this foreign country, they might lose it.

"If we are told to go," growled old Matt Crowe, "we won't have a leg to stand on."

The German post, now strategically established at Morobe, besides keeping an eye on unauthorized prospectors, was a base for the German geological expeditions. An officer named Klink was in charge, a smart man who, with strongly organized patrols, penetrated inland where possible with military precision. He brought all the Lower Waria under control, and must have found out something about the farther Bulolo country, for one day when he and Frank Pryke were fellow passengers aboard the *Prinz Waldemar* between Samarai and Sydney, he tried hard to get Frank to make a big expedition up the Waria, branching off into some unknown area.

"I know the gold is there," he insisted; "not in perhaps the precise locality where your Australian countrymen venture to enter, but not so very far away. In that area I know your practical experience must eventually locate the gold; what you call the real 'big stuff.'"

Pryke shook his head.

"I know it's there too," he replied, "somewhere. But it will take a lot of money and time to locate. The country is terrible to cross and we have not the same power to press the natives into our service as you have. No, I am returning to Papua." And he sailed on the well-known trip that was to end with his discovery of the Lakekamu.

To Matt Crowe, Arthur Darling, and Shark-eye Park, Germany said officially:

"You can enter the country as bird of paradise shooters as well as prospectors. Your boys can be shooting the birds while you are prospecting. Then, if you find no gold, you will still make much money out of your trips, by the sale of the birds' skins. If you find gold, you will make a fortune; never fear that we will be hard on you. You can peg out prospectors' claims just as you would in British New Guinea (Papua). And the gold you win will be yours, less a very small royalty such as you are charged in British New Guinea. We are thinking of adopting the Queensland or British New Guinea ordinances in the event of discovery of a goldfield. Whether or no, you men, as the prospectors, can rest assured that whatever you may find will be yours."

So, at different periods through the years, these three Australians, in different expeditions, sometimes in the one party, sometimes split up, tried to penetrate deeper into the country. Sponsored by the German authorities (until they kicked over the traces) they attempted entry into the mountain systems mainly by means of the Markham, Snake, Waria, and Bulolo rivers. Up these grass- and jungle-screened rivers they went by launch and canoe where possible; then penetrated farther by means of native carriers. They got tantalizing traces of gold towards the headwaters of the Waria and in the lower waters of the Watut and Bulolo. But the source of the gold they could not find. The other Papuan prospectors returned, or were driven back, to Papua. Of the three stayers the cold, grim determination of Shark-eye made him last longest.

Papua, where these men came from, is much the most civilized portion of New Guinea. This is due, principally, to the work of its district and patrol officers—a body of men whose romantic achievements probably eclipse anything of the kind in the world. The Papuan coastline, where geographically possible, and the adjacent island archipelagoes, are dotted with beautiful plantations. The large native population has been brought under control, except in portions of the interior and the upper reaches of the Fly River. This sullen, brown waterway is navigable by launch for five hundred miles. Many islands dot its stream, while its banks overflow into mysterious grass swamps and flower-covered lakes.

Dutch New Guinea, covering nearly half the island, is the world's most mountainous and primitive area. Its Snow Mountains are thought to rise in places to seventeen thousand feet. Its population of wild men is estimated to be two hundred thousand, probably considerably more. In another hundred years, if Dutch New Guinea is as it is to-day, Holland will own a living museum of the primitive world and primitive man.

The Dutch have not been eager to colonize their possession; there is "lots of time." True: time and nations last though the individual dies. The sole revenue to the Dutch, until the bottom dropped out of the market, was bird of paradise feathers. The shooters were generally gangs of Chinese, Malay, Javanese, and Indo-China men. These fought their way inland and were fought against, sometimes falling to the Tugeri, who are such experts with the bamboo head-hunting knife. Women overseas have worn feathers that were bought at the price of a man's head. And the birds lost their lives too.

There is gold in Dutch New Guinea; we know of two widely separated gold-bearing areas. But why should we tell?

The Digoel in Dutch territory is a great river, although not so great as the Sepik in the Mandated Territory. During the war, an Australian destroyer (seeking a raider) steamed up the Sepik for three hundred miles, non-stop, at fifteen knots, and back again without a bump—and without a chart.

Swift and broad that mighty river hurries down from the Victor Emanuel Mountains and the southern Torricelli, six hundred miles away, near the Dutch border. In parts the Sepik is really an inland sea, a sea of "lakes," of sometimes fantastic beauty, peopled by thousands of head-hunters. These virile fighters build enormous tambaran houses and carve weird figures half-man and half-beast, half-bird and half-fish, inlaying them with shell with the artistry of the cultured savage. But skulls gape down from the "dovecots" up in the house-tambaran.

German New Guinea comprised the north-eastern portion of the great island. Germany also held the Bismarck Archipelago (New Britain, New Ireland, the Admiralty Islands, and various smaller groups), and the two northern islands of the Solomon Group. The Germans planted their main activities in the Bismarck Archipelago principally because Queen Emma, traders, tenacious missionaries, and other adventurous diehards had got a start there, and also because New Britain has finer harbours than the mainland. Rabaul, the present capital, is nearly five hundred miles from Salamaua, the port for the present goldfields.

New Britain is three hundred and seventy miles long and about fifty miles broad. If you are sailing along that rugged coastline at night, and in the right place, you may hear a nasty rumble and perhaps catch sight of a deep red flame leaping from a volcanic crest.

Germany hurried ahead with her plantations while she hoped more and more for a gold discovery on the apparently untameable and distant mainland. In 1913 rosy hopes were held throughout Germany that her pet colony was to become the golden Queen of the Pacific. But the Great War was brewing.

CHAPTER III

SEEKING A NATION'S GOLD

Gold talks a language that is carried by the wind. Hence the rumour in distant Rabaul, and the whisper in Papua, that the three Australian prospectors were "getting gold."

Again, odd men slipped over the border, only to be challenged and hastened back. Lucky if they escaped by losing only the gold or bird of paradise skins in their possession.

Crowe, Park, and Darling did not always play strictly fair to their invitation. Prospecting away from their allotted district, they occasionally found trouble. Darling, quietly sneaking along in a whale-boat up-river into forbidden country, was spied and chased by officialdom back to the open sea.

Of course, it could not be expected that old Matt Crowe would do otherwise than run foul of the German authorities:

"I'm no bloomin' parrot in a cage," he said. "They're not going to pin me down to one district." And they couldn't. But they confiscated his feathers and gave him a flying start to help him along.

"Not a damn feather to fly with," he growled. "An' I was going to play hell in Samarai."

But old Matt cruised back again vowing he would "take it out of Germany." He got his chance when a German cruiser anchored in the mouth of the Waria. The prospectors, sailing into the river-mouth not in their district, were nicely caught. In no little trepidation they accepted the invitation to "come aboard." Old Matt's hair bristled as the whaleboat cruised up to the man-o'-war.

"For heaven's sake," whispered Jim Preston. "Go steady, Matt."

"I'll show 'em!" growled Matt.

"Hush!" admonished Pryke. "These men have been decent to us; it's our fault if we are prospecting here without a permit."

But old Matt glared up at the grey vessel, at the guns poking out over the sides, at the disciplined sailors:

"I'll show 'em!" he muttered.

With apprehensive feelings his mates followed him up the gangway.

"I see you've got steam up!" Matt said as he climbed to the deck.

"Yes," replied the officer civilly. "We always keep steam up; we are always prepared."

"Always prepared, eh!" growled Matt triumphantly. "Well you weren't prepared for that hurricane at Apia!"

Readers may recollect the big hurricane at Samoa when the British gunboat escaped destruction by steaming out to sea in the teeth of the hurricane, while the German and American vessels were blown ashore.

The natives of all New Guinea (estimated at over a million) are a fascinating ethnological study: from the swamp "rat" with muddy claws and bat-like appearance as he flits through the reedy maze, up to the fine upstanding savage who builds his huge war-canoes, carves beautifully in woodwork and shell, weaves his native fibres like an expert, and builds communal houses three hundred feet long. Interesting varieties are the shy little pygmy, who often lives in trees to protect his hide, and the dreaded Kukukukus, who flit like bark-clad phantoms among the trees, with fibre bags around their necks in which to carry the heads of the slain. These uncounted tribes (except in the well-controlled areas in Papua), acknowledge the jungle law only: "an eye for an eye." The coast people sometimes build their communal villages over the water the better to avoid foes.

Mandated Territory Natives.

(Top) A motu travelling craft. (Bottom) Jim Pryke (standing, centre) with his prospecting party at Lakekamu 1913 (Charles Kerry)

Yet other tribes live in trees, or away up on the craggy heights of precipices, or in the heart of miasmatic swamps. They speak a babel of tongues. To end this confusion, that quaint but highly useful language, pidgin-English, has come to stay. Brought by the seafaring wanderers of very early days, the New Guinea coastal man picked it up and rapidly "modelled" this lingo to his own tongue. In course of time it has penetrated some distance inland.

The New Guinea native has a queer mentality. To him the white man is long-long, a fool. Although the native lives under the jungle law, and the ever-present dread of the sorcerer, he would not live as the white man lives, or not until he is taught, and often not then.

Those who for the first time saw the white man pushing his laborious way inland, sneered from their heights in scorn. Sometimes they attacked. Then the rifles rang out, and the New Guinea men retired in dazed stupefaction at something they did not understand.

Anything not understood is a tambaran. A man who, by cunning or otherwise, can surprise or frighten his fellows, does so by means of his tambaran—his personal devil which works for him and is obedient to his command. This fear of the tambaran is ever present in the daily life of the New Guinea man.

Arthur Darling hated to be detailed to a given district. Besides, he planned a trip from knowledge of the country, gained before he and Park had dissolved partnership. He determined to ascend the Markham to the Watut, then up along that wild watercourse to its head, and eventually climb across into the Bulolo head.

Had he succeeded, as he nearly did, world history may have been changed. For he would certainly have discovered the present goldfield in the then German territory. German New Guinea would have been well populated by 1914; a German Pacific fleet would certainly have been stationed there; and—?

In Papua, Darling recruited thirty Orokiva boys, most of whom had marched before under him and Crowe. The Orokiva were notorious fighters, warriors of the Binandele tribes, restless raiders for centuries past. There was nothing these husky, chocolate-brown Papuans loved more than a fight. Darling's boys had been trained to the rifle and they would follow him anywhere. He sailed from Papua for German territory and brought his whaleboat into the mouth of the Markham River. Near by he passed a German Lutheran mission station, recently established. An "outback" station it was, with a courageous man in charge. Darling pushed up-stream into No-white-man's Mountains, congratulating himself that he had dodged all official authority. Soon the river shallowed and he was compelled to hide his whaleboat and march up-river into rugged country with his thirty armed braves.

Now, the right or wrong of the case is not debated in this story. The simple fact is that Darling, one white man, was seeking a goldfield in a district inhabited by one hundred thousand fighting savages. He was completely cut off from civilized help, and from stores. He had to push on or be pushed out. He pushed on until he was pushed out.

Thirty-one hearty eaters take a lot of feeding. So to help replenish the commissariat, the boss boy, a fine giant of a man alive with initiative, and as faithful as a collie-dog, would march with twenty men to the nearest village. There they would trade, and return loaded with vegetables and fruit and pigs. But sometimes the scowling villagers refused to trade; instead, they ambushed the party. After the fight, providing they were successful, the twenty men would enter the native gardens and take what they could carry, returning to Darling who generally remained with ten men at the camp.

Naturally, as the little band pushed grimly on, swift vengeance closed around them. With the booming of the kundus shadow figures came until it seemed that every jungle tree hid a tribesman burning with the lust to take back a head to his village. The Adzera alone numbered twelve thousand; fierce fighters all. They could have eaten those thirty men over and over again had it not been for the fear of those rattling rifles and the spirit that worked them; for this terrible little band fought and worked as one man, welded together by life and death.

Darling reached the Watut and hacked his way some distance up it. A morning came when they must have more food-stuffs. The boss boy and what remained of his twenty braves filled their bandoliers and set out to procure the necessary while Darling with eight boys held the camp.

That afternoon Darling was lying down, drowsy with fever. The eight men were squatting around, careless as always when the *Taubada* (master) is ill, or careless himself.

In an instant the very trees seemed screaming; hundreds of painted warriors howled at them, stabbing with spear, smashing with club. Automatically, Darling swung up his deadly rifle, firing from the ground with two spears through his shoulder. Still firing, he tried to rise, but another spear tore into his hip. He kept on firing and those of his men not dead fired up into the bodies of the maniacs hacking down at them. The place was a butcher's shop in a minute. But the attackers vanished leaving Darling and four men still alive.

The boss boy with his men burst back on the camp just in time. The tribesmen had planned well but had attacked a few minutes too late.

"It is all over, Taubada," said the boss boy sorrowfully as he bent over Darling.

"I'm not dead yet!" gasped Darling with gritting teeth. "Cut these spears out of me!"

They hacked and pulled them out, and out of three men who might live. It was a bloody surgery, while the remainder of the boys kneeled by their rifles and peered into the growing darkness. A chill was in the hearts even of these Orokiva fighters, for the Taubada was down!

"It is no use, Taubada," declared the boss boy late that night. "We must return. To-morrow we make a raft and float and fight our way down-stream."

They did so. One glowering morning as the raft swept around a bend there was a sudden cry at sight of a timber-jam—hundreds of trees all locked together in the river. In a moment the raft hit it and crumpled up; the current dragged it under the logs. The wounded men went with it but the others leapt on to the rolling trees, jumping from one to the other right across to the bank, where they disappeared into the jungle.

They were never seen again—except the boss boy and one other who leapt from log to log straight down-stream; over three hundred feet of flying leaps before they landed on the last log. Clinging to the branches, the boss boy peered into the water: a warrior, descended from a line of warriors, he was almost crying.

"Ah well," he said in Orokiva, "the poor old Taubada is finished." Then with a wild cry he plunged straight into the water.

"Not yet," gasped Darling, as the boss boy helped him up to his companion on the slippery tree. Those were the very words used. The current had taken Darling under those three hundred feet of trees and, although almost unconscious, he told afterwards how clearly he had heard the words of his boss boy as his own head emerged to the surface.

The Orokivas got Darling down to the Markham, then to the whaleboat. They had one rifle between them, and needs must travel in haste and silence. They fed themselves and Darling with fat white grubs chopped out of rotted trees, and finally reached the mission station near the river's mouth.

The missionary was kindness itself, and placed at their disposal all he had. They rested there a week. Then Darling had a fright; he was very weak. One afternoon a crowd of coastal kanakas came along dragging a prisoner. Darling weakly tried to interfere. They motioned him to mind his own business. Then they clubbed out the prisoner's brains. The executioners explained what the boss boy already understood; it was merely a "pay-back." This man's people had caught one of their people and clubbed him in the bush. So when they caught this man—"an eye for an eye."

Darling and his two men crawled into their whale-boat and floated out to sea. In raving delirium they were picked up by Les Joubert in his launch *Euna*.

But it was the finish of Darling, although nearly a year later he and Bob Newcombe were getting ready for another attempt. He was actually dying at the time, but he was a man who refused to die until he was quite dead. And his boss boy was killed down in the hold of Whitten's famous old island steamer *President*. The boss boy was a splendid man in bush or jungle, but he did not understand the slings in unloading a ship. He was helping to unload the Taubada's stores when a case fell and broke his back.

Newcombe later went to Darling to discuss the boss boy's burial expenses. Darling cried. He was near his last breath from those old spear-wounds, but he did not want his boss boy to die.

A notoriously quiet man was Park, tireless and thoughtful. He listened to others, but always knew his own mind. An invaluable man to his mates, for at a glance from him truculent natives simply did as he willed. A man who never broke a promise; when he said he would do a thing he did it, though at the risk of his life. The natives always admire those traits in a man. But he was a cold, steely devil if aroused; they knew that if ever, in that cold voice of his, he threatened to kill a man he might do it.

Strangely enough in a man leading such a life he had one great dread—that of dying with his boots on! He never wore them when it was possible to do without; he never entered a canoe with his boots on, nor forded a deep mountain stream leather shod.

Sometimes with a mate, sometimes alone, he pushed ever farther in. Intuition had long since brought him in tune with native mentality in Papua. That intuition was worth more than an army to him here. It saved his life; it fed him; it carried for him; it gave him news; it placed what the natives knew at his service. He presently began to take longer and longer trips entirely alone. He could dispense with white man's company; could go where he liked, stay where he liked; live where he liked. He found himself independent of civilization; unfettered by the need for civilized stores. Then he became quite independent of German authority; he could go and live where it dared not go.

In 1913 the German governor granted a mining-concession to an Alsatian named Kaempf, who, after some wildly adventurous experiences along the Waria, located what looked like a dredging proposition. At last it seemed that German New Guinea was to produce gold on a large scale.

In 1914 Captain Detzner and Lieutenant Baum led an expedition into the Mount Albert Edward area in an attempt to break through to the Markham valley. Detzner's force consisted of a large number of trained native constabulary, well disciplined, and armed to the teeth. One day his little army, tired and unsuspecting, pitched their camp right against the Papuan border. From the shrubbery on the hill above, Patrol Officer Chisholm and a dozen police boys, reinforced by a score of miners from the Lakekamu goldfield, with a few armed carriers, looked down on them.

A Papuan native police sergeant carrying a white paper approached Captain Detzner. That sergeant was game, but his eyes were bright with fear at suddenly finding himself right in a "white man's war." He expected to be immediately shot. He handed the surprised Detzner the paper, then stood at rigid attention. Detzner read:

"War is declared. Surrender."

Detzner stood one startled moment then shouted an order. In an instant his coloured soldiers had disappeared into the jungle leaving their little white tents and the Papuan sergeant all alone in the sun.

In Berlin, shortly before the outbreak of war, a mining-concession was granted to Rudolph Wahlen, who also had located promising areas on the Waria.

Meanwhile, Detzner was king of Central New Guinea, trying hard to save the land for the Double Eagle. He fed his "army" on the country, and some hostile native tribes suddenly realized that there was a real war on. The Lamanai swarmed down from the Bubu heights and tackled Detzner tooth and claw. A very big war it was, according to the tribesmen's account.

Baum, after several years, became ill with fever and staggered down to Morobe to surrender. But Detzner held out and did not surrender until after the war.

Shark-eye Park, alone, away up on the misty heights of the Bulolo listened to the kundus sullenly booming as they had never boomed before.

Detzner was drawing very close. Shark-eye silently stole away, and crossed right through into Papua. Impossible to find, impossible to stumble across, a jungle-man!

(Top) Native Troops at Madang, 1920.
(Below) Native ceremony at Madang, 1905

CHAPTER IV

SHARK-EYE PARK

Australia seized German New Guinea and, after a sharp little fight for the important Bita Paka wireless station, occupied Rabaul. An incident of historical importance was the reading to the natives assembled at Rabaul on 12 September 1914 of a proclamation in pidgin-English, dealing with the annexation from the German Empire of their possessions in the Pacific.

It was a unique proclamation. Thousands of natives gathered at Rabaul to watch proceedings and listen to every word. An imposing display of military and naval forces marshalled under the lazily waving Union Jack, surrounded by the closely packed ranks of natives in gala attire, and many groups of warriors in full regalia of marvellously fashioned feathered trappings. After a military salute of the flag this proclamation was solemnly read:

PROCLAMATION

All boys belonga one place, you savvy big master he come now, he new feller master, he strong feller too much, you look 'im all ship stop place; he small feller ship belonga him. Plenty more big feller he stop place belonga him, now he come here he take all place. He look out good you feller. Now he like you feller look out good alonga him. Suppose other feller master, he bin speak you "You no work alonga new feller master!" he gammon. Suppose you work good with this new feller master he look out good alonga you, he look out you get plenty good feller kai-kai: he no fightem black boy alonga nothing.

You look him new feller flag. You savvy him? He belonga British, he more better than other feller: suppose you been make 'im paper before this new feller master come, you finish time belonga him first, you like make him new feller paper belonga man longa new feller master, he look out good longa you, he give good feller kai-kai. Suppose you no look out good alonga him, he cross too much. British new feller master he like him black feller man too much. He like him all same you piccanin alonga him. You get black feller master alonga you, he alla same Police Master. You look out place alonga with him, he look out place longa with you. You no fight other feller black man other feller place, you no kai-kai man. You no steal Mary belonga other feller black man. He finish talk longa you soon. By and by ship belonga new feller master he come and look out place belonga you. You look out him now belonga place belonga you, you speak him all the same.

Me bin talk with you now. Now you give three feller cheers belonga new feller master.

NO MORE 'UM KAISER
GOD SAVE 'UM KING

That era was a busy time in pretty Rabaul, and an historical epoch for Australia. Then she arrived at maturity and took her place as an active colonizer. She had to fit out quickly a tropical service, complete with administrative headquarters, medical service, and staff of native affairs. She had to find and appoint experienced men as district, patrol, and medical officers. The youngest of nations, she had quickly to form the machinery to govern a tropical kingdom.

Burleigh Gorman was musing on the whims of fate. Well known on the Western Australian goldfields, here he was, beginning to get on in years, tossed by the god of war into a government billet in a wild tropic land. Like an old war-horse, he had twitched his ears to these rumours of gold.

If there was gold over there the Australian prospector would find it when affairs settled down. Gorman decided to "make every pound a prisoner," in case a rush came. If that came he was determined to make a last bid for fortune. These thoughts were interrupted by an explanation on high finance developing outside his office window.

One kanaka, in pained disgust, held a chit on the Commonwealth Bank, recently started. He was dumbfounded that he had been paid with a slip of worthless paper instead of the treasured marks (shillings). His friend, wise in his generation, pointed to the Treasury:

"You savvy this feller? He house-money gammon. You savvy this other feller place?" and he pointed round to the Commonwealth Bank, "he house-money true!"

As with a very relieved expression the paper-money man hurried across to the bank, Samsu came bounding into Gorman's office to thump a parcel on the table. Gorman had promised this boy a clock when he could tell the time. Evidently the clock had arrived. The boy's eyes were like walnuts as he excitedly explained:

"Master, master, me like talk longa you! Now me go longa house *kong-kong* (Chinese store). Me give him paper belonga you (purchase note). Kong-kong (Chinaman) he catchim something longa top (shelf) now he rouse him lap-lap belong him (tore the paper off the clock). Clock he die! (It was not wound up.) He fightim behind longa him (the Chinaman wound the clock up). Now he cry big feller too much! (the alarm had gone off). Now he die (the alarm had stopped). Now he talk *lik-lik* (little bit). Me savvy him tick! tick! tick!"

Gorman laughed. That boy was as delighted with his clock as Gorman would have been had he found a gold-mine. He wished some good genie would present him with the kind of clock he wanted.

Until the ownership of the country should be definitely settled, newcomers were not admitted. A definite period of seven years was fixed. Prospecting was forbidden. Many of the Papuan prospectors had died out, as their generation did in Australia. Some went to the war, and never returned. Old Matt Crowe, Arthur Darling, and others were hastened into the Shadow Land by the cumulative effects of malaria and spear and arrow wounds.

There were few to take the places of these old hands. Of those unsuitable for military service Shark-eye Park was one. When he actually returned on his golden quest no one knows. But the laws of nations could not stop him; he disappeared from Papua, and melted into the jungle as he had often done before. Time passed, and again that elusive whisper spread over Papua to the few ears attuned:

"Shark-eye has gone bush again!"

Wherever scattered gold-diggers met, they asked: "Any news of Shark-eye? Is he on gold?"

No one could say, definitely. There was no chance of tracking him, or of learning his whereabouts from returning carriers, for he employed none. He travelled from village to village, living native; a friendless wanderer if ever there was one. He was a man in a nationless country; no one, then, knew definitely who owned German New Guinea. He survived because of dogged pluck and that queer mental mastery of the kanakas. Their gardens were open to him; their banana and yam patches, sugarcane, sweet potatoes. He even had tobacco, for some tribes cultivated and smoke-cured their own leaf.

Men can only surmise what he went through. He himself would never tell. This sinewy, grim-faced man with the shark's glare in his eyes, but who could smile finely when he wished, climbed the razor-backs right up to the craggy peaks where the villages cling like beehives; passed unharmed while demanding food and attention as his right; and taking it, but taking it in the native way. He respected the customs and beliefs and laws of these warring tribes, while his strange personality exercised a seemingly mesmeric influence over the minds of *luluais* (hereditary chiefs) and sorcerers alike.

The natives felt, even in the most superstitious of their mystic ceremonies, that he was with them in the "making" of their young men, in their spells against their enemies, and in their propitiation of the god-spirits that ruled the fate of their fights, crops, and life. He could walk into the stinking gloom of a charnal house, glance casually at the skulls around and not notice anything except as it ought to be, while the human vultures squatting in the shadows, watching, and, with acute minds, waiting for but one mistake, would intuitively realize that he understood.

Sometimes as he travelled he heard the war-drums booming and read, in their harshly throbbing tones, the messages of this savage wireless used for ages past. Often he would meet on the path befeathered warriors running with the lust of the man-hunt in their eyes. He would stand aside as they sped silently by. They knew he was there; had been told of his coming by the drums.

Occasionally he entered a village where the man-hunters were dining on the bodies of the slain. That was the test. They snatched the baked limbs from the cooking-fires; but the curl of their bestial lips betrayed no revulsion in him. The flicker of an eye-lid would have sealed his fate. They sensed his understanding with its mastery. He must be one of them, the spirit of an ancestor, reincarnated under a white skin, who had brought his tambaran with him!

And so Shark-eye Park climbed once more to the heights of the Bulolo. His feelings thrilled him every hour of the day and in his dreams at night. He was the only prospector in all inland ex-German New Guinea; alone in a golden country forbidden to him and all like him. The Military had said: "Keep out!"

And he had found gold, the big stuff that rattled in the dish long before the dirt was washed out! He had succeeded where Germany had failed. Shark-eye had found it in a bend of Koranga Creek beneath the shadow of giant Kaindi, from whose shoulders the waters of Koranga, the Watut, Namie, and of another creek (later to be called the Edie) splashed down through the trees to fall into the Bulolo River which, with its great sister tributary, the Watut, hummed and tumbled and roared down the range into the Markham, which spread-eagles slowly down to the sea.

It is known that considerably earlier than 1922 Shark-eye Park had found gold, the really "big stuff."

The small prospecting pick he wielded, picking like a bird in the silence of the jungle, was the forerunner of civilization. That three-pound piece of iron was to be the forerunner of two thousand-ton dredges made in Australian and Canadian workshops with white man's Capital and Labour.

CHAPTER V

CECIL JOHN LEVIEN

Cecil John Levien was stationed at Buka (North Solomons) as a government patrol officer: a shrewd, calculating, courageous, and determined man, possessed of almost inexhaustible energy. Moreover, he had a will-power that made him face any obstacle once he was determined to carry through an idea. Now, he had a feeling that this Mandated Territory of New Guinea was destined to make history within the Empire; that in this last big unexplored and unexploited country there was incalculable wealth.

Levien was a stockily built, broad shouldered, restless man, with more than average strength, a cheery, determined face, and calculating eyes that could also twinkle irresistibly. He had far too many important things on hand and mind ever to dress well. He was, as often as not, seen flying around in an open-necked shirt, khaki trousers, and frayed canvas shoes; ready with a cheery laugh and joke before he hurried by, though ever willing to grab the tools and give a hand with the job.

His mind worked like lightning. As he worked he might be thinking days, weeks, months, even years ahead. While cutting a path through trackless forest he could see the road it would be in five years' time. He could sail into a land-locked bay and visualize the savage lands beyond under coconut plantations, the native village a white man's town, the throb of the tomtoms a wireless melody.

Levien had, too, extraordinary organizing ability. Above all, he had that feeling—priceless to any man—the feeling that he would like to, and that he *would*, do something big before he died; no matter how long the chance was in coming.

As a government official he carried out his numerous duties with characteristic efficiency, while on every possible occasion seeking to know what little had been learned of the mainland during the German regime. He inquired of old-time traders and planters, of recruiters and island wanderers, warily sounded German interpreters and missionaries, for any fact, any whisper, of what the Germans had done on the mainland. While at Rabaul he had searched through old records, old German papers, scientific and other-wise, to which he could gain access. He found authentic information so scarce that he redoubled his efforts and soon concentrated on the probability of great mineral wealth in the Territory.

Gold! That was what would open up a new country. Granted a gold discovery, not only would the country boom, but a man would grow with it. Not only could he help his nation, he could grow rich and powerful with the rapid development; be a force that counted.

Levien thought of his age. Fifty-one! Grimly he smiled and banished the thought. He did not look his age: he rarely thought of it. But, owing to a run of bad seasons on his farm in New South Wales before the War, he was still in debt, and that is a killer.

His feeling of a golden country grew into conviction. In imagination he saw a rush of men; steamers converging on a New Guinea transformed; capital coming from all over the world. Feverishly, but in apparent gossip, he collected the reports of the activities of the more venturesome Papuan prospectors. He narrowed his attention to five men—Shark-eye Park, Matt Crowe, Arthur Darling, Jim Preston, Frank Pryke. Finally he concentrated on Shark-eye Park. Where was he now? What was this mystery prospector doing? Easily Levien fixed upon Morobe as the probable district and apparently the Waria area, but not exactly the Waria. Morobe was a huge district, anyway. Shark-eye must be in the mountains somewhere behind Morobe—if he was not dead!

Levien swore that somehow and some day soon he would be stationed at Morobe. It should be easy. Fancy any man in his right senses asking to be stationed at Morobe, the most lonely post in the Territory! A desolate, fever-stricken hole away out heaven knows where! In uncontrolled country, too!

He fought his way step by step. When, eventually, he was stationed at Morobe, he knew he would have plenty to do taming the wild bush kanakas, and carrying out dangerous patrols up the big river-systems, the Waria, Markham, Bulolo, Ramu, and others.

He would lead his own patrols into the country that had attracted the big German surveys; then up rivers and into country they had not penetrated. He would go through this country himself; prove, if he could, whether it was gold-bearing or not. Perhaps impossible with numerous official duties to perform. He must find that wild-man prospector in there somewhere, living kanaka.

The conviction grew that this man was neither dead nor gone native. He was a genuine prospector. The more Levien thought of it, the more certain he became that Shark-eye was on gold. He would find him and his gold. He determined, too, that he would put all his energies into opening up the new country "over there."

Levien took the plunge. It was the beginning of seven years' battling. New Guinea men know some of those battles. They guess at others. He was a secretive man when he wished. He was lively, hail-fellow-well-met when you met him in Rabaul or Aitape or Madang or out on patrol; but when he left you, you realized that you had told him quite a lot, whereas he had told you nothing that mattered very much.

In 1921 the military administration ceased. Civil administration under Brigadier-General E. A. Wisdom was established throughout the Mandated Territory. Rabaul, on New Britain, was the capital. The former German posts on the larger islands and New Guinea itself were administered by district officers. A district officer generally had a patrol officer under him, sometimes a medical officer or medical assistant, and squads of native constabulary. Each district officer was responsible for the administration of a large district. He was a little king with autocratic powers but expected to rule humanely and for the benefit of the country; to treat his white "subjects" with tact and justice, while bringing the laws and ideals of civilization into the life of the head-hunter.

C. J. Levien, ex-lieutenant of the A.I.F., was appointed district officer at Morobe. Looking back, it seems that Fate had deliberately placed the right man in the right place.

Levien soon turned lonely Morobe into a first-class station; his patrol officers were keen; his constabulary disciplined, and keyed up to the highest pitch of efficiency and endurance. He was easy going when on the station; "snappy" when on a job.

His job was to put the country under control; to enter country that had never seen a white man, to pacify the villagers, to teach them that head-hunting is a crime, cannibalism worse, and that murder is not a pastime but something to be shunned. Withal, his job was to make the way possible for peaceful penetration.

It sounds easy enough. But it required infinite tact, patience, dogged determination, and physical fitness. He was an unwelcome visitor. The war-like tribes, especially, did not want the white man nor the white man's rule. And when they tried at times to keep their country to themselves, who can blame them?

Always on his trips of penetration and pacification, he searched for a bom-bom who was hidden away deep within the mountains. (In some dialects *bom-bom* means the frond of a coconut palm. But the double report of guns in certain valleys earned there the name bom-bom for the first white men.)

Sulkily the tribesmen held the secret of Shark-eye Park. Every mountain torrent that Levien crossed he scanned keenly, watching the icy waters for any sign of muddiness, the banks for any debris or grass that might have been sluiced into the stream by a man working miles away above.

If only he could locate that mystery prospector, he was positive he would find the gold country.

There were lonely nights at the station, but not for Levien, engrossed in his map. Heaven knows where he got that map. It was a large one of the presumed Morobe district, made by some German officer. The mountain systems and innumerable waterways were filled in with precision in those areas which a survey had patrolled. But the bulk of it was surmise and pure guess-work. And there were many spaces still to be filled in. Maps must grow, like everything else. On this map, Levien coloured red a little fringe around Morobe. That represented the controlled area. In his patrols he had already filled in a range here, a tributary river there. But even to-day, ten years later, when we know so much more of the country, that map is very, very far from being finalized.

Levien's hours, when off active duty, were devoted to finding a man in a map. He was patrolling this country as swiftly and efficiently as he could. Those places where he found no trace of the man, he enclosed by lines on the map. As time went on he hoped to narrow down that particular locality in which Shark-eye must be working. Then a patrol through that area must sooner or later locate him.

On that map Levien had marked the course of the German expeditions and the results attained, so far as he knew. In different coloured ink he drew wavering lines to mark the tracks of the prospectors coming in from Papua. On several rivers, the Ono and Waria particularly, were little red dots marking where the more venturesome prospectors had won gold. But those dots were specks on a broad expanse of white. He had marked, too, the routes of his predecessor and *his* patrol officers. These had seen no sign of Shark-eye and he marked their routes blank.

Thus, from his store of knowledge, collected with great pains, he marked the map, adding to it after the completion of every patrol.

Many months later it was completed, and he sat back grimly, aghast at the task before him. The marked portions were like posts in a wilderness of mountains.

And in that wilderness he had to find one white man.

CHAPTER VI

THE GOLDEN CALF

The district officer finished his official mail; then, with a thankful thump on the table, turned to his private correspondence. He wrote a long and cheerful letter to his wife, and finished with a sigh. Several business letters followed. Then he carefully added up a column of figures. That wretched debt! Month by month, year by year, he had been paying it off, ever since the war. The little home in Victoria had been an awful drag; practically all his salary for years past had gone into it. Thankfully he finished the last letter and leaned back in the big chair, hands clasped behind his head. Gradually the worry eased from his face; his eyes grew bright with the vision of the dreamer.

How to turn the savagery of this land into energetic white towns, prosperous homes, big trade, and ships? Gold only would do it. Somewhere in this tangled maze was one white man who could put wings to Levien's vision. And he sat alone away back there, like an old man of the mountains guarding his hoard, not caring.

With an exasperated frown Levien wished he would turn up, as he had occasionally done throughout the years, without a moment's notice, at some tiny outpost, such as in the Madang or the Aitape district, or maybe at a mission station; even, at rare intervals, in distant Rabaul itself. He would stay a week or two, quietly talking and enjoying conversation, appreciating civilized food and company. Then he would go; probably not to reappear again until men thought him dead.

What a queer position Shark-eye had been in. Apart from his extraordinary wanderings among savage tribes, he had been a lone man playing a game against nations. Had he found rich gold under the German regime, he might have hesitated to report it, fearing confiscation. Levien wondered how much the Germans really knew of the strange prospector's activities. Then, when the war broke out, Shark-eye had been in a peculiar dilemma. Worse still during the military occupation. In a sense this was No-nation's country. Prospecting had been prohibited; a man would not have been legally entitled to gold had he found any. Even now, under the civil administration, the mining ordinance had only just been passed. But now, if he wished to, he was safe to come in and report his find.

Levien was jolly sure he wouldn't—except at his own sweet will.

"One feller master he come!"

Levien pulled himself erect with a jerk as a white man entered the room. Implied secrecy in the man's fixed stare caused Levien to dismiss the orderly. With curt formality he motioned the visitor to a chair. The unkempt man accepted defiantly, his clothes all ragged and torn.

"Levien, I have found gold!" he said with a sneer. "Got" you, did I? Thought so. Well, we won't argue the point. You are a Jew and I am a missionary; gone wrong. Gold has queer welding powers."

Levien's eyes narrowed, his face tightened in nasty lines. He was a bad man to bait, was Levien.

"You are not over communicative. Out with it!"

"Right!" The man leaned forward, his face transformed, thin hands trembling, his speech coming faster, as huskily he said:

"Levien, I've found a river of gold! It's full of it; its sands are gold. Levien, give me your protection against natives and whites alike and we'll go fifty-fifty!"

Levien stared at that excited face with fever-bright eyes but not from malaria. This man who had found a river of gold was nearly beside himself.

"Where is it?"

"Of course you would ask me that!"

"I am district officer here!" replied Levien harshly.

"Of course you are! And I'm the man who has found the gold! You are Levien, too. That's why I've come to you. A word from you and the tribe I'm sheltering with now will work for me instead of eating me! Then you can pass the gold south through the shipping company and arrange for all my stores. You can keep the find quiet so that Rabaul does not hear about it! There need never be a rush! You can work here while I work up there. We can both be rich men! Fabulously rich! Without the combination— well, I clear out and bide my time until another district officer is appointed to Morobe. Now, what do you say?"

"Show me the place. I'll give my definite answer then."

The man stared wolfishly. Levien glared back. They looked more like springing at one another's throats than entering into a partnership. Suddenly the stranger laughed.

"Right! I'll show you. A river of gold! I know what your answer will be, Levien."

Levien called Sergeant Bewa. The patrol officer was away on duty, but there were ample police boys left for a hasty patrol. It *was* hasty, too; up the Waria River; their guide daily pressing on well into evening. Levien could not sleep, for his guide with the familiarity born of a common objective and companionship in loneliness dilated on his river of gold until Levien's mind was throbbing.

Levien ceased to wonder now at this renegade from the missionary ranks. He knew the man by rumour. He had had charge of a mission station for years; but had broken away and "gone native." Levien thought of the Golden Calf as he hurried behind his ragged, eager guide. Here was a worshipper, with a vengeance!

"We won't be long now!" the man gasped, turning his thorn-scratched face. "It's a little river in here at the foot of those peaky razor-backs. The village is about three miles ahead, up the Waria. Send your police boys on alone."

They came to it very quickly. It was a little singing river with sandy banks brown with ironstones, and with little white quartz ones dotted here and there like plums in a pudding. Pretty trees shaded the banks but the man ran to the water's edge and dropped to his knees upon the sand.

"See it!" he cried in delight. "See it glitter!" And he ran handfuls of the stuff through his fingers.

Levien stared, his heart beating with blows that slowed down painfully.

With a bitter curse he turned his back and strode away. It was mica! Newchum's gold.

Only in the quick years to come, when he had gained wider experience in gold-mining, did he realize that perhaps, after all, there might be gold in that river—not in the sands on top, but on the bottom under them. It was not the shiny mica which told him that. It was those valueless-looking brown ironstones and white quartz that the mission man had never noticed.

But he never went back there.

The little mission trading-station at Singawa looked dreamily peaceful in the gloom of a New Guinea evening. Isolated from all white habitation, this place was like others of its kind. The mission boys had just hurried away to the village for there was going to be a ceremonial "sing-sing" to the tambaran (in this case, "good" devil) of the crops that night.

The missionary lit the lamp, his slow and careful fingers not wasting a match. He was a quiet, serious-minded man who lived only for his job, and never concerned himself with other people's business. He could have been a wealthy man to-day, had he chosen. He glanced up from the lamp at a rustle in the doorway. A gaunt, haggard man leaned wearily there, with the devils of malaria glaring from his eyes.

The missionary helped the stranger to a chair. With the efficiency of experience he dosed him with quinine, boiled him soup, and insisted that he "drink in strength." Smiling grimly, the man obeyed, then sagging back closed his eyes and sighed.

The missionary made ready a warm bed. The sick man glared with teeth chattering, fighting to keep his good Samaritan from growing into a black bear. Clumsily the bear rolled about, then advanced with great teeth champing to an evil grin.

"Come, come! You must go to bed. You have a temperature, you know. But you will be better in the morning."

Shuddering, the man pulled himself together; wearily he shook his head as with fumbling fingers he undid a stout canvas belt, double rolled and bulging, and threw it on the table. The missionary looked questioningly as it fell with a dull heavy thud.

"There's three hundred ounces in it," croaked the man. "It's yours! Give me a Christian burial—with my boots off! I've lived among natives for years, but I want a white man to bury me."

The missionary placed the belt under the pillow of the bed. Then he lifted the man and wrapped him warmly in blankets.

"I refuse payment," he said soberly. "You would not offer it to me if you were not half delirious. But you are not going to die. You have come here just in time: I understand the treatment for malaria."

The man lingered on the border-line for many days. When the day came that he was strong again he hesitated by the doorway in farewell, his face thinner, more lined, but with the same grim eyes that softened as he glanced at the missionary. Casually he nodded towards the mountain peaks; told the missionary of gold there, and gave an invitation. But the good Samaritan shook his head.

"My work is here," he said.

The visitor nodded understandingly. Then he turned and walked away. The missionary looked from the doorway to where the rolling clouds joined vague peaks to the sky and wondered, momentarily, to what fastnesses away up there his strange visitor would go.

He watched Shark-eye until he vanished into the jungle, then turned inside to his work.

CHAPTER VII

WHILE THE VILLAGE BURNS

District Officer Levien stepped along in sprightly fashion, yet with the jungle wariness. The moist path betrayed no sound of his light tread or of the bare brown feet of his police and carriers.

Yet, unseen ahead might be a crouching savage with his ear to the path. Wild men know things. Nature has taught them secrets about vibrations; possibly secrets that even we do not know.

At the rear of the file Sergeant Bewa strode ahead of the district officer, a military haversack strapped across his broad back, a rifle clasped in his big brown hand. The district officer admired this splendid fearless figure in front of him; of such a type must have been the gladiators of old.

Sergeant Bewa later retired, when his beloved district officer retired. He founded Bewa village on the Neumir River; collected thirty-odd men and women and kneaded his progressive spirit into them; and laid out a model village "as per government regulations," ruled by Bewa the luluai.

But the police-call with its travel and adventure came again to Bewa. He is now Sergeant-Major Bewa, of Aitape station. Meanwhile, his village is growing.

In happy mood, for he thought he had solved the secret of Shark-eye Park, the district officer was attuned to the silence, the gloom, the crowding trees all around. A smell of old New Guinea was in the air. There hardly seemed to be air. The police and carriers might have been phantoms passing through a world where everything stood motionless.

But things moved other than phantoms, and well the police knew it. Their wide-awake brown eyes scanned the path for the razor-sharp splinter that might be hidden under a fallen leaf; eyed the foliage, ready for a sudden spear-thrust, and glanced up at the branches for the climber bowman waiting to speed an arrow to their chests.

Particularly did Corporal Boassi watch out lest his be the foot that would kick a trigger-vine (like a tripwire) and release an arrow into his stomach. Cunningly the foemen conceal those hidden bows with the long arrow set. Touch such a vine and "Twang—ugh!"

So Corporal Boassi, padding on silently, out of sight ahead, clenched his rifle and used his ears, his nose, and his ever restless eyes. The imprint of a toe or a heel upon the path, a fallen leaf, a vine swaying unnaturally from the branches, an animal-like odour, the muffled call of a bird—all might mean lurking death. Rather frightened, but all the gamer for that was Corporal Boassi, in that he hid his fear. At any cause for alarm the district officer would come up and take the lead.

The white-man leader is always the first target for waiting bowmen in New Guinea. Corporal Boassi did not want his district officer to take the lead. That officer was on punishment bent. The wild Adzera had raided another village and carried off ten heads. By peaceable means the district officer had done all that was humanly possible to stop these forays. Now he would clean up this particular village and restore order and confidence in the terrified area.

And he might gather news of Shark-eye, for this was the Markham River, new country; he had never been so high up here before. He frowned. This was the last river. If he got no news of Shark-eye here then the man could only be on one of the mountain summits. His map had convinced him at last. In future patrols he would follow up river after river to its head, then climb to the very summits. The water carried down the gold, so it must be richest up on top; and that was where Shark-eye must be.

So the map said.

An immense velvet-black butterfly with green and orange wings flitted by, almost touching the district officer's nose before it lit upon a leaf, to be instantly seized by a hunting spider.

"That's a symbol of this country," he thought. "Beauty and life and death everywhere: tremors in solid mountains, winged death in the mosquito, a python in the night, an arrow in the back; crocodile and shark in the stillest of waters. Perhaps that is its fascination; listening and expecting the unexpected to happen at any moment." Instinctively he halted at the sergeant's outstretched hand, then moved up along the motionless file.

It was there all right—the *tambu*, hanging down over the track in ominous warning: "Come no farther!" Corporal Boassi stood staring at it, overcome by an inborn superstition stronger than his physical bravery.

With a contemptuous tugging the district officer tore the direful branch aside and marched at the head of the file, realizing the fear that had spread down along the carriers especially. But Sergeant Bewa was guarding the rear. Presently the leader halted and the long file stopped as if he had shouted an order.

He was looking into the foreboding mouth of a branch path, wondering if he might safely take advantage of the deviation. The element of surprise often spells victory in New Guinea. He turned into the path and almost into a giant spider-web, its silken cables stretched from branch to branch, completely blocking the path. The district officer drew back from the hundred hairy spiders crouching amongst those strands, their bloated bodies brilliantly speckled in green and scarlet. He threw a stick. As it bounced back the spiders champed their hairy legs upon the vibrating web.

"Fancy walking into that in the dark!" thought the district officer, as he turned and signalled Corporal Boassi.

That night they camped by a jungle creek moistly warm from a billion leaves. It was so dark that the enclosing tree-trunks looked unguessable forms. The sentries crouched wide-eyed, motionless, ears straining to distinguish the whisper of a footfall above the burbling of unseen water. As a flying squirrel volplaned through the air to land on some branch with a soft thump and scratching, a timid coastal carrier nearly fainted. A fire-fly, like a green emerald, floated by, to dissolve in the night; a snake slithered across the district officer's blankets; a huge green centipede with burning claws wriggled over Sergeant Bewa's toes; something of the night momentarily rustled a leafy creeper above. In that velvet blackness all things seemed listening.

Suddenly a scream tore the silence; then scream after agonized scream. The district officer's hair slowly lifted, to subside as he settled back on his blankets, his hand trembling on his revolver. He could almost hear the leaves trembling too, just there where his servant boy was lying. The police and carriers had not moved; they had listened, then, reassured, turned to their listening again.

In a hidden village somewhere near by they were roasting a pig. From a tripod of black palm-sticks he was suspended by a twisted vine above a slow fire. As the vine slowly untwisted so he slowly roasted. After many minutes the vine would, momentarily, come to rest; then the pig would slowly begin to spin again and roast on the other side as his kickings twisted the vine up. So he would roast and scream his life away.

Three days later the tiny army was marching up a valley, hastened by the harsh thrumming of the kundu drums. The district officer growled good humouredly at this native wireless, though it warned of his crafty approach. At the double he sent a file of police running through the grass to the right, another to the left to flank the village, while his main force ran straight up the well-beaten path. With police pattering behind him he ran out of the grass on to the village stockade, with thatched roofs peeping up inside. The constabulary closed in at the rush and leaping at the stockade swarmed up the poles like monkeys and jumped down inside.

The village was silent as death.

The district officer had expected it: he knew New Guinea. His men ran rapidly from house to house, applying the firestick. He hated to do it, but it was the only way to make these people realize that the white man meant it when he forbade head-hunting and cannibalism. These people would be compelled to rebuild their village. By and by, probably, after it had been burnt several times, they would pause and say:

"Is it really worth all this labour, just for the sake of a few heads?"

Upper Markham Women with the husband's skulls.

A native of Nakanai wearing a shell money head-dress.

C.J. Levien.

Jim Pryke among the Kukukukus
The belt around the native's waist is the thighbone of man.

The dry palm-thatch on house after house burst into flames, crackling into a leaping red that was immediately overwhelmed by acrid black smoke. The houses were built on piles five feet high, with floors of bamboo and a bamboo platform at the entrance to each. As the bamboo floorings caught fire they began to crackle harshly; with the ventilation below and the enclosing stockade the place would soon be a furnace. Dense smoke came sweeping over all.

The district officer wheeled round and shouted fiercely, angrily waving his arms. Corporal Boassi, a shadow form there in the smoke, slunk away to his job. The officer was amused, though grateful in his own rough way for the corporal's affection. But he wanted every man on his job now; he wanted a quick finish and "Line up!" so that he could march clear of the blaze and be ready for a counter-attack should it come. Besides, he had often felt embarrassingly boyish with this brown shadow continually at his heels lest harm befall him.

He turned back to the fire again. The house before him was now blazing merrily and out of this burst on to the smoking platform a big brown figure, all groping arms and spluttering mouth.

With bloodshot eyes, so rudely awakened from sleep, it glared at the man below, then leaped straight down, hurling him to earth. With sinewy hands squeezing his throat, the white man smashed ineffectual fists against that snarling mouth, then wrenched himself double as teeth met in his cheek. He gripped the bulging throat and pressed back with the fury of a madman, making animal noises as he bit at the sinewy wrists hurting his jaw. They rolled; that awful back-wrenching, stomach-twisting roll of men each struggling to straddle the other and force him to earth until his eyes bulge out of their sockets.

But the savage had magnificent strength and with hysterical joy tried to kill this thing that fought and gurgled and wrenched and rolled and kicked with a madness like his own. Those straining brown legs felt like a horse's shanks as they twisted around the white man, but he jerked his knee into the brown stomach and the gurgle was music. They rolled under the platform and fought wedged there, with burning thatch falling upon them, while their fingers tightened—content to die if only each could take the other with him.

And so they would have done, choking under the acrid thatch, had it not been for Corporal Boassi. In an agony of fear he crawled under, terrified to strike lest he strike his master. Then a burning bamboo pole hissed across his back; with a cry he shoved his rifle-muzzle hard in between the two bodies and, pressing the muzzle into the brown, fired. He dragged his master out, but the convulsive brown body came too. The white man stared at the dying thing in his hands. Suddenly he understood and staggered up, covered in blood from head to foot, his breath wheezing.

Levien knelt beside his dead foe. He wished he had done it himself— but not that way.

CHAPTER VIII

SHARK-EYE SEEKS A MATE

In the gloaming of a tropical evening Jack Nettleton stared at the forbidding mountains, their crests emerging from the clouds, their bulk rapidly blackening under the evening shadows. Somewhere within there must be gold and Shark-eye Park.

Nettleton, tall and soldierly, stood, a deepening silhouette against the coming night. Mosquitoes hummed around him; frogs croaked from the swamp; a little lullaby of wavelets tinkled from the beach. It was a very lonely spot, here at Bukuaship, this small trading post on a palm-clad inlet near the mouth of the Markham River. Beside the trader there were no white people here; only loneliness, the waters of the Huon Gulf, those old black mountains—and memories and longings.

As Nettleton looked, fires leapt up across the inlet, and with their gleam came the thrum of a kundu drum. He had savage company, anyway. How well that stamp of feet and barbaric song blended with the silent blackness! With a sigh, he turned and walked into the palm-thatched house.

A well-liked man, this Nettleton (recently sergeant in the New Guinea constabulary), in the few places where men meet in New Guinea. A roamer, as many of those men are, he had served his time in the Northwest Mounted, had travelled in strange places and lived among strange scenes. A big rawboned fellow, quiet and steady; a typical sergeant. They say of him in Madang:

"Jack Nettleton would rather do a good turn than a bad one." True, he had helped many a man.

Now, he almost needed help himself. His little trading station was not turning out too well; and it was rather late in life to make yet another start. When a man realizes that, his thoughts are seldom cheerful. This particular evening Nettleton had to fight against melancholia.

This whisper of gold! He had heard it wherever white men congregate throughout all New Guinea. He had heard it far up the Sepik, up the Ramu, at Madang, at Rabaul, away out on the Admiralty Islands. Whenever he met a white man on mountain trail, in lonely village, even out at sea, the whisper was often of gold—and Shark-eye Park.

And yet there was nothing tangible in it. Native rumour said that Shark-eye had been eaten long ago. Nettleton himself had prospected the wild country between Bukuaship and the Markham; had battled his way among the fierce Adzera and the tall Laewomba fighters. He knew Park, the lithe, quiet jungle-man with the steely eyes. They had met in Madang, and several times when Nettleton was far back on lonely patrols with his police. Each man had silently liked the other, as quiet men sometimes do.

Very late, Nettleton climbed in under the mosquito-net. The dancing men had gone to rest. A brooding quiet that one could almost feel surrounded him. He fell asleep, and dreamed of mountains of gold, and of Shark-eye Park, and of cannibals dancing around a feast. And through it all boomed a kundu drum.

What urged him to do it, no one knows. But Shark-eye came down from his mountain retreat and sought out Nettleton:

"We have not met often," he said gravely, "but we have liked one another. You are doing no good here. Put all your stores behind the two of us. I know of gold in the mountains. To work it properly means stores; above all, axes and iron, rice and tobacco to induce the kanakas to work. Come in with me if you like."

Nettleton did not hesitate. In due time they disappeared into the jungle, heading towards the mountains, and a long string of carriers went with them. So Nettleton's trading station vanished.

Shark-eye showed him gold.

Nettleton was thrilled with a joy far above the value of this yellow stuff. This would bring to life his dying dreams, a country home in England, entire relief from worry, the life of an English squire. That was what this yellow stuff was saying—that and other things.

He turned to Shark-eye and offered his hand.

Only two years, say, of this. Then fortune! Two men—no, say three—Levien, the district officer down on the coast at Morobe, though he did not know it: three men controlling a goldfield. If they could only hold it awhile! Work it until they located the richest claims! A rush was inevitable, but it would be held off a long time in such a place as this.

It was a thrilling position.

Apart from the golden gain of keeping the field to themselves as long as possible, Park had other reasons for not yet wanting the discovery broadcasted to the world. Such immature news might well bring misery to hundreds; ruined health, even death, to scores of men. He did not know whether this creek was rich enough to return a dividend to many.

Koranga was simply a jungle creek, covered by nature with rocks, trees, and roots. His ground and Nettleton's was rich, they knew; but to prospect the surrounding country would mean many months of work. None knew better than Park the difficulties and heartbreak in that work;

he had done years of it. If a rush came now, hundreds of men might find themselves stranded here far from help, surrounded by savages, the nearest store hundreds of miles away, and no gold other than that in a few fortunate claims. No, it was advisable to keep the discovery as quiet as possible. Before long the Papuan prospectors who were left would be sure to "smell gold." They would drift in by ones, and twos, and fours; experienced men all, who would do their own prospecting and so test the field.

The two men set to work systematically. It was imperative now to have a supply of civilized food, of tools, and of presents for the kanakas. Tomahawks, beads, knives, trade goods would delight them as payment; rice and their own native foods, bought from their own gardens, would feed them. There was an unlimited supply of willing labour, for the time being, at any rate.

After his own stores were used up, Nettleton would go straight down to the coast, then canoe to Morobe, and arrange for stores from Rabaul. Rabaul, five hundred miles away, would wonder what the stores were for—exactly. Park would stop on Koranga and keep the claims working. Nettleton, just as occasion required, could be going to and coming from the coast with his string of carriers.

What an advantage now was the personality of Park! The thousands of tribesmen on that dangerous eight-day trip to the coast would never be actively hostile; while up round the Bulolo the tribesmen, sufficient of them at least, would be eager labourers for the white man's steel, the wonderful tomahawk, and that wonder food, rice. Gold in the ground; plenty of it; big stuff; labour to get it out! Only Time and no accidents or sickness were now needed.

A tremendous advantage in the prospectors' favour was water, running water. Harnessed in sluice-races, it will do the work of many men. Easily worked timber was abundant, sluice-boxes were chopped into shape by tomahawk. Soon the ground sluice-races and boxes were rushing away their muddy water and tailings; the creek was echoing to the tinkle of stones thrown from the races by many black and brown hands; the working of the claims was in full swing. Rude but surprisingly efficient methods, as the clean creek-bed and the yellow gold in the boxes showed evening by evening. All the labour had to be patiently trained it is true. It takes a long time to train some varieties of stone-age men in the simplest things; but the supply of labour made up for the lack of skill.

Gold—big stuff!—was being won at Koranga.

CHAPTER IX

THE BUBU PATROL

Sunlight streamed on Morobe station, bathing in light the bungalow with its beautiful garden and well trimmed paths on the hillock by that lovely island plumed sea. Directly behind the old station towered the mountain wall. Near by, the Morobe lagoon shimmered in peace. But no tropic palms graced this lonely scene.

Apart from the substantially built patrol officers' quarters, police barracks, and the store, the district officer's bungalow stood in dignified isolation. It was built for strength, but its bays and encircling veranda, its restful blinds, and windows like wide doorways, gave its strength a homely touch. The substantial furniture was in keeping with the building. The district officer's bedroom was almost filled by the double bed, with its enormous red-duck mattress stuffed with horsehair, on which that officer slept under the Double Eagle, carved heavily in the woodwork, at the head of the bed.

The mattress was in sections so that portion could be snatched up and thrown into launch or canoe in the event of a sudden patrol by sea or river. Large, heavy chairs were in dignified waiting in the main and guest-rooms, while a big sideboard and office furniture frowned over all. The Germans had certainly built their station, and all in it, to last.

An air of military efficiency well fitted Morobe station. It had been strictly military in the German regime; it was military now, in Levien's. That station has a history, with adventure, sudden raids, exploration, punitive expeditions, and quick romance written large on its pages.

The police master was busy at the store. On the shelves rations were arranged in order so that an issue could be served to any constabulary force at a moment's notice. The medical orderly was attending to an arrow-wound in the thigh of a native constable, while his trained native orderly was busy attending to such sick of the proud Suweni tribes that had deigned to seek aid.

The parade-ground, swept clean as a billiard-table, looked to be awaiting the roll-call. Those native. constabulary not on duty sat in their barracks cleaning side arms, chatting and laughing. Over all floated lazily the Australian flag.

The district officer sat in his office sitting-room, studying his beloved map, spread out on the big table. He had decided on a long, perhaps dangerous, patrol. He was looking for a man; but he would patrol at the same time.

The powerful Lamanai were again loudly boasting they would "fight the Government." These fierce Bubu tribes had been a nightmare to the German Administration. Their strongholds were on the heights inland, above a fertile valley where the Bubu tears down from the upper heights into the Waria. The Lamanai were the people who had attacked Detzner a dozen times. Now, they terrorized the people, not only in the valley, but down into the Government's controlled area. Friendly luluais urgently sent the district officer word that they could not hold the respect of their people much longer if the Government "still sat down at Morobe like a woman."

In grim delight Levien pored over the map. Shark-eye Park, Matt Crowe, and Arthur Darling had located gold in the Upper Ono, just where the Sini and Repu people were fighting now. By a successful peaceful patrol he would improve the *mana* of the Government and pave the way to the taming of the savage Bubu tribes which would eventually lead to the pacification of the entire valley. And possibly learn news of Shark-eye Park! He leaned back to think and dream.

Park must be in there somewhere. He had sought him in so many places; along the rivers, in the lower valleys, wherever in a wide stretch of country gold might lie. Could the man be actually working on the very summit of the mountains? Well, the Bubu were nearly up there! He would visit the Bubu. He would need especially efficient, well-equipped police boys. Arrangements must be made for carriers. He would start at daylight the day after to-morrow. He thumped the table smartly. Instantly an orderly appeared from the veranda.

"Callim sergeant!" snapped Levien.

A quarter-minute later and the sergeant's feet thumped on the veranda to hurry into the room and smack smartly together as he stood at salute.

A fine figure of a man, Sergeant Bewa. Keenly intelligent; over six feet tall; erect as a cedar; he was the picture of virility and readiness. Upon his thick, coal-black hair sat a peaked cap; over his loins was a well-fitting blue *lava-lava* with red stripe; around his broad waist was a whitewashed belt with polished fittings and bayonet; and on his huge bare arms were the three chevrons of a sergeant.

"Bewa! To-morrow me feller go walkabout longa bush-me feller go longa lookim Bubu! Now, me like catchim ten feller police boy. Me like you-you come. Now nine feller police boy. Two feller bokis (box) tobacco; two feller bag rice; one feller bokis meat."

"Yessir!"

"You go six o'clock longa morning time (to-morrow), catchim alla police boy, go longa store, waitim police master belonga catchim cartridge; now altogether something." (Meaning to collect all stores, equipment, etc.)

"Yessir!"

"You catchim feller boy savvy too much!" (Meaning, highly capable police boys only to be selected.)

"Yessir!"

"Arright! You send him 'talk' now along kanaka belong pick him up altogether something." (Send word to nearest village for carriers to come.)

"Yessir."

"Arright!"

Smartly saluting, Bewa wheeled on his heels and was gone. A minute later his stentorian voice was heard lining up the constabulary, selecting his men, and issuing orders with an efficiency that would have been a credit to any army sergeant-major.

The patrol set out at the appointed time, Corporal Boassi in the lead of twenty carriers, a police boy marching behind every second carrier. In hostile country this protection would hearten the carriers while placing every man of them under a police rifle should any be inclined to bolt. At the rear of the file marched the district officer's personal servant, proudly carrying his master's shot-gun.

Levien prized that gun. Though reserved for shooting pigeons it was really the "big gun" of the patrol. The snatching of that gun, its reverberating roar in a rocky gorge, followed by the howls of a foeman peppered with shot, had more than once averted a pitched fight.

Behind the servant marched the sergeant and the district officer. If the patrol should enter hostile country, then the district officer would take the lead with the corporal, the sergeant being responsible for the rear.

In the event of an ambush, the district officer would be the target for the first arrows, it being the primary law of New Guinea bush-fighting to spear or arrow the white leader first.

Inland from Morobe, up the river-mouth, and through the Suweni country, the patrol travelled easily along the broad, well-beaten paths leading from village to village, across verdant river-flats and grassy slopes, and between heavily timbered hills.

The Suweni owned the first few days' "travel" in this lower country. They had been driven from adjoining Papua by the fierce Binandele; but being virile people they had scattered the local population and seized their lands and country. When past the Suweni area the patrol marched up the fertile flats of the Lower Waria, passing the villages of the friendly Zia tribes, right up to the Gomena where the river swirls in snappy wavelets, churned by whirlpools.

This country had all been brought under control, and a luluai given the government cap. Hence each village had its "house-kiap," especially built and reserved for the use of the visiting district officer. As the patrol advanced, each tribe supplied carriers to as far as the tribal boundary, sending word on ahead from village to village as to the object of the visiting patrol. But as the patrol wound its way up into the head-waters of the Waria it began to climb into uncontrolled country.

And the country looked uncontrollable. Huge mountain systems clashed and split into rugged gorges down which streams rushed; and in their squeezing they threw up ten thousand jagged spurs. At high altitudes were long and narrow valleys, savagely beautiful, their fertility proved by the numerous villages that, like eagles' eyries, dotted the crags around. Those villages were almost impregnable. In the evening the tribesmen climbed up and bolted themselves in behind their palisades; in the morning they descended into the valleys to till their gardens. No wonder that similar eyries had defied Detzner.

The drums began to beat. Sergeant Bewa and the police attuned their ears. The district officer listened, too, but felt no especial uneasiness. At every village halt he conferred with the luluais, then sent explanatory messages on ahead; and he was careful only to travel into country which was peaceful to the particular tribal carriers he had with him.

Soon the patrol was climbing up the razor-backs. Typical of New Guinea, these almost sheer, narrow spurs can only be climbed "along their backbone;" at times the almost indiscernible path is hardly two feet wide. On either side of many of these razor-backs, was a sheer drop of thousands of feet. Misty views one gets up there.

To the climbing patrol there now floated far out overhead the clear, yodelling call of the mountaineers, calling out news of these strangers toiling below. From other crags where villages nestled came answering calls, clear-toned and effortless, carrying an immense distance.

Gazing from these razor-backs, with the carriers resting in a line behind him, the district officer would actually stare into the stockade of a village on a crag ahead. He would eye the people, the warriors arrayed in befeathered head-dress and handling their long bows, the women and the children, all staring across at him. The parties were hardly ten bow-shots apart, but it would take the patrol half a day, perhaps a whole day, to reach that village. It must climb far down, then far up, to do it.

Their every movement was noted and yodelled from crag to crag.

While climbing they never knew when a huge boulder might come thundering down or when the rolling, spinning, screeching trunk of a tree would sheer the path clear as a razor shaves a chin.

The marvel is that the few men of the New Guinea Service have brought under control so much of such a country in so short a time.

The district officer advanced cautiously, holding "court" every evening, waiting for luluais of surrounding villages to assemble, then making presents of salt, for which the inland kanaka will travel long distances. He bought vegetables and conferred with the luluais of the villages directly ahead, while the tribesmen with childish delight blew the mouth-organs and played the Jew's-harps issued by Sergeant Bewa.

In this way he learned the attitude towards the patrol of the tribes immediately ahead and was able to advance from allied to friendly tribes.

Soon he entered villages that knew not the Government; some indeed had never seen a white man. After the delaying parley necessary before entry, these crowded around him in shouting mobs, jostling one another to touch his skin, attempting, in guttural excitement, to handle the rifles of the frowning patrol.

These were the true mountain people, well-built, fierce-eyed, light-skinned, and strong. Quite arrogant some of them, many with noses like huge beaks pulled to their lips by heavy ornaments. An alert people, with head-dress of clipped cassowary feathers; their hair in greasy pigtails plaited with bark or reeds, and with a forehead fringe from which dangled coloured seed-pods. The chattering women especially displayed these fringes and ornamented their necks with squirrel's-teeth and dog's-teeth necklaces. Some wore necklaces of human bones with little, smoke-browned, grass-plaited bags of charms. Gruesome charms! In easy fashion they wore a thin strip of tappa-cloth bark around shapely thighs, the belles adding fringe ornaments that swished to every lithe movement. The native police glanced dubiously at the younger women, who laughed back in primitive excitement. Big-eyed children cowered back from the crowd around the patrol, and peered from the huts at these mystic strangers. The men laughingly encouraged their wild cubs to come and touch the white man. Several of the men wore handsome head-dresses of the red bird of paradise. All were garbed in a girdle of twisted cane, and never walked a yard without their bows and arrows. In the chill of evening and bitter daylight each wore a light cape of tappa-cloth bark that gave a very bizarre touch. Squatted round a fire, hunched under the bark capes, they looked like huge-beaked birds.

These villages were heavily stockaded. The houses within, arranged in two rows facing each other, had sloping roofs thatched with pandanus palm strongly laced to the ground, and dark little entrances about three feet by two.

The patrol camped one bitter night in such a village perched on a crag which overlooked a precipice. Shades of evening were fast dimming the narrow spur up which ran the one and only track. The precipice overlooked the valley with the gardens far below, now hidden under a rising mist. The gaunt poles of the stockade had been enormously strengthened by a living semicircle of fig-trees whose cable-like tendrils, years ago, had been knotted to one another. These living ropes now grew in a tangled fretwork, jamming fast the poles of the stockade. All formed a maze-like defence of intertwined roots and cables nine feet high, with the stockade poles and trees towering above. Some distance outside were the dark shadows of the bamboo clumps that concealed the initiation house. No woman was ever allowed to pry into the dark secrets of that sacred place.

The stockade entrance was defended by hidden pits and barred with great logs rolled so that even should an athletic foeman leap upon them he would be immediately silhouetted for arrow-fire. Just inside, like columnar approaches to a gate, towered a framework of giant bamboos. Thigh bones were interlaced among these, while the smell hovering over the village suggested a charnal house. Capping a chopped-off tree at each end of the village "street" was a lattice-work "dovecot" of split bamboo from which white skulls grinned down. Running through each gloomy house was a deep trench in which the cooking was done. The floor, lined with bamboo, was like two benches raised two feet above the cooking-trench. On these benches the families slept with millions of fleas.

These people quickly got over their distrust and surrounded the white officer, bringing their children to touch his skin, believing that thus the mystic power of the bom-bom would enter into them.

These people, like numerous others, earnestly invited the district officer to co-operate with them in exterminating villages near by. To which he sternly replied that, now the Government had come, all murder and head-hunting must cease. If there was any fighting to be done the Government would do it, and would also protect weaker tribes against their enemies.

This ultimatum was always received in sullen silence, with an "I told you so!" look on the face of the sorcerer.

Keenly Sergeant Bewa noted the expressions of all these people as the patrol penetrated farther into uncontrolled country, while his constabulary kept their ears and eyes alert and their rifles ever handy.

CHAPTER X

THE AMBUSH

Cautiously, as he passed on, with the aid of interpreters the district officer sought information of a bom-bom, a white man in the mountains who was looking for a gold stone. At every village he inquired, keen for their answers as he climbed farther among the peaks. But all denied any knowledge of a bom-bom. Sullenly they answered "Bush nothing!" By which they lied that there was nothing farther ahead in the bush, so he might just as well turn back.

When Levien climbed into the wild Ono his heart beat fast as he saw ironstone and diorite and quartz—gold country! He stared up at the valley sides, at the majestic grass slopes merging into the duller line of jungle which spread upwards, ever darker, to fade with the summits into mist. Silver scars, under the midday sun, were waterfalls. Where in all this tangle of mad nature could Shark-eye be?

Near Sipa Levien was very nearly at the limit of his patrol. Here he gazed up at the Sini villages like eagles' nests on needle-pointed spurs. The ragged edges were the stockade poles against the sky-line. He estimated some of those dim villages to be eight thousand feet above the precipitous Ono. He went warily here, for these people were at active war against the Repu. The vigilant Dewa reported that the antagonists were watching his every movement with the keenest suspicion. Levien stared at those schistose rocks by the tumbling river. Here prospectors had won gold even before Detzner's time. They must have been men, those fellows. How on earth did they manage for food, so far from any civilized post? What trouble they must have had, getting carriers through this hostile country. And when here, how had they managed to survive? Exciting times Detzner must have had too; isolated not only from Germany but from all other white men; alone with his little army, and all these savage tribesmen swarming down upon him.

To his intense disappointment Levien could learn nothing here of Park. And yet some of all the people he had visited must know of the man. What compelling power was it that this mysterious prospector exercised throughout all these savage valleys?

Well, the district officer would visit the Lamanai—Levien's last hope, in this district anyway. Besides, if he could only sow the seeds of peace among the Bubu tribes his official trip would not have been in vain.

Like ants scaling a peaked rock the patrol warily climbed to a Mismisi village. These people and the Saiko and Gavagutta were allies, and friendly (so they declared) with the Bubu tribes, especially the powerful Lamanai. The Saiko people in particular were enthusiastic about the Lamanai; they were not nearly so bad as they were painted. The Lamanai were really easy people to approach, too; the Saiko would willingly supply carriers. The Goluga and Manilofa villagers of the Gavagutta people growled acquiescence to the words of the Saiko.

This looked like straight ahead work for the district officer. The main Atuatak, Tiugatai, Lamanai, and Kiwutai villages of the Bubu were within easy reach—as the crow flies. He sent two Saiko warriors with messages of peace and goodwill to the Lamanai people. The messengers departed so willingly that they at once attracted Sergeant Bewa's suspicions. Craftily he eyed those messengers when, considerably later, they returned bearing an amiable invitation from the Lamanai for the patrol to proceed.

The Lamanai villages were situated four thousand feet up on the side of the valley. On its first climb the patrol was escorted by a long line of Saiko warriors, heavily armed with bow and arrow, spear and club. Levien glanced back several times at these eager warriors, but he had no especial misgiving; often village people so escorted the patrol some distance on its way.

But Sergeant Bewa had noted the number of armed carriers who had eagerly volunteered. He glanced up at the towering heights and was not surprised when many little figures appeared upon them, waving spears and dancing. Presently far above, from all sides, floated the mountain yodel with a thrumming of drums. Bewa knew that every village on peak and cliff around was being kept fully informed of the number, direction, and progress of the patrol—and of those armed men coming up behind.

It was a tough climb, "cat-walking" along a narrow, ascending ledge that clung to the bare cliff face: on one side a plunge of thousands of feet for the unfortunate who should slip. Then instinctively the patrol halted— a tambu was hanging out across the track. Levien stepped forward, reached up and broke it down, then sent the branch of ill omen spinning far below. He hid his uneasiness under the sharp command, "March!" Unhesitatingly, Corporal Boassi stepped forward; the patrol followed.

When the path left the cliffs and joined the valley edge proper it twisted and turned and corkscrewed until often the men above were climbing back over those toiling below. Then the track joined a steep spur and snaked dizzily up to what appeared a flat summit. A nasty place in which to be attacked, thought Levien. He was glad that the Saiko had explained his visit to their friends the Lamanai.

As the patrol climbed higher, Levien saw many tribesmen in battle array outside their stockades. Occasionally, from village to village floated a burst of kanaka war-song, deep-throated, with a hoarse, nasty menace. Uneasily he looked back. Coming from below like a winding brown snake were those Saiko warriors.

Levien called to the sergeant to order the Saiko men to lag back until the patrol had entered the village above. The sergeant promptly obeyed; but later, as the head of the patrol wound up out of sight he looked down and there, wherever the track was visible, were the Saiko men quickly following. The sergeant felt the patrol was going to be attacked. His beloved officer was in danger. Bewa was now almost certain that these Saiko were no friends of the Lamanai. If so, well, when the trouble started, so much the better for the patrol.

On top of the spur a halt was called to allow the patrol and carriers to climb up and get their breath. The spur top was long but broad, with a patch of stunted scrub entwined with long grass spreading across the centre of it. Over those low trees, the track could be seen narrowing again as it climbed straight to a village, evidently of great strength, with a double stockade. The logs at the stockade entrance had been rolled aside, which was a jolly good sign anyway. A crowd of Lamanai men stood there, gazing down. From stockaded villages plainly visible on crags around, big groups of Bubu were now silently watching. Even the drums were still.

Levien gave the order and took the lead. The patrol moved cautiously forward, the police nervously gripping their rifles and scowling at these carriers so unusually eager to push on. Levien decided that as soon as they got through this scrub he would advance on the last climb with the patrol alone, until all doubt of the Lamanai being friendly was at an end.

Sergeant Bewa, bringing up the rear, noted the eager movement of the carriers' weapons, the shifting of their loads, ready to be thrown off at a second's notice. He glanced behind, but the crown of the spur hid the Saiko men from view.

Levien entered the scrub with Corporal Boassi at his heels. Sergeant Bewa hissed an order and, striding forward, hurried up the patrol until each man's toes were on the heels of the one ahead. As the sergeant entered the scrub the heads of the Saiko warriors were bobbing up over the spur.

With a roar the terrible kanaka war-cry burst out to the rumble of feet and answering roars from crags around. A mad Saiko war-cry surged up from the rear. Levien staggered back with an arrow in his chest, shouting as the corporal's rifle cracked:

"Fire! Patrol, fire!"

He whipped out his revolver as the sergeant rushed the police straight up with the carriers who, throwing their loads, pressed forward, howling the Saiko war-cry as yellow painted Lamanai burst upon them from all sides. To thrusting of spears, rapid rifle-shots, whizz of arrows, both crowds joined in a mad struggle among the swishing branches. The roar of Sergeant Bewa rose above all, as, standing over Levien, he shouted the police back to back.

Levien tore the arrow from his chest as the sergeant pulled him to his feet, his ears ringing with the howls of the Saiko and Lamanai. The Saiko rush saved the police; several were down with arrows in their bodies, but were firing as they crouched or lay. The sergeant took command. Levien was rather badly hurt but, reloading his revolver, he stood fighting back to back with the sergeant until the Lamanai were entirely engaged by the Saiko who, to Levien's intense relief, were suddenly reinforced by Mismisi and Gavagutta warriors.

The police fought their way back, bringing their wounded and the wounded carriers. Splendidly did Sergeant Bewa fight that rear-guard action back to the lip of the spur. It was impossible to stop the fight raging behind, nor did the sergeant make the slightest attempt to do so. He seized the chance to get the stricken patrol back down that narrow spur to where there would be plenty of Saiko help in the valley below.

All had been well organized, from the Saiko point of view. They, the Mismisi, and the Gavagutta people were really deadly enemies of the Lamanai, and had seized this chance to even up old scores. They had planned on buying a fight for the patrol against the Lamanai and then rushing in themselves, side by side with these innocent allies. That it almost cost Levien his life was a matter of no moment to them.

When eventually the patrol struggled back to Morobe great news was awaiting Levien. Eagerly the police boys there told him. Kanakas had told them of the white man Nettleton disappearing with the strange man from the mountains.

Levien knew he had his man—and a goldfield. Shark-eye could disappear alone; but Nettleton with carriers? Impossible.

Lying in that big bed, with a nasty hole in his chest, Levien vowed that he would track Shark-eye from village to village, from razor-back to razor-back, mountain to mountain; climb above the clouds if necessary. With an irritable impatience he waited for his wound to heal, attending to his official duties as best he could meanwhile. At last, in wild delight, he marshalled his patrol again and set out to find Shark-eye.

And he did.

"Where is Shark-eye Bill?" they were asking again across in Papua. The fields there were producing very little gold and the remnant of prospectors were now hopefully discussing the mining-ordinance, which allowed prospecting in that new country, the Mandated Territory. So they were remembering with redoubled interest those old tales of Shark-eye Park. Later, with increasing curiosity, they asked:

"Where is Jack Nettleton?"

And they thought their own answers.

Wherever men talked gold in Papua the greetings invariably were:

"Hullo, old mate! How's things?"

"Not bad. How's yourself?"

"Not too bad. Heard anything of Shark-eye Bill?"

"Not a word. He's away out in his old haunts for certain. A thousand to one he's getting gold, or he'd be 'back in' long ago."

"That's what I was thinking. If it's true he's killed and eaten, then where has Jack Nettleton disappeared?"

"Dunno. He was down on the coast towards Morobe, and Shark-eye is supposed to be somewhere away back of Morobe!"

"H'm! How do they get their stores? Rabaul is five hundred sea miles from Morobe. No one's heard of any stores being shipped from Rabaul for Shark-eye."

"No. But I'll bet stores are going through now. Nettleton is not a jungle-man."

"Looks as if Shark-eye and Nettleton are on a big thing; stacking up the gold and keeping it quiet."

"Looks like it. Shark-eye always was a 'silent' prospector. No wonder the Germans picked on him. He might have been a bit too silent for them."

"What is it about him that bluffs the kanakas?"

"Oh, some tambaran stuff or other. Seems to mesmerize them. The sorcerers reckon he is the reincarnated spirit of some old-time sorcerer who was familiar with all sorts of devils. They're windy of him right enough."

"Well, Nettleton is no sorcerer anyway. If he's really gone in with Shark-eye we must hear of stores drifting in there sometime, somehow or other."

"I wish we'd hear soon. There's tons of gold in Papua, but there's all Papua mixed with it!"

Thus the talk in the Papuan mining-fields, and in its two little coastal towns, Port Moresby and Samarai.

Port Moresby is the picturesque little capital on the south-western coast. It is a healthy dry place of white bungalows built on small hills that run down to the sea. It has its port for shipping, its electric light, telephone service, picture show, and four hundred white people. The prospectors from the inland come to town occasionally to recuperate, buy stores for another trip, and find out "what's doing" in the island mining-world.

Samarai is the other little town, on Samarai Island at the south-eastern point of the Papuan peninsula adjoining the necklace of little islands that runs out to sea to the northernmost point of the Great Barrier Reef. Samarai has its wireless and electricity, its hospitals, its up-to-date hotels, and cheerful shops; and with its tall palms down the main street, its vivid and tropic shrubs, it has beauty too. A pretty track sentinelled by palms calls one to walk round the island. This bright gem of the Pacific can be encircled in twenty minutes. About a hundred and twenty white people make it more or less permanently their home. Samarai is the port for the east coast of Papua, and a rendezvous for the mining men who periodically disappear into the big grim mainland only a few miles across the water.

But it was in the historic coffee-room of Port Moresby that a crowd of miners on a certain day were having dinner—men from the Yodda and Lakekamu, the Mambare and Ikori. Of course the talk was of gold—and of Shark-eye Park.

"The coons must have got him!" declared a man from Cloudy Bay. "Even he could not stay out so long."

"Nettleton!" said another. "Where is he? Have they gone in mates?"

"What's the strength of this mining engineer Barton going over to the Waria?"

"Dunno rightly. He's sailing from Rabaul by schooner. It's those Kaempf leases, pegged out in the German time. But Shark-eye's somewhere away inland where the gold is thicker than on the Waria."

"If the Barton crowd find anything we'll know anyway. The mouth of the Waria is right near Morobe station, and that district officer is a wide-awake chap."

A woolly-headed serving boy on big brown feet came into the room, proudly bearing a steaming bowl of soup.

"You dirty pig!" growled a miner. "Take your thumb out of it!"

"'E alright!" protested the boy, "'e no hot!"

"What do you think of it Joe?" asked a man from the Keveri. "Where's Shark-eye?"

"In the Mandated Territory."

"Getting gold?"

1. Gold from the Day Dawn Mine.
2. Wally Digby with gold for shipment.
3. Staff of Day Dawn Mine.

"Ask him!" smiled Joe.

Joe is noted for that smile; and now men hung on his answer. For he is "Lucky Joe Sloane," a lanky six-foot North Queensland bushman. They say he can "smell gold." During his thirty-five years in Papua he has always been one of the very first men on every new field. He has an uncanny instinct for realizing when some far-distant prospector is "on gold." And from somewhere in the Mandated Territory gold had been calling Joe for some time. That was why he was in Port Moresby now, on the way to Samarai. But he did not say so: secretiveness is a Papuan trait.

It was Joe who found the osmiridium on the Gira, was it not? A nice little patch that; but requiring imagination and grit to go in and get it and return!

Joe has stopped an arrow or two, has leapt around to see his mate tomahawked behind him; but came through it all smiling, winning and spending a string of little fortunes in order finally to land a big one. It's a great life—when a man is born lucky.

Thoughtfully the crowd proceeded with their dinner, with a smile now and then at a man who growled, "He's a billygoat butcher, that's all *he* is!" referring to the butcher, and that worthy was very wroth. What if the "mutton" chops *were* for the "big" room, *he* couldn't help it. And if the mutton *was* goat, well, it was the "big room" people who were paying for it anyway.

A Papuan stalked in from the kitchen bearing a tray of mutton chops. As he passed by, *en route* to the big room, a man reached for the tray but missed, and a chop fell to the floor. In a moment the Papuan reached out his leg and retrieved the chop with his big toe. Replacing it on the tray he glanced haughtily at the assembled diners; then, holding the tray out of reach, stalked into the big room.

Again the talk drifted to gold in the ex-German territory, with men wondering "Is Joe going?"

If so, what then? A wild-goose chase, probably, in a country without stores, full of unexplored mountains and probably hostile natives. Only two rumours to go upon: that the Germans had found gold somewhere inland; and that Shark-eye was somewhere in there now—in uncontrolled territory.

When officialdom puts "Uncontrolled Territory" across the map it means "Keep out. We will keep you out if possible. If you enter unauthorized, and are killed, then attend to your own funeral."

That afternoon as the men adjourned to the bar for a drink an old resident came hobbling along for a yarn and sympathy. An old-time official, his legs looked pretty shaky.

"What's wrong with your pins?" they inquired sympathetically.

"I dunno," he growled irritably, "the doctors call it rheumatic arthritis, whatever the blazes that is. They're treating me for it, but I don't know whether the treatment is doing me any good or not."

"Why don't you ask them?"

"I did. 'How the blazes do *we* know,' they snapped. 'You're the first we've tried it on!'"

Joe laughed. "Have a drink?" he invited.

"Well, the doctors told me not to drink whisky. But I'll have a rum."

Stores for the Goldfields, Salamaua, in the early days.

CHAPTER XI

THE FINDING OF SHARK-EYE PARK

Joe Sloane did disappear; but all saw him go. He sailed from Samarai in the launch *Shamrock* bound for the Mambare with Jack Nelson. (Later Jack was blown up by dynamite, and recently the craft went sky-high when a native lit a cigarette while pouring benzine into the tank.)

The several-hundred-mile trip up that Papuan north-eastern coast is an experience to be remembered. Majestic heights inland, the coast densely wooded to the water's edge and dotted with palm plantations that give a checkered impression of civilization and savagery. Towards Cape Nelson the bold headlands and deep fiords suggest memories of the Vikings. Villages on stilts are visible here and there. Islands dreaming in a blue sea make you long to step ashore and explore. An outrigger canoe with grotesque "crab-claw" sail skims along before the wind, and on the canoe platform are the Papuan and his family, his fowls, dog, bananas, and beloved pig.

But Joe was not admiring the scenery; it was part of his world. He was trying to "fix" Shark-eye's locality in his mind while wondering if carriers would be available when he arrived at Morobe.

When the launch entered Mambare Bay, Joe unloaded his stores, recruited a few boys, hired a native canoe, loaded up, set sail, and—went bush.

It was a quaint craft, a serviceable burnt-out outrigger, scudding along under a leg-o'-mutton sail of plaited coconut matting, steered by a fuzzy-headed savage manipulating a paddle. The crew were a mixed lot of cheerful copper-skins, of good physique and gigantic appetite. Two well-dressed fellows among them wore a lap-lap, but the proletariat were content with just a *cuppertree*, otherwise a pandanus leaf. However, they knew how to handle a boat. Joe kept them cheery; he has that gift with the natives. His smile, when he wanted it to, would make a cat laugh.

The Mambare River is quite close to the ex-German border, and from there it is only a fifty-mile run to Morobe; in good weather, a pleasure cruise.

The half-dozen little white buildings, against a sombre background of mountains, shone brightly upon a point running out to sea. Joe landed, to find that District Officer Levien, was absent on patrol to Lae village, eighty miles farther along the Huon Gulf. Lukin the magistrate,

Macdonald the clerk, Morris the medical assistant, and several patrol officers usually away on patrol inland, constituted the complete force of Australians administering that huge area of untamed savagery.

Sloane learned what he could, then shipped with his dusky crew to Salamaua, some sixty miles farther along the Gulf. Here on a sandspit with wind-blown palms, the only sign of white man was the palm-thatched "house-kiap."

Joe landed his stores on what was to become the famous "beach" where so many golden hopes were born. But now all that a visitor would note were the house-kiap, the wind among the palms, a large native village on the shore-side, and the mouth of the Frisco River farther along.

The stores were stacked up on the beach while Joe donned his recruiting smile and strolled across to the village. He made friends with the luluai and *tul-tul*, the two most important personages in any Controlled Territory village. The luluai is the hereditary chief; the tul-tul a chief appointed by some passing government officer. These gentlemen wear the air of a blasé lord — occasionally nothing else.

Things went well and Joe had a crowd of carriers around him in a few days. One morning he awoke to the sighing of the palms — and silence. The carriers had vanished. The village sat in sulky silence.

So Joe smiled in the old Papuan way; left his stores in charge of half of his Mambare boys; then, with the others well armed and carrying a little food, set his face to Mountain Land. For five weeks he trudged up and down one razor-back after another, following village paths, combing village after village. He was coldly received. The villagers simply did not want to carry heavy loads up mountains. Why should they? But he kept on until he found people to whom the lure of bright steel tomahawks proved irresistible. Then he got his carriers.

Joe loaded up on the beach and with his long string of amateurs set off into the mountains. He was in great spirits. His shrewd grey eyes twinkled as he followed behind his singing boys. He was on a scent he loved. The villagers ahead had told him that two white men were up in the mountains somewhere; their carriers actually came this way to the coast for food! The party toiled on, following the trail, camping at village after village where the mysterious white men's carriers had camped. Joe smiled at the beat of the drums thrumming his coming far and wide. Gold! He *knew* he was going to get gold. He had followed the trail too often to be mistaken, the Rainbow Trail which had so often lured him right on to the yellow sands.

Near Lambura village he stopped in startled surprise, while a lively little Englishman, clad in a growth of whiskers and rough bush clothes, stood staring wonderingly at him.

"Ernie Dover!"

"Lucky Joe Sloane! You'd smell gold if it was up in the mountains of the moon!"

A bamboo flute ceased its wailing. The carriers threw down their loads, glancing half-scornfully, half-fearfully at those shaggy mountain men squatting so silently and eyeing them within Lambura village. And Yabbi, the luluai, brave old savage with the cruel smile, watched them craftily.

A grim village was Lambura; a noted "fighting" village for centuries past. Its low, thatched houses were built enormously strong. They needed to be, when furious attackers tried to pull them to pieces in order to drag out the defenders within. Bones lay about the village, a skull here and there adorned a post. Men and women have been eaten in Lambura. One of those very carriers now grinning in contemptuous fear was to be eaten there.

"Gold! Of course there's gold," said Dover with a laugh. "They're digging it out by the bucketful. Heaven knows what Shark-eye has got; he must have been in there alone for years."

Joe's smile spread from ear to ear.

"I suppose you'll be on it soon," prophesied Dover ruefully. "My wretched luck followed me. Gold all around me and I couldn't strike it. But I'll strike it at last!" And the fires of desire laughed from his eyes. "I didn't have the stores to hang out anyway. Shark-eye gave me a job—he's got the stores. I'm taking a message for him now down to the coast. He gave me fifty ounces, and I'm sending it away for a supply of stores."

Joe pushed on across the Bulolo. He came out on to Koranga Creek, and met Nettleton there, standing by his sluice-box with the boys throwing out the stones. As Joe strode up his eyes automatically glanced at the ripples in the box. What he saw widened his smile.

"You got the news!" said Nettleton as the carrier came filing out of the big timber.

"No," replied Joe with a smile, "I guessed."

"Are others coming?"

"Not a soul knows where I've gone."

"I wonder how long before the others guess too?" mused Nettleton.

Lying by the box was a dish, its bottom gleaming with gold. Joe glanced across at the camp. He could just see into a few meat-tins—they were filled with gold.

"They say gold talks!" drawled Joe.

"Well, they ought to hear a shout in Papua."

Joe tried the creek above the workings of Park and Nettleton. He got gold in the very first dish; he was on payable gold the very first day.

His carriers, paid off, returned to their villages. Joe hurried down to the coast and took canoe to the Markham, then trudged inland, recruiting for a labour team. He brought twelve skinny, bushy-looking boys back to the beach, where they "made paper" — signed on for two years' service. It took six months' training before they were much good; but during that time Joe was making on some days from twenty to thirty ounces per day. Koranga gold is worth approximately £2 16s. per ounce; the low price being due to excess of silver.

Down at Morobe, District Officer Levien was busy leaving the station in apple-pie order for his successor. Levien's chance had come. It is a wonderful feeling when a man sees a chance to put a country on the map. Levien would have rushed straight to the field had not his coldly reasoning mind told him he was going to be ill. He decided to hurry to civilization; be "overhauled" by expert doctors; then return reinvigorated for the task ahead.

Mining-engineer Barton, returning unimpressed by his investigation of the Waria River areas, called in at Morobe. Levien told him of Park and Nettleton, and of his belief that a Company could successfully venture where as yet a rush of men might be disastrous. Barton sailed for Melbourne, and eventually returned to Morobe to travel up into the mountains for a new Melbourne syndicate.

So Levien's hope of getting the field quickly recognized, though without danger to individual adventurers, was disappointed. He sailed for Rabaul and tendered his resignation, which was unwillingly accepted. Then he sailed for Australia.

Meanwhile the field was kept quiet for a further seven months or so. Shark-eye, Nettleton, and Sloane set teams of kanakas to work, box-sluicing the golden earth. As soon as a meat-tin became empty it was filled with gold. Gold was lying everywhere about the camps; tins of it; bags of it, then boxes of it; shovelfuls of pure gold could be dug out of those boxes. Digging out a fortune of pure yellow gold in that way is madly fascinating. So very few ever do it. The lure of trying to do it has led thousands to despair and many to death.

Levien, after his recovery, lost no time in learning the city side of mining and picking up all the information he could about mining-plants and syndicate expeditions.

Before leaving Melbourne for New Guinea this time, he dug up a war-time friend, C. V. T. Wells, and made him his attorney. Then, with definite plans laid for the future, he returned to New Guinea in 1923 and took out the first miner's right ever issued for the Morobe district. He was taking no chances. He knew the mining game and the laws that govern it.

Upper Waria men, Bubu River 1923.

CHAPTER XII

BATTLING THROUGH TO A NEW LIFE

Levien climbed that eight-day mountain trail, feeling like a man granted a fresh lease of life for the new career beckoning ahead. He was burningly eager to do things, big things, and he sensed the chances all around. Cheerily he heartened the carriers as they toiled up those terrible tracks, but never hurried them; he was too "New Guinea wise" to do that. These were all selected men, loaded with stores and tools; they carried all his fortune on their backs. Koranga Creek was his bank and he must reach it with every pound of rice intact. As many of these men as he could persuade he had engaged to sign on as a labour team. When they reached journey's end he camped near Park and Nettleton; then quickly, but with care, prospected the unoccupied ground near by and selected his claim. If he made a false step now he might never make his fortune, let alone hurry on to much bigger things.

And he needed money quickly. The first £1000 would be the hardest to get. After that, the thousands could look after themselves.

He made no mistake; and he was lucky, too, for there was *rich* ground left and he pegged the last of it. Abundance of poorer ground remained for those who inevitably would begin to drift in soon. He wished newcomers would find another and larger field. If so, his dreams would be assured.

While his labour-gang were busy clearing the creek of boulders he felled a cedar-tree, and the first swings of that axe made a sawmill. For he thought of whizzing saws as he felled it; every blow of the axe spelt time, money, energy; and he had so little time to do things. What time and labour would be saved if only a sawmill were here! A mill would surely pay.

From the tree-trunk he split rough slabs in quick, practical fashion, teaching several boys how to use the axe so that for the future this labour would be saved him. He was making a sluice-box. From this rough beginning his fortune would start. He chopped those slabs into boards, boards that would run with gold. Each board was about a foot wide and ten feet long. Two boards made the bottom of the box, one each the sides, while the "head" was a short board. For ripples (the bars which catch and hold the golden grains), he made flat basket-work of lawyer-cane, which fitted snugly down upon the bottom boards. His boys carried the box to the claim. He set it in the ground at a gentle slope, then diverted a stream of water over and into the head of the box. While some boys were digging the washdirt from the creek, others shovelled it into the box, where the running water sluiced it down in a muddy stream over the basket-work ripples and, splashing out of the "tail" of the box, carried the dirt away. Heavy gravels remained, particularly at the box-head, and pellets of gold if any; the finer gold was caught in the ripples. As boys shovelled in the dirt, so others flung out the stones with their hands. The days of the sluice-fork had not yet arrived.

It was a simple process, but surprisingly efficient. It was Nature's way too. In just that way, using the creek as a box, she had washed the gold down from the higher mountains and concentrated it among these creek stones that acted as ripples. But Nature had taken aeons of time to collect and concentrate her gold. Man, by using his brains, would take that gold from her in much less than the lifetime of one man.

To the primitive men now doing the labour work, it seemed a wonderful task, a process above their reasoning. But why these strange white men went to all that trouble over a yellow stone was quite incomprehensible. They laughed at these men for fools.

On the first morning that Levien set his box, as he supervised, explained, and toiled, he cast eyes now and again at the muddy water gurgling over the ripples. Would the clean up show gold? How much? He knew the ground was good by his dish prospects; it *must* pay well in actual work. But he was excited. At *kai-kai* (food) time he stopped the boys working and dumped a rock in front of the box-head. The water soon cleared; then, as the lessened flow carried the remaining sands away he stared into the box and then sprang erect in laughing delight, for yellow gold gleamed at him from the head of the box while many yellow specks were caught among the ripples lower down.

With shaking hands he helped the water as it carried away nearly the last of the gravels, then turned the water off, lifted up the ripples, turned them upside down in the box and threw water over them, poking loose the yellow specks that here and there had wedged in the basket-work. Laying the cleaned framework aside he placed the dish at the tail of the box and ran the water through it, thus washing the concentrated sands and gold down out of the box into the dish. He dished the concentrates, thus freeing them of sands; and then, too excited to dry it, weighed the gold wet.

Fifteen ounces! Koranga gold was only worth £2 16s. per ounce, worse luck; but that represented £42 for a morning's work.

Smilingly he strode to camp and issued an extra tin of meat to each boy. It was a frightful extravagance, for that meat had been carried there under harassing labour conditions. But, hang it all, a man must christen his claim. Never had he enjoyed a meal as he did the one that followed. That night he wrote a long letter to his friend in Melbourne.

Presently, at Rabaul, news leaked out that gold in quantity had been "going through" post and shipping office for quite a time. From Rabaul the definite news spread across to Papua. There, an occasional man of the more adventurous sort dropped his tools and started off on the long trail, seeking Joe Sloane.

Levien worked with a methodical haste that, under the circumstances, would gain him the quickest results. Though dead tired in the evenings, he generally strolled over to have a chat at Shark-eye's camp. Nettleton and Sloane and Dover would be there. The kanaka labourers, outside their quarters, spent the evenings telling of tribal feuds, of the ambush and chaos, of love as they understand it, and occasionally, in whispers, of sorcerers.

The talk in Shark-eye's hut was nearly all of gold and gold-hunters. A fortune was lying there in loose gold; the fire played on the yellow-red stuff gleaming in tins and boxes. There were a couple of thousand pounds' worth in an old pair of trousers. The leg ends had been tied and the gold poured down into the "bags." What an advertisement those toil-stained, patched old trousers would have been in a tailor's shop!

The men would talk of "boys," too; of staunch fellows who stick by the white man through thick and thin; of fights with wild tribesmen, and the thrill when the war-song roared upon the air. Three of those men had felt the bite of an arrow. Occasionally they would speak of Sydney, and Brisbane, Melbourne, and Adelaide. But those places were in another world.

Physically, Levien worked harder than any dozen of his boys. Again and again he almost hurled himself down that terrible track to the coast when his own going would speed up the work of his plans. The *Marsina*, sailing from Rabaul, used to land the stores and tools at Finschhafen mission station, some miles along the coast. From there, a small mission vessel generally carried them along to Salamaua beach, where one of the white men would be waiting. He would load the carriers and escort them up the mountains. Besides the sometimes month-long wait on the beach, it meant a three weeks' trip. Once, the vessel was six months overdue, and when it did arrive their ton of rice was rotten.

Levien set his axe boys to make another box; he was eager to lay hands on that first £1000. With two boxes working simultaneously he should clear £50 per day. Not quite! It required a team of ten labour boys to work one box, and twenty carriers to feed that team. Thirty men to keep one box continually working! Phenomenal expense.

Leaving the box boys in charge of a boss boy he hurried down to the coast and took canoe to the Markham River, recruiting. Travelling almost night and day he returned with another complete team and started his second box.

The physical work, the responsibility, and the ceaseless thought that planned everything (as well as the expense) were terrific. But Levien was in the seventh heaven of delight when he saw the sparkling gold in the second box. That was the box which made the difference. Its added production soon made the first £1000 — but not clear. An awful lot of it went in stores as payment to the as yet inefficient labour of his new recruits. He noted a likely area of flat jungle; he would clear that soon and plant gardens. Native foods would help feed the teams and partly solve the time and transport problem. Shark-eye had realized that long ago; but time to Levien was too precious. No matter how high the cost of food there was more than enough gold here to pay for it. So he slaved to dig out his capital before "the rush" came.

Levien spared no expense in feeding his boys, knowing that the well-fed horse is the willing horse. And he saw that they were well housed; he attended personally to their sicknesses, and judged fairly in their disputes and troubles among themselves when he was called upon to adjudicate.

Shark-eye, Nettleton, and Sloane took things much easier; but only as their outlook differed from Levien's. Shark-eye had found the field. Right! Let other men develop it. Nettleton and Sloane wanted their fortunes. Right! They worked all the boys they could and had already secured those willing from the nearby tribes. These they supervised, each team under a boss boy. For the rest they were content to let the future take care of itself. They did comparatively no physical work themselves; there was no need; nor is it "New Guinea fashion." The gold was rolling in, had been rolling in for a long time now, and they were content. Their one anxiety was sickness. Park and Nettleton, especially, had undergone prolonged hardship; and living where they were, and under such conditions, illness was a menace.

Their deep delight was to see their tins and bags filling up with gold. That strange metal carries a delight of its own far above what it will buy. These men felt, too, the need to win their fortunes and get clear away before the country got them. Many a man in New Guinea has stayed too long.

"It creeps into your bones!" remarked Joe Sloane one sultry night.

"And your bones stay here!" answered Shark-eye slowly.

Nettleton moved uneasily.

"May as well be here as anywhere else!" said Levien dreamily.

A fire-fly glowed past the hut door, and vanished

A little later and the boys began to straggle in: Fred Smart, Travers Black, Peter Burke, Bill Anderson; then Herb Wilson and Jack Livingstone; then Burleigh Gorman, Wilton, and several others—just a dozen or so of them.

The invasion stopped at that for some time. These were the real adventurers, the men who will travel anywhere, at any odds, at the first whisper of gold. The tiny outposts of distant civilization waited, not taking rumours too seriously. They awaited news of some big find, something definite, that less experienced men might rush to. Australia did not know of this gold at all, except for an attuned wanderer here and there, and Levien's close friends who received news every few months by mail.

Levien wanted a group of city men to be ready to act immediately, with finance, organization, and technical skill, should the dream which was rapidly taking practical form in his mind warrant it.

New-comers at Levien's camp were heartily welcome. He recognized these as the vanguard of what he hoped would be many hundreds. It would crown his hopes and plans if one of these men or anyone else found a new and larger field. Although these men did not know it—never dreamt it—they were actually working for Levien, toilers for his thoughts. When they arrived, they enjoyed a spell and a look around for a day or two, then scattered, prospecting adjacent creeks; thus spreading in twos over twelve miles of country. Shrewdly Levien watched results; eagerly he listened. For the local country was now a map in his mind; the rivers, the creeks, the larger flats in the valleys, and the terraces—all these, in a considerable area, he had explored. When a new-comer located gold in a creek, no matter if unpayable to his pick and shovel, it was instantly on the map in Levien's mind. It meant another "gold creek" to prove the theory on which he was basing his dream. So, every new-comer unwittingly worked for him, proving or disproving country probably miles away.

This country would be modernized quickly, not by the individual richness of a few claims, but by returns from huge areas of comparatively poor ground which he believed existed far down in the valley flats.

When he had his camp established, his boss boys trained, his labour teams efficiently working, his carriers coming and going methodically, Levien extended his explorations. He walked many miles in quick, restless strides over the surrounding country, recording its geographical features on his mental map. Through jungle and bush, through forest and scrub and kunai grass he pushed and cut and climbed his way until the features of the country within a twenty-mile radius of Koranga Creek were indelibly mapped on his mind. One day he stood by his camp, summing it all up.

Where Levien stood was three thousand feet above sea-level. Behind the camp towered Kaindi Range, mists on its shoulders, and its peaks in the clouds. It must rise in parts to nine thousand feet. Down that range fell tumultuous creeks, to broaden and flow more evenly around him. Koranga, apparently, was on a great irregular ledge jutting from Kaindi Range. He glanced across at the Wau plateau, bright green under many acres of kunai grass, like a green field three parts enclosed by jungle trees. He stared at where that grass slope shelved, apparently, into the sky. Would it be suitable? Could aeroplanes land there? Would that Wau ever be a mountain aerodrome?

His thoughts were flying fast!

Levien turned again to the creeks that, from ravines which like twitching fingers clutched far and deep across the face of Kaindi, came tumbling down into the Bulolo and Watut. Wau Creek, Koranga, Namie, Lower Edie, all flowed into the Upper Bulolo which sped along its bouldery bed to plunge into the Bulolo Gorge.

He knew now that all those creeks carried gold.(the new-comers had prospected them) —had been a channel for golden sands these ages past. And all came from Kaindi Range. He held his breath, gazing up towards the giant brooding in its mists. He had a queer feeling that his fate was wrapped up in that old mountain.

What if the main gold had come down from there! What if a richer goldfield were far up in the mists! If one were discovered, Levien's plans would be ready for action.

He walked down Koranga Creek to where it flowed into the Bulolo, and pondered a long time over those travelling waters. Each drop as it hurried past had come from Kaindi. Companion drops had stayed by the way, been caught and absorbed by the creek bottom and banks. Each uncaught drop would still hurry along; some drops would be caught and held by the river-bottom and banks, but most would hurry on until they tumbled into the Bulolo Gorge.

So had the gold come from Kaindi! Many of the grains, especially the heavier ones, had been caught and held by the creek-beds and terrace sides. But in the course of ages countless lesser grains and dust must have come down swirling into the Bulolo and been swept down the river and over into the gorge. In that longer and easier flowing river below, those fine grains and that dust would settle on the miles of terraces that lined its banks.

That was it: a huge dredging proposition!

Up here on the field, and higher still, perhaps, individual miners could work content. Theirs would be the pick-and-shovel ground, the ground that would pay to work with a miner's tools; while miles below, along the Bulolo, giant machines would churn out gold from ground far too poor for the miner's pick to work.

With his mind revitalized, Levien hurried back to his sluice-boxes. Urgently he would need funds to start capital working if his unknowing workers proved that gold was up there on Kaindi.

The gold values, miles away in the Lower Bulolo, existed, as yet, only in Levien's imagination. He didn't know if those big alluvial terraces contained gold, much less did he know whether gold existed up on Kaindi. Only time, and the results gained by men over a wide space of country, seeking gold for themselves, would prove that.

Meanwhile he slaved at his ground, accumulating the thousands necessary to put his giant-machine schemes into operation should events justify them.

But there came a great worry: "How could his dream machines be carried over the mountains?"

CHAPTER XIII

WHILE THE CARRIER SLEEPS

Jack Nettleton was satisfied. He had made enough thousands to keep him in comfort for the rest of his life. Now he was ill he decided to quit while he could. Shark-eye bought his ground. Nettleton went around all the camps and said a quiet farewell; then he walked out.

Despite sickness it was a happy walk. He hardly noticed its roughness, knowing that each day brought him nearer the coast. His carriers were lightly loaded—with his gold!

It was a lovely day when he walked on to the beach and gazed over the blue waters of the Huon Gulf. How sweet the sea smelt! Jack Nettleton was going home. A little place in England: he would call it "Nettle Park."

But he would always remember Shark-eye. At little Madang, and later at Rabaul, he quietly remembered old friends. Then he sailed for home.

There were hardly more than a dozen men, in addition to the originals, up on the Wau at that time (July 1924). They found it a desperate struggle to hang on. They were scattered over the mountain top, along Koranga and Namie creeks, the Watut and Bulolo rivers. Gold was in all those places. It would have been payable under ordinary transport considerations, but not under the present. The rich gold so far found was on Koranga Creek, and the richest of this was naturally taken up by Park, Sloane, and Levien. The last was now watching a team of carriers as they plodded down an open forest slope opposite. He had been watching their bobbing heads for an hour. During that time they had travelled a distance he could easily have walked in twenty minutes. True, each man carried a pack which originally weighed fifty pounds. But each man had now eaten fifteen pounds of the contents.

When they reached the mountain foot they slung off their packs and enjoyed half an hour's spell; their voices came up to Levien in ribald jokes. A spell was pleasant, and they had one at every available excuse. They had lazed along now for ten days.

It was late indeed when they came dawdling up the last grassy slope. The boss boy carried a rifle, but no pack. Levien stepped just within the jungle edge. The carriers loafed by. The last man stopped by the jungle edge, loath to leave the forest grass. He threw down his pack with a grunt, squatted beside it, lay back and used it as a pillow.

Levien stood there among the lianas, thinking. This was a carrier, the sole means of transport for the field. If this transport failed them the men up there must starve or walk out.

This man sleeping before him had cost his master £25 in a recruiter's fee. Added to that came government dues and the man's own few shillings per week, and probably £2 per week to keep him, even before he had carried a single pack. On top of that, the miner had to sign papers and be responsible, under a heavy fine, for this man's health and well-being; had to care for him; doctor him; had to look after him as he might a prize stallion. In return, the earner did—what?

Loaded up with a fifty-pound pack of rice, bought by the white miner at an exorbitant price, the carrier would eat fifteen pounds of it before he got to the field; and would throw a precious ten pounds of it away to lighten his load if the boss boy were not vigilant. He would arrive on the field carrying about thirty-five pounds of rice. The white miner would have to spell him there a week, still feeding him, then send him back to the coast for another load, feeding him on the way. The rice out of that pack which the miner would have for his own use and to distribute among the boys working his claim might be twenty pounds—if he was lucky.

And here was this sample fast asleep, night coming on, and in head-hunters' country too. Besides being an unreliable and expensive proposition, he was going out of his way to be a total loss.

Levien stepped from the lianas and landed the sleeping man a kick in the ribs. He leapt up screaming, with arms outflung to ward off spear-thrusts as he fled. He stopped, trembling, as Levien shouted; then returned, seized his pack and ran on into the jungle track.

Levien slowly followed. Even a rich goldfield, no matter how rich, could not live after the first cream of its gold was gone, under such conditions. It must be abandoned; go back to the jungle. Here was a mighty transport problem. How to solve it? Roads? Out of the question. Up and along and over those tiers of razor-back mountains, a road would be a task for giants of labour, and capital, and time. The mountains would probably beat all. Great landslides might come crashing down and sweep the road away.

Transportation must be by the air, if the field was to live. That would mean aerial problems of heavy-weight lifting, clouds, air-currents, heights, and several queries new to the aviation world.

It was very late when Levien reached camp. He thought far into the night. He found thinking the hardest work of all. His first thoughts came just like a lazy string of slow, rebellious carriers.

Down at Salamaua beach, time brought Bill Royal from his boat-slip in Rabaul, anxious to try his luck at this new gold find. Schooner-Captain Bill Stower was with him. Another man who soon followed was Dick Glasson, Royal's mate.

When they landed at Salamaua, a white woman smilingly welcomed them. She was Mrs Doris Booth. A lonely spot for a white woman to be.

A terrible track lay ahead, one which was to prove the last track for a few men later on.

There were half a dozen men on the beach; dour Herb Wilson (old Papuan pioneer), Dave James, George Arnold, Peter Burke, Fred Smart, and Young Collins. Collins was cheerily building a little sago-palm store-depot that Captain Will Money had decided to erect. Money had just sailed away in the tiny *Manam* little dreaming that that palm-thatched store-shed would soon be the centre of a prosperous Salamaua with its stores, its modern hotel, its refrigerators, its electricity, its *Marsina* and *Melusia*.

An eager little crowd were these, held in enforced waiting by the imperturbable brown man. For the kanakas were unwilling to carry, and without carriers the white men were helpless in Kanakaland.

Fate must have been smiling down at those half-dozen men on the beach, knowing how she had already loaded the dice for each. They thought only of the track ahead, and of gold. Practically all were to have their wish, in part; after many struggles they were to win a few thousands quickly. The lone woman amongst them was to be lucky too. Captain Money, now sailing away, was to win a big fortune. So was Royal. Cheery, whistling Collins, did not know that for him the dice were heavily loaded. Before long he was to fall beneath the spears of the Nakanai warriors in New Britain.

Several of these men, now going into the wilds of the most primitive land on earth, were in the next few years to dine in luxury in big cities; dress in evening-suits; own their motor-cars; and float big commercial schemes. But now, they only thought of one luxury—a team of kanakas to carry their precious stores.

They scoured the bush in all directions seeking carriers, offering to buy them, pay them, bribe them. The brown men listened disdainfully; they did not care whether they carried or not; they would never carry were it not for the magical "iron." Axes, knives, iron hoop and wire—magical material for making spear- and arrow-heads. The white men invaded the country seeking gold, and they bought their way with iron.

It took these men weeks to get carriers. Later arrivals were months in getting them.

As each man secured carriers he set out, struggling up from village to village. "Yorkey" Booth secured a few and hurried on ahead, anxious, like the others, to peg a share of golden ground away up "on top." He would peg out a claim and pitch a camp into something like home shape by the time his wife arrived. She had resisted all persuasion to return to Rabaul. So she saw her husband off, then started recruiting with the aid of a few boys. By degrees she battled along with the stores; an epic struggle against mountains and gorges, jungles and rushing torrents, sometimes pouring rain and ice-cold winds, primitive kanakas and awful loneliness.

With indomitable pluck she carried on; the first white woman to trudge the terrible track to the Bulolo. She won through only to find further struggles awaiting her. She had more than earned a fortune when it came at last.

Shark-eye Park carried on serenely. His dream was realized anyway; he had found a goldfield; he was a rich man; he could retire when he liked. So, just to get accustomed to independence, he imported a Chinese cook. There was keen competition in Rabaul for that job, despite prophecy that the kanakas would eat the cook.

The lucky Celestial blandly smiled at such dire forebodings. Millions of Celestials would be willing to cook for the Man in the Moon if he had found a gold-mine up there.

The boys looked askance at Shark-eye when the Chinese cook arrived. "Why not?" challenged Park grimly. "I've lived like a kanaka for years; now I'm going to enjoy a bit of luxury."

"Good lad," said Sloane as he bent to his poker hand. "We're beggars to-day, millionaires to-morrow. Spend to-day, for to-morrow we're broke."

"Not me," replied Shark-eye. "I've cut my wisdom teeth."

"What are you going to do with your gold, Shark-eye?" asked Sloane curiously.

"I don't know," replied Park quietly.

"Aren't you going to paint Sydney red?" inquired Arnold with a smile.

Shark-eye shook his head, but the light of unusual reminiscence twinkled in his face.

"I'm afraid of Sydney," he admitted slowly. "It is a wonderful city. In a way I feel proud of it; and I've helped build it too—that is I've laid a bit of tram-line. But it frightens me. I was sandbagged there!"

They looked their surprise.

"Yes, many years ago. I had been out back of Moonta, prospecting. Times were bad. I came to Sydney in desperate need of a job. Had seldom done wages work before. Got a job digging up King Street, for the tramline you know. It was hard work—a ganger standing over you every minute—the real old navvy days. I chummed up with an old man in Woolloomooloo. We used to play dominoes every night; the poor old chap didn't seem to have anything else to live for. One night, coming home near St Mary's, I was sandbagged—and I only had eighteen-pence in my pocket. No, I don't think I will like Sydney again."

That was one of the longest speeches Shark-eye had ever been known to make. He refused to be drawn again.

When Christmas Day came, Park invited all on the tiny field to sample the dinner of his Chinese cook. They were a happy lot at that dinner. Several there thought of all that was behind it. Those grim years of battling alone up among tribesmen as untamed as the streams that tore down the shoulders of Kaindi; then that little pick of his first striking the golden earth. Now dinner in the wilderness, cooked by an imported chef.

Old Ned Coakeley was in Samarai when word definitely dribbled through that Shark-eye had struck it rich. Ned started out. He had been starting out all his life; as a lad he had started out to Johannesburg; then to Kimberley. Those were stirring days. He had been chased out of Lobengula's country at the run. He had started in again to be chased out by the Matabele; and since then he had started out to, and been chased away from, half the countries on the globe. He started out to and was chased all over the big Western Australian fields for twenty argumentative years. Now he started out for Salamaua. He didn't know that was his destination and didn't care. He was seeking his fortune, wherever that might be. It was really at the foot of the rainbow.

Ned was a grizzled, cantankerous old Irishman. His delight was trouble; and he found it easily enough, although he swore it followed him.

"'Tis a banshee," he growled. "Never left me since me birth, bad cess to it!"

Ned is the man who was always "agin the governmint." But he had a rough principle of his own. When later he reached the Edie and found there the trouble he loved, he was doing a perish. Dick Glasson said:

"Come and have a cup of tea, Ned."

"I will not!" refused Ned stubbornly. "I'm up agin ye—an' I will not eat your kai-kai."

Glasson had a share in the leases which were then in dispute. However, we are getting ahead of the story. When Coakeley arrived at Salamaua only Collins and Money were on the beach. Next day Shark-eye arrived from the mountains with three thousand ounces of gold.

How Ned's eyes glistened! He battled his way through the "haythen" villages along that awful Gadagadu track. It was nothing but the gold fever that gave strength to his gnarled old limbs and eventually pulled him through.

Ernie Banks was the only man at the Wau then. Joe Sloane and Cecil Levien were farther out on the Koranga; while Mrs Booth was working Shark-eye's boys on the lower Koranga. Ned went on to the Namie where Burleigh Gorman, Burke, Sharpe, and Bill Anderson greeted him right civilly.

But Ned went farther along, passed Chisholm and Royal, and climbed down into the Bulolo. He sank a shaft, spitting on his hands from habit while growling at the cold. He washed a dish of dirt from the bottom of the shaft. There was a pennyweight piece of gold in the dish!

Ned did an Irish jig. But he kept the secret all to himself; it would have meant a rough trip to go and tell anyone. That night he went to bunk in wonderful humour; not a growl in the world, at least not before the rain came! It rained all night. Next morning there was six feet of water in the hole. Ned saw it would be the same with every hole he sank—just there. He swore at the country, at the "governmint," at everything! Then he abandoned the ground and went higher up. There he glared at Levien who casually strolled along and inquired:

"Get any prospects in the Lower Bulolo, Ned?"

"Indeed I did not! An' if you want to know, go an' dig for yourself!"

Several years later, when mining engineers proved payable gold in that lower ground Ned realized what a fortune he had thrown away. But that only made him growl the more.

Odd men came drifting along to Salamaua in any old craft; some came in canoes, some by cutter and lugger. Several had made venturesome voyages of considerably over a thousand miles, dodging uncharted reef and sandbank, nosing their way among a maze of islands, fighting the "black squalls" all alone, well out to sea. All aboard were gold eager: the tiny holds, the cabins, the little decks, lashed with foodstuffs and belongings and swags. Men slept anywhere they could, and hung on by the skin of their teeth when she rolled at night. Two venturesome voyages were made by whaleboat for seven hundred miles. The voyagers got there and got a bit of gold, too.

John Mitchell was one of these whaleboat adventurers. He sold £40,000 worth of ground for £700. He, of course, didn't know the gold was in the ground. It was one of Darby's leases. But that nomad was still at Rabaul, with a vague idea of trying his luck at Shark-eye Park's find.

All the craft that set out for Salamaua did not arrive. Some from Australia only got as far as Thursday Island. Several were sold there for a song, and the owners returned to Queensland.

The 21 October 1925, when the *Marsina* (Captain G. E. Williams) with sixty-one tons of cargo, called for the first time at Salamaua, saw the birth of a new Australasian port. Wherever the British flag has gone, the trader has gone with it or followed it. Burns, Philp & Co. Ltd., is one of the empire-building firms which are serving the outposts in the Pacific, linking them together and joining them up with the great trade centres of the world. It carries on business in all the important ports of the South Pacific, and many others. It deals with people of almost every race and colour, and handles goods of an amazingly varied character. Like that of its great prototype, the East India Company, its history is full of romance. It was natural therefore that this enterprising firm should be quickly on the scene.

Burleigh Gorman's store, Salamaua, 1925.

CHAPTER XIV

THE MIDGET AND THE STAR

Levien was deep down in the Bulolo Gorge; he felt so small he almost lost his individuality. He clung to that in almost a frightened way; he felt he was Levien, Levien! He gazed up at those cliffs towering for thousands of feet; he looked higher still, and there shone a star. Though broad daylight, it glittered like a huge diamond. Crowning the heights were pine-trees and cedars that had grown there probably for hundreds of years. But that star shone down now as it had shone from the beginning. Coldly he felt its meaning: "Live and die, you pygmy!"

Levien laughed—as men had laughed through hell and death in the old A.I.F. days. On clear days stars are always visible from the bottom of the Bulolo Gorge. With a thrill Levien gazed about him. There were the waterfalls that could be converted into hydro-electric power to work a thousand years if necessary. Here were the terraces, stretching for miles, with gold-dust in them which the hydro-electric power could extract for the benefit of man. For days now he had been down in the gorge, with one carrier. In calculating haste he was trudging those miles of river-flats, wary, but fearless of the wild men he occasionally saw. He was all eyes and reasoning. Through his mind flowed the river that had sped there ages ago. He saw it all. These flats had once been the bed of the river, a much greater river. All these terraces and flats on which now grew grass and scrub and trees were actually debris brought down by those ancient waters from up above, around the Wau and Koranga, the Namie, and Edie; and, yes! through them, from far up on the summits of Kaindi! These alluvial flats had come from the gold country. There *must* be gold in them, too poor for the prospector and miner, but probably rich enough to be worked by the huge concentrating machinery of modern mining methods.

In those days of hard physical surveying, Levien marked mentally eighteen miles of river-flats. And he fixed in his mind the localities where he could quickly drive his pegs to enclose those flats in dredging leases—provided he could prove gold in them.

He dumped himself down with a sudden, unexpected sigh. He felt such a midget down here in the bottom of the world. He had so much to do, too, at Koranga. It would be a man-size job to work his own ground, let alone even prospect these lower flats. That would be a huge job for a company. And here was he— He stared up and down the river, at the bouldery watercourse, at the flats covered in grass and scrub. He gazed up at the great walls of the gorge, with the mountain summits receding away behind, at the clouds, now overhead, moving like a rolling sea...

He jumped up and swore he would beat it; he would tear the very insides out of this great gorge; he would strip these eighteen miles of flats bare to the very bottom of the old river-bed. He would put these millions of yards of gravels through the dredges, just as his labourers were putting Koranga Creek through sluice-boxes. Nature had taken millions of years to deposit these gravel banks down here. Well, he would churn all up again to the very last yard, and extract the gold from them in less than the life-time of a man.

He was on a ledge half-way up the side of the gorge when the ground shook. He clung there, the soft vibrations tingling his fingers as he clung to the rock, looking down. It was not much of an earth tremor; it felt and sounded as if the gorge away down there had coughed and cleared its throat. In panting exhaustion he was just clambering over the lip of the gorge when he suddenly dived straight among the trees. A mighty boulder hurtled down, and, striking the gorge edge, exploded, to whizz in fragments into space.

Levien and the carrier rose, shivering, staring up along a spur which led down from Kaindi. Right up the spur broken scrub and smashed trees marked the path of the boulder. A fifty-ton piece (at least) of solid rock had come hurtling down out of the mist.

"Might almost have been meant for me!" murmured Levien.

When, wearily, he returned to Koranga Creek he could not think. He slept for twelve hours.

To Levien's delight, a few weeks later two parties of new-comers, despairing of finding payable gold near by, climbed down into the gorge and commenced boxing, each on a river beach. Each party had a team of seven natives. Weeks later they climbed up out of the gorge and reported an average of eight ounces per day per box.

This confirmed Levien's reasoning that there was gold in the river. He was enthralled. But how about those flats? For the men would only work on selected beaches.

He equipped a team of boys, clambered down into the gorge and set them sinking a line of shafts for miles along the flats. He proved a depth of wash and gold in each.

Hurriedly he returned his team to work again at Koranga. Then he sat down and wrote another voluminous letter to his friend in Melbourne, some extracts of which are:

Bulolo,
6 April 1925.

Dear Wells,

I wish you to interview A. & B. in confidence on my behalf and find out if they would entertain a really good gold-dredging and saw-milling proposition here.

I could peg out more than 2000 acres of river-flat which would average approximately 2s. per yard value of gold contents on an approximate yardage of 20 to 23,000,000 yards[1]. (There arc other huge areas.)

He described the depth of wash, the ground, the country, the difficulties to be overcome; then went on to say:

A road could be found up the Markham and Watut ... it should be possible to build a light narrow-gauge railway or motor road; the cost could be borne by the timber trade; pine is everywhere in enormous quantities, being 3 ft 6 in. to 4 ft 6 in. diameter with 8 ft to 140 ft milling timber; cedar being about four trees to the acre, 4 ft 6 in. to 6 ft, about 70 ft to 120 ft milling timber. Pine predominates and is over thousands of acres as far as one can see over mountain and gully.

...A thorough test could be made for £3000 ... I have no objection to you telling them what Park and I are making on a small creek shedding into this area ... it seems a pity to see £2,000,000 or more of gold go begging when at a cost of a little over half a million it could all be in someone's pocket.

... this is not an underground mining proposition that one has to take on trust, but it can be sampled and proved and brought down to absolute mathematics.

... the main and only difficulty is transport of machinery and dredge; it is of no use anyone thinking of this business without going thoroughly into this matter and being strong enough financially to make transport reliable ... aviation possibilities might be all right ... there is ample water available at any head quite handy for hydro-electric power ... if A. & B. are interested I would suggest they form a syndicate of about £6000 or £7000, sending two reliable men over, one to be a dredging and sluicing expert and the other a good engineer and surveyor.

I think for a start this is about all you require in information, but I send you a rough diagramatic sketch of position to enable you to better visualize the business.

Yours sincerely,
C. J. LEVIEN.

When Wells received this letter he sat a long time, thinking. "The Three Musketeers," that was what they had been jocularly called in the

---

[1] Note: Years later, Bulolo Gold Dredging mining engineers actually estimated the proved value of this ground at 2s. 1d. per yard.

officers' training-school at Duntroon—he and Levien and Lapthorne of Adelaide. They were inseparable, a quaint mixture too. Lapthorne with his quiet ways, his ready wit, his eagerness to do anything useful even if it might be the wrong way. Levien with his loud laugh, his quick boisterous manner, his physical strength. By Jove, how he could work! Dig a trench, and in just exactly the right place, while another man would stand wondering where he should start. But Levien hated arithmetic and theoretical study of all kinds. Wells smiled. How often he had helped poor old "C.J." with the clerical part of his studies, while in return Levien had dug his trenches for him! That was the way they had won their commissions. Not one of the three would have passed his exam, without the help of the others. But how funny the old major was, and how he disliked Levien! The major, a typical Imperial Indian army officer, straight as a ramroad, as military as the traditions of the British Army. Levien, an energetic, untidy Australian, either hurrying about and joking in that loud voice of his or digging a trench with a grunting energy. The major ignored Levien when he could and disliked him always. But there came a Saturday afternoon when the major stood helplessly beside a motor car, softly cursing a puncture. Just out of Canberra, too, during a cross-country ride, far away from a garage. The major walked round and round that car. He was absolutely helpless.

"Hullo, major! What's the trouble?"

The major wheeled round at that loud, detested voice, and stood rigidly erect. Levien brushed him aside. "Here, let me at it," he ordered cheerfully. "I'll soon fix it; I understand these things. You'll never get it off that way this side of Christmas."

He threw off his tunic (that was only buttoned on parade), wrenched the tyre from the rim and tinkered about for twenty minutes. When he had finished he was all smiles and grease.

"She'll go like a house afire now," he said, with a cheerful laugh. "Hop in, major, and buzz off."

The major thanked him stiffly, stepped into the car like a soldier, and drove away. But he recognized the practical man in Levien after that and grew quite tolerant. Levien would never have addressed the major so on the drill-ground. On parade, Levien was always a good soldier.

Now he was in New Guinea amongst natives and cannibals and things. And he had written to say he had found a gold-mine. And he wanted his friends to float it! Well, Levien was in his right place, he certainly was pioneering stuff. But Melbourne is a big city, presided over by cool business men to whom an unknown man in a far away island was—Well, what was he?

Wells did his best. With misgiving in his heart he took Levien's letter to some of the financial magnates of Collins Street. He explained to them what a fine, capable, practical, honest man Levien was. They listened politely, and held the letter to study it. A few days later it was returned, with a brief note to say that the proposition was regretfully declined.

Frank Pryke and Les Joubert's first camp at Koranga, 1926.

CHAPTER XV

THE FINDING OF EDIE CREEK

Bill Royal was feeling desperate. From a rock that jutted out over the Bulolo Gorge he stared up at Kaindi Range. He stood on top of a mountain but others towered into the mists four thousand feet higher.

He was practically penniless. His mates were so nearly so that they had barely a month's supplies in camp. For nearly two years now they had roamed these gorges; battled their way through forest and scrub; tried dishes in the bouldery Namie, and in the jungle-shrouded waters of the Watut; forded the restless Bulolo at point after point, seeking in its rushing stream the elusive yellow metal. They had lived like kanakas; toiled like slaves. And all they had seen was other men's gold. Gold by the dishful won from Park's claim, from Sloane's, from Levien's. They saw it in the sluice-boxes on many an afternoon's clean-up, shining under the brown hands of the kanakas. They had seen it cleaned and dried, had felt the weight of the heavy little parcels sewn up ready for transport to the coast. Other men's gold!

Several men among the scattered score or so over the mountain were also winning gold; not like the rich fortunes that were being won from the Koranga, but good payable stuff all the same. But Royal, Glasson, Chisholm, and Money had not made tucker. He stood there, gazing up. A strong man, stockily built, with the grim lines of a battler upon a face that was now all longing as he stared up towards Kaindi. A whispering wind was around him but all else was silence. Royal turned abruptly and trudged down to his camp. Push on or push out! He decided on a forlorn hope; one desperate prospecting trip right up Edie Creek, to its very source. It would be a frightful climb. But he had frequently got provocative traces of gold in the Edie. It must come down from somewhere. With the last of the food, he and Glasson would push right up the creek to its source. If unsuccessful, well—a hurried scramble back to the coast; then farewell to this "land of gold."

Good-natured Dick Glasson was agreeable. A roamer, a solidly-built man like Royal—he had been pearler, buffalo shooter, soldier, trader, planter, prospector; he had "taken a chance" all his life. Chisholm agreed to hurry down to the coast and send on by the boys what supplies they had left, and keep them travelling. Bill Money would help with the stores.

Levien heard the news with delight. At last! Could Royal do it, he wondered? Had he the grit to storm giant Kaindi? Fervently he hoped Royal would find gold, rich gold. A new field would be the consummation of Levien's dreams, the trigger touch that would set his plans moving, just like that boulder rolling down from Kaindi.

He often gazed out towards Kaindi. He had just about sufficient thousands ready now to set the ball rolling. A new field up on Kaindi would confirm his belief that gold in quantity had come down from there and was now distributed in the Lower Bulolo flats. A new field up there would imbue Australian capitalists with just that faith necessary to back him up. While not seeming directly concerned, he knew all that was taking place, and his wishes for Royal's success were rich ones.

Royal and Glasson set out with half a dozen carriers. They crossed the Bulolo, joined the Lower Edie, and had kai-kai at Archie Whitbourne's, the last white man's camp. Whitbourne did them splendidly. Food there was worth its weight in gold, but he put before them all he had.

"I'm going to find a field," declared Royal, half in despair, half in earnest, "that will make the name of New Guinea ring throughout the world!"

"That's the way to talk!" encouraged Whitbourne. "There's plenty of gold for all of us in these mountains."

"Well let us find it then," said Glasson with a smile, as he stood lazily erect and nodded to the carriers.

As the forlorn hope disappeared into the jungle, Whitbourne watched them go rather longingly. He had given a meal, a helping hand, and words of courage. Little did he think then that he was to be given the chance of a fortune in return. He was the first man to set his sluice-box in the fabulously rich Upper Edie.

But things happen like that, when men are battling in "gold country."

Royal and Glasson scrambled out into the stupendous Edie Gorge, then climbed in earnest struggling against a thousand arms of the jungle, against rain and mists and gloom. A network of roots entangled their legs; hawser-like cable growths looped from the trees against their chests and waists; lawyer-canes gripped their ankles and coiled in a stranglehold around their necks. Slowly and painfully they plodded on and upward; the only sound the vicious slash and hum of the scrub-knife as it bit through root and vine, the "drip," "drip," "drip" of rain from sodden leaves, the startled cry of some dazzlingly plumaged bird. Wet and shivering, as the cold grew intense with height, they struggled up amongst the tree-trunks, seeing no sign of the sun, only a wilderness of dripping vegetation. Up past the four-thousand-foot level there grew a muffled, wind-blown roar. Moss now appeared, thick and treacherous, carpeting the roots of trees. Their feet slipped straight through and they snatched wildly at the foliage in awful fear of a broken leg. That would have meant hell for a man, up there seventy miles from the coast with a hundred mountains in between.

They hacked their way up out through the jungle into a clearing of mist and sound to stare at grey rock ramparts whose tops were lost in mist. A torrential stream poured over with a steely crash. Clouds of water-vapour drifted into the foliage which lined the walls of a gorge that hemmed them in.

Royal looked at Glasson; Glasson looked at Royal. The carriers grinned and squatted down.

The prospectors camped, in awe awhile at that stupendous beauty. The sound, too, of the water, plunging down twenty-eight hundred feet, held their eyes and minds. They reconnoitred the cliffs that blocked their way. No hope of recovering gold from among the mighty boulders of the gorge; they must seek the very summits, where the waterways might run easier.

They tackled the job with scrub-knives and bare hands; they crawled and slipped and struggled up barriers of rock until they came to a sheer precipice. This a kanaka climbed; with his monkey-like toes and fingers he climbed a twisted root growing down the face of the cliff. Then he cut a long rattan of lawyer-cane and lowered it as a rope. Tools and provisions were first hauled up; then they hauled each other. A pause for breath, on the ledge, then on again, scaling stage after stage right up into precipitous jungle.

The mists settled down thickly upon the jungle and tickled their throats. Mosses were growing up the tree-trunks now—sodden green and brown over-coats many inches in thickness. It became bitterly cold as they struggled up into a world of moss; moss everywhere; moss hiding the trellised roots in a carpet four feet thick; moss that appeared like solid green earth until they plunged through to their waists. That clogging moss, under which their legs were sometimes kicking, tangled in unseen roots, was gripping in soggy strength around their belts. It squelched water as their timid feet gurgled down into it; coldly clammy, it tore away in their hands as they snatched at the trunks. The lawyer-canes were icily slippery; their fingers pained as they pushed aside the heavy cables and felt the coarse-edged bark under the moss. Moss, feet in depth, carpeted unseen ravines. They trod in momentary fear of plunging through and down, down, down! They edged forward with shoulders hunched, toe-feeling step by step, ready instantly to leap back should the "ground" tremble. From somewhere through the lush green came a murmur of wind and water in symphony with the perpetual "drip," "drip," "drip;" otherwise no faintest sound except the sudden gasp and shower from rain-drenched leaves when a man slipped down. The carriers crept forward, on legs trembling like their lips. As their feet dragged up from the puddle-holes, their soles gleamed clean as sliced turnips. Shadowy timbers hedged them in; sometimes when the mists settled thickly upon the tree-tops it grew quite dark in the silence below.

So, by a series of scarcely negotiable stages, they climbed, until one day they reached the seven-thousand-foot level. There the exhausted carriers collapsed. Glasson stayed with them and made camp. They would push on next day, or the day after; it all depended on whether they could find a possible route.

There were a few hours of daylight left. Royal was eager to push on, mad lest they be forced back when almost at the summit. He would cut his way ahead and search for a route; it would save time on the morrow.

He did so, with one native carrier, and to his wild surprise almost immediately broke through. Torn and bleeding and ragged he pushed out of the jungle. The panorama of mountain peaks and open forest and tumbling waters that met his gaze fairly took his breath away. The summit just below him mothered a flat tableland and through this tinkled the narrow waters of the Upper Edie.

Royal's hands trembled as he washed the first prospect, his eyes staring at the wet earth sluicing out of the dish. The carrier squatted there in wondering contempt of this white man who would risk his life over a yellow stone.

But it was a song of destiny that tinkled from the dish. Heavy scratchings from gravels made aeons ago; then a little rolling sound like leaden pellets moving, sweetest music on earth to a prospector. Royal held his breath; tremblingly he canted the dish and the water rolled the gravels aside. He stared, transfixed, at the yellow gold. Then jumped up, trembling, the dish in his outstretched hand. Wildly he shouted, "Gold!" "Gold!" "Gold!"

He turned and raced back for Glasson.

CHAPTER XVI

THE FAREWELL OF SHARK-EYE PARK

There was gold "everywhere." No matter where they washed a dish there was gold, ounces of it to the dish. It was thick on the creek bottom, thicker in the rock bars; it was even up in the wash and among the roots of the trees. They tried dishes up and along and down the creek. Gold everywhere! They could dig out a shovelful of washdirt from the bottom and get an ounce on the shovel blade!

A few days later Royal, wild with excitement, almost fell down that four thousand feet to spread the good news below. And the first man he sought was Lucky Joe Sloane.

How Joe's eyes glistened! How that smile spread from ear to ear! How those long legs took him straight into the jungle to start climbing!

Royal spread the news by word of mouth and by native runners to the Booths, Archie Whitbourne, George Arnold, Robertson, Wilton, and Taylor. He hurried up Koranga Creek. Shark-eye gazed at him; stared at the gold. Levien came hurrying across; he stared at the gold.

Thus the news spread to all the scattered few; native runners sped from camp to camp; excitement spread like the whispering among the pines. Men from the scattered creeks downed tools; ran to their camps, shouted to their boys to get "packs up!" and stampeded to face the big climb. The find the prospectors had made was magnified many times. Later events were to prove it had not been magnified at all. Ernie Dover, the unlucky, downed tools and started straight away. He entered the gorge too low down and got bushed. In mad desperation he fought his way to starting-point again; then climbed and climbed; he failed, staring up at cliffs that towered black and cold and wet. He tried again—and climbed until his knees trembled and his eyes smarted from the slap of vine and displaced dirt when his hands snatched the creepers on the slimy rock sides. Years of hard luck had dogged his footsteps, and now gold, big stuff, was calling away up somewhere in those coiling clouds of mist. He tried yet again, despair pulling at his heart as he scaled moss-covered ramparts that had never seen a white man. He gained the top in almost crying exhaustion, his clothes almost torn off, his body red with blood, his finger-nails torn and broken. When his trembling knees could support him he staggered upright and pressed forward across the broad flat summit—to peg a little fortune.

When old Ned Coakeley heard the news he simply dropped everything and ran for it, as he knew he was already a few days late. He was so busy growling mentally that he hardly noticed the fatigue, the cuts and bruises, and the thump when haste brought him crashing to his back again and again. But that climb soon steadied him, although he followed the now well broken track of those who had gone before. He was all-in when he climbed wearily over the top, to lie there awhile gasping for breath and wiping the mud from his eyes. His eager ears heard ahead the ring of axes; a shouted voice now and again; then the swirling of gravel against tin as some man in among the trees washed a dish of dirt. That sound was a bugle-call. Ned staggered to his feet and plunged forward.

The first man he saw was Lucky Joe Sloane, sitting beside a sluice-box. The suspicion of a grin lurked on Joe's face as he stared solemnly at the derelict.

"There's no gold here, Ned," he volunteered glumly. "Y'r a liar!" gasped Ned. "Anyways don't trouble to tell me whether there's gold or not. I only want a flour-tin full!"

Yellow gold was gleaming from the ripples of the box. Ned staggered angrily on followed by Joe's laughter. Ned could have twisted the long galoot's head off. He got his tinful of gold; but not all at once though. Oh dear no!

All hands set boys to cutting the track, while from down below on the Wau their labour teams, very lightly loaded, carried up the camps and stores; a slipping, sliding, falling string of human ants harassed by the wild excitement of the whites. No doubt these white fools were mad. And the boys hated this new field; they shivered as they struggled desperately up, to crawl over the top exhausted, not buoyed up by the lust for gold that strengthened the whites.

Soon, rough camps sprang up along the creek whose ice-cold waters were rapidly muddying. Rough-hewn sluice-boxes were set by the water's edge; picks thumped into the ground; shovels rasped and tinkled as they dug into the wash. Axes rang out where axes never sang before; trees crashed down to a sharper axeman than the wind; the shout of voices echoed over brooding Kaindi.

The few excited diggers found gold beyond their dreams. There were fortunes all along that smooth, peaceful creek. Each man only needed to peg his claim; it was like signing a rich cheque on Nature. But Fate, later, cashed some of the cheques!

Those men needed the gold. They were seventy miles within mountains among the wildest in the world, at an altitude of seven thousand feet, over five hundred miles from. Rabaul, and they had only carriers to depend upon.

And away down in the lower mountains, and along the gloomy gorges right to the coast the kundu drums were beating; slow and sullen; vibrating with a nasty message slowly forming.

Levien bought out Shark-eye Park, then hurried down to the coast and took canoe to Morobe. From there he radioed to Wells, now moved to Adelaide, then hurried back to the excitement by Kaindi.

Shark-eye Park was happy, in his own unfathomable way, as he climbed down that long Gadagadu track for the last time. He paused awhile by Salinkora and Lambura and Kaisinik, taking his farewell of those age-old villages. Long he gazed at Lambura. New hands were already calling it "Old Rabal" village. He had seen things happen there that men do not talk about. At the same time he had lived among these people and they had treated him well. Regretfully he stared across the valley at the tall palisades of Kaisinik. In the changes that would inevitably come he hoped these people would not lose their wild independence.

As a long string of carriers filed past him *en route* to Garagoda, he turned and gazed at the grass patch, like a huge golden cloth under the sun, away across on the Wau. His pick had started this—his little iron pick—with his grit and something else in him, that "something" which has lifted the human above the beast. He wondered where it would all end, this now ceaseless activity, these files of carriers, like black and brown ants coming and going along the track wherever it was visible. On the Wau now were many tents; shacks were already appearing; the surrounding timber was falling in swathes; daily came the crash of great pines and cedars as men felled them for sluice-boxes and water fluming and houses. Mountain streams, usually crystal clear, were muddy from the workings. Over all the Wau, Koranga, the Bulolo, Watut, Namie, right up to the Upper Edie, the country echoed with the ring of the axe, the sharp, rasping song of the saw, the chorus of picks and shovels and sluice-forks. Truly the bom-bom had come!

Park turned to the coast. Though a sick man he felt no fear, not as when, long ago, he had crawled to a missionary's place to die. He knew he had only to get away from this country to get well again. If necessary, he could lie up in comfort with doctors and nurses to attend him.

And he was going to be married. Only he and she knew. Others would not have believed him had he told them. He was going to Rabaul, then Sydney, then Canada: a rich man. He walked down the long, long track with almost a smile on his face. But he did not hasten. He felt as if he was slipping through the jungle and it was vainly whispering him back.

Park, like Nettleton, when he reached Rabaul, quietly gave old friends a helping hand.

The "Big Six" of Edie Creek were Bill Royal, Dick Glasson, Frank Chisholm, William Money, Joe Sloane, and Albert Royal. The leases of this party proved to be phenomenally rich. Sloane set to work putting a box in while the others consolidated the leases, attended to recruiting and labour, and the transport of stores.

Sloane's first box on its first day's operations returned sixty-eight ounces of gold, working a team of six boys. Later on, in easier ground, the boxes returned as much as two hundred and eighty ounces for one day's work. Edie Creek turned out to be an extraordinarily rich, but small, alluvial field. If it had been found in Australia, in an accessible locality, it would have been overwhelmed in a few days. Its distance and inaccessibility meant fortunes for the few who were able to get there very early.

Burleigh Gorman had won just enough gold to make him want to look for more. But on a trip down to the beach for supplies he met Money, who was in a quandary; he had to go up "on top" and join Glasson. Would Gorman take over the store depot in his absence? There was money in it!

Gorman did. Time lengthened into months. He bought the depot and started to build, after coming to an agreement with the distant miners to store and look after their supplies, pack their carriers as they arrived, send their gold away, and transact all business for them with any vessel that might call in. Each party was to pay him £5 per month.

So Gorman laid the foundation of his own prosperity; and thoroughly earned what the future brought him. During 1926-7, three and a third tons of gold were boxed and dished from this small field; a phenomenal return considering the small number of men working. Such returns could not be kept quiet. The *Marsina* anchored off Salamaua one day and a crowd rowed ashore, littering the sandspit with hundreds of cases of provisions and bags of equipment and stacks of tools; all in a noisy confusion.

The vanguard of the rush had come.

Wells walked through the streets of Adelaide on a stifling day in February 1926. He was troubled. He had a radio in his pocket, worded: "Phenomenal alluvial gold has been found at Edie Creek. Get busy. Levien."

How like Levien! But how absurd! This staid city, these orderly-minded people, expected to sit up and take notice just because a man named Levien sent a radio from an island called New Guinea.

This radio was really worrying Wells. How could he respond to its cryptic command? He had only been in Adelaide a few weeks, sent from Melbourne to open a branch for his old firm. He was unknown, and knew nobody. If he, a total stranger, began his professional career in the city by asking people for money to finance a gold-mine a friend had found in New Guinea, his reception might be polite, but it would certainly not be cordial. It sounded so like the Uncle-from-Fiji trick that he might imperil his career at the very start. The struggle might well be severe without this handicap.

But Levien would be waiting and working, expecting him to do something. What on earth could he do? He thought of the old days and of things Levien had done. Small things perhaps, but not easily forgotten. Levien as a junior officer in the troopship, fussing around his young soldiers like a hen over her chicks, seeing they got the best food possible, harassing the cooks to cook it well; seeing that the lads' quarters were all "comfy," looking after their welfare by night and day. But that stormy day, though, when he proved that a ship's officer was issuing inferior quality food to his boys! How Levien had raged up to the officer-in-command! What a frightful row when Levien told him exactly what he thought of him! Levien was temporarily relieved of his command and put under open arrest for the remainder of the voyage. That was old "C.J.," with his heart and soul in his work; anxious to do anything for anybody under his charge and tempestuously ready at any time to brave "the Heads" should he think they were not doing their duty, too.

And now Levien wanted something done for him.

For days, without a soul to confide in, Wells went about Adelaide with that message in his pocket. What could he do? What if, by a fluke, he raised money, and then Levien's gold-mine turned out to be no mine at all!

But the bonds of old comradeship are strongly cemented by memory. One hot day Wells stood outside the post office hesitating whether to cable back: "Sorry cannot help you." He pictured Levien's face when that message reached him. No. It must not be sent. Could nobody ... Why, of course, there was old Lapthorne! Wasn't Adelaide "Lappy's" city? In a flash he remembered. He would dig up the third musketeer! If only he was still here, he would know somebody of course. Wells turned on his heel and hurried back to his office to see if he could trace the name of "Lap."

He did. And "Lappy" had many friends. He was delighted to hear of the other two musketeers and immediately believed all about Levien's gold-mine. He called a meeting of his friends and made Wells read them the letters, then the sensational radio. They too believed, to the surprised relief of Wells. Several shrewd business men were soon chosen as co-directors of a small syndicate to investigate things. They named it, "Guinea Gold, No-Liability." Plans were quickly laid. Funds were to be ready immediately Levien could send something more concrete to go on. It soon came in the form of a carefully reasoned letter.

Wells radioed him that Mining-engineer James Hebbard was on his way to the field.

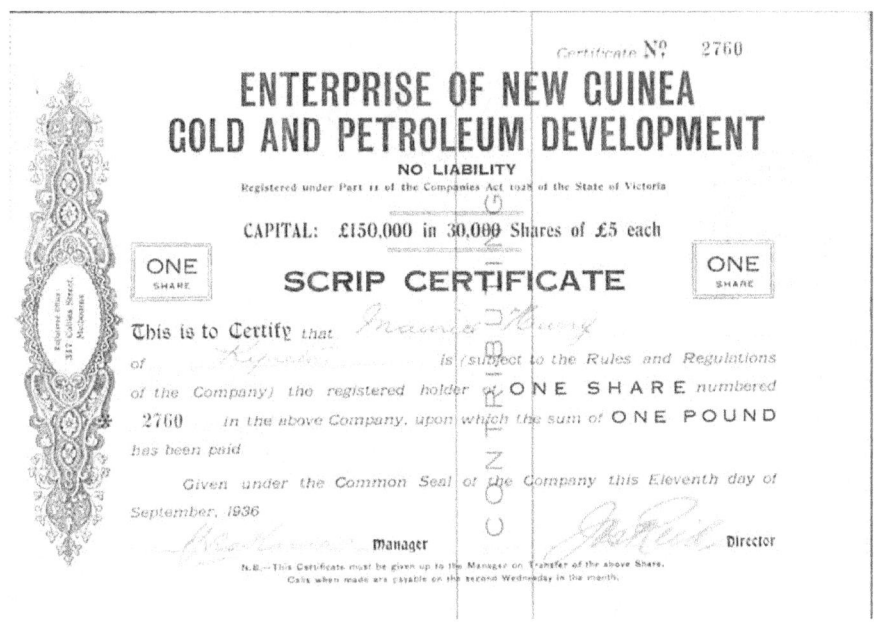

CHAPTER XVII

THE BOM-BOMS COME!

In Koranga Creek the gold was three thousand feet up, while the Edie field rose another four thousand feet higher. Scattered over both mountain-tops appeared little white tents, like flowers set deep in the scrub. Palm-thatch huts, too, were rapidly appearing.

By the greatest of good luck the auriferous country was above the fever-belt. There was fever at Salamaua and sometimes the far more dreaded blackwater. But fever did not appear on the fields until considerably later.

And the mining activities did not interfere with the native rights, for their ancestors had abandoned all this ground to the Curse of Kaindi. The top field was hardly seventy miles from the coast but one had climbed twenty-nine thousand feet by the time one reached there. An awful eight days' walk along a native pad up and down the razor-backs leading from village to village; a track that began to be more definitely worn by the increasing carriers as, more quickly now, the "mad bom-boms" began to drift in. The primitive men looked on contemptuously at first, then in sullen resentment; for these carriers passing through their villages belonged to other tribes; sometimes to hereditary enemies. To add insult to injury some of them were the despised coastal men.

But the carriers, with the exception of the wild Adzera from the Upper Markham, the Laewomba, and certain Sepik River boys, were fearful and behaved themselves—until later on their numbers swelled to four figures! The Adzera gave scowl for scowl as they carried their loads past the glowering villagers.

Crouched within his gloomy hut, old Yabbi, the luluai, sneered his thoughts of friend and foe. A notorious man this chieftain of Lambura; soon to be notorious to white man as well as native. Wizened and greasy and evil, to our way of thinking he was a man-eater, but a patriot according to his lights. Craftily he awaited the time to strike and completely demoralize both these foreign carriers and their white masters.

(Top) Pryke's mine at Koranga showing 30 foot tail race over the gully and 300 feet of pipe. (Below) Native labourers in the gully, prepare for sluicing (both photographs Frank Pryke).

Sluicing at Pryke's mine, Koranga 1926.

The men who arrived up at the field in the earlier batches, before the "Big Rush" set in, mostly won payable claims. Still, the rich ground above was of very limited extent, and most of it was quickly taken up in leases of large acreage. Consequently, new-comers found that they had to strike out for themselves or return to the coast; their money, time, and labour all gone for nothing. In Australia, a new mineral field is generally pegged out in claims of much smaller area.

The trouble of the leases question came within an ace of being another Eureka Stockade. Had the Miners' Association not been well managed, and the miners not been a remarkably patient and law-abiding body of men, it would have done so. This trouble, after much dreary waiting, led to a Royal Commission, appointed by the Commonwealth Government.

Salamaua was now very busy when boat day came. Crowds of kanakas carried innumerable mats of rice, bags and bales and boxes of provisions of all kinds, from the jetty to the store. Camps grew up under the palms and farther along towards the mainland shore. Strings of wild-looking natives were coming in from the mountain track shepherded by pompous kanaka "head" boys. These natives were being brought in by the recruiters to "make paper."

Shacks of sago-palm, of hessian, of palm slab and corrugated iron, began to appear. The primitive men from the village near by looked silently on. The white man had come.

But the new-comer had to battle to keep his foothold. Dumped on the beach, many new hands gazed about them in bewilderment. What to do next? Behind them the sea, ahead the mountains. No roads, no trains, no motors, no horses, no shops; only some grinning kanakas.

Those natives proved worth their weight in gold—to those who got them first. Fortunes were won and lost in that rush; won by the men who secured their carriers, lost by those who didn't. Numbers of the old Papuan hands went straight out into the bush, battling from village to village, securing a carrier here, a couple there. They returned perhaps, with sufficient carriers in a month, more often in two. Then a feverish loading up and away towards the Frisco River heading for the Gadagadu track. And already a little wooden cross or two was appearing on the beach at Salamaua.

Men not used to the country simply had to wait on the beach until a new batch of carriers arrived. A heart-breaking wait for them, watching the lucky ones start in their tortoise race to peg the golden ground. But fortune for the recruiters! There are more ways of winning gold than by digging it. At first, boys could be secured at £1 a head. Soon they rose to £5, then to £10. As Burns Philp's boats poured more eager human cargo on to the beach, the price of boys rose to £15, then £20. Some recruits actually brought £30 a head. There was a feverish demand; money did not count when it meant getting up to the goldfield quickly, or else losing all chance.

Every man needed, at least, ten carriers. He must load them with stores correspondingly expensive. And he must have his steamer fare to New Guinea and back.

The authorities debarred anyone leaving Australia for the field unless in possession of at least £550 capital. It was a wise law; otherwise thousands of men would have flocked to Salamaua and found themselves starving on the beach. Maybe half a dozen men found their way to the field without the proverbial shilling in their pocket. But theirs was only the tough exception. Old Man Luck of course was in his element, and he chose one favourite from these battlers to win an Eldorado. Wally Digby was another who battled in so, and just got back to the beach, almost dying of fever. Indomitably he pushed in again to reap the reward of pluck as one of the finders of the Day Dawn.

It is all a matter of grit and luck.

The recruiters were tough men of necessity, venturing into uncontrolled country wherever the natives were thickest, bargaining with savage luluais for recruits. Sometimes they had to fight; always they risked fever and blackwater; privation of numerous kinds. After a three months' trip the recruiter, grim of face and perhaps shaking with fever would emerge from the jungle hurrying to Salamaua with a hundred savages trooping at his heels. These would sign on officially as recruits. In batches of tens, twenties, and thirties they were handed over to their new master, perhaps a man who had never seen a kanaka in his life. No wonder that numbers of these men presently found themselves absolutely out of place, deep in the jungle at the mercy of a string of heathen to whom he was, in slang idiom, a "mug." Some tribesmen among the kanakas, even if they have seen their first white man only a few months before, are surprisingly quick at picking up things—undesirable things. Some of the new-comers woke up alone in the jungle, the remnants of their stores around them, but of carriers—not a sign. They had silently stolen back to the beach again to "make paper" a second time, and securing their money in precious shillings and their yet more precious trade goods, pick up their new master's bundles and march away, ready to desert him, too.

On the other hand Levien was in the seventh heaven. Mining-engineer Hebbard would soon arrive to report on his cherished scheme. Meantime Mining-engineer Clark visited the field and was loud in his opinion that someone ought to start an aeroplane service.

Levien hurried to Adelaide wanting everything done so that he could rush back. He wanted a bigger company formed, money subscribed, and mining engineers and machinery packed on the *Marsina* all in one breath. And why not? He had brought the goods!

"Go easy," advised the city friend. "There will be lots of explanations to make; the proposition must first be thoroughly investigated."

"Investigated be blowed! I've been investigating for the last three years. Isn't Hebbard's report good enough for them?"

Wells nodded but felt uneasy. This hustler would not show to advantage before a group of cool business men used, not only to weighing personality, but to testing every statement made. And the proposition needed weighing and questioning, sifting and discussion. An unknown man with mining-leases in some unknown portion of the unknown Mandated Territory, vaguely presumed to be in New Guinea, and with not much more than his own word as guarantee, demanding finance to work the bigger proposition too. For Hebbard had only been asked to examine Koranga, and in the time allotted him, could do no more than look at the great Lower Bulolo flats from the top of a hill.

Levien talked a hundred to the dozen as they walked along to the office, Wells trying to answer cheerily despite his apprehension that, within the next hour or two, Levien might meet a serious set-back from coldly-critical financiers. The coming introduction was going to be his first enterprise in a strange city, and if events miscarried it might ruin him. Tactfully he tried to tutor Levien, emphasizing the need for patience, the long and painstaking explanations that would be necessary before these men fully grasped the significance of all he claimed for his proposition.

"Oh I'll manage this crowd!" declared Levien confidently as he leapt the steps two at a time.

"Hold hard!" remonstrated Wells, impatiently. "For heaven's sake don't imagine you are bossing a gang of kanakas!"

"I'll put them through all right," said Levien, laughing. "Never fear. Anyway I'm bringing a fortune to their doors—what more do they want?"

"Yes, but—"

But Levien was already at the board-room door.

It was a momentous meeting that. The fruits of it in a short five years were to enthral the mining and aviation world. But the dreamer of it all nearly wrecked it. First of all, Hebbard gave his report and made a very favourable impression. Then Wells, hoping for the best, introduced "Mr Levien" and called on him to address the meeting. He stood there and told them everything as he knew it from the very start. How Park, Nettleton, and he had each made a fortune; how his own had gone into the buying of Park's ground. It was this ground now, Park's, Nettleton's, and his own which he offered to the group, to be the basis of a far larger scheme, huge dredging areas on the Lower Bulolo. He explained those areas, and his reasons for believing that gold was there. He explained the transport difficulty; declared that it would be solved in the near future by road or aeroplane. He explained how, in the meantime, the ground he offered could be worked by hydraulic machinery, transportable by kanaka labour: The hydraulic plant to be installed as quickly as possible to work his ground. The gold won to be spent in taking up leases on the Lower Bulolo, in the systematic prospecting of those leases, and the eventual flotation of a powerful company to work them by modern dredges. He was right! He *knew* he was right; and every penny he possessed would back his words!

They listened in silence, keen faces of keen men all around that big, shining table. They gave him a sympathetic hearing, a long hearing; and he gave them plenty of details, emphasized by thumps of a hard fist upon the table. When he had had his say, he looked round steadily at his audience, then sat down with a grin of defiance.

Wells sat still watching. There was a faint change of expression upon those faces. They had been thinking as they listened; now their thoughts were put into queries.

A slight man, alert of face and grey at the temples, reached across the table and dropped his burnt-out cigar in the ash-tray. Then he looked at Levien frankly, and in a pleasant voice asked the first question. Others followed.

Levien answered question after question with rising gusto; answered them in the quick, decisive manner of the practical man. But he became cautious when highly technical questions arose. He described himself as a rough "bush engineer," not a scientific man. He was quite at home to the mining questions, and gave practical "all round" answers to engineering problems; but several highly technical questions floored him. Shrewd old Jeffrey, sitting all hunched up there with his bright eyes unwaveringly on the speaker was thinking:

"This man is quite sincere. He believes every word he says. But he probably has deceived himself."

Wells heartily wished the meeting would end. But he hardly cared to close it yet. Everything had gone splendidly so far, better than he dared hope. He was beginning to think there would be a favourable decision if only the end would come quickly enough.

It did. A big man fired a question in such a way as to throw doubt upon Levien's gold samples, all laid on the table. It was one of those take-it-as-you-like-it questions.

Levien sprang up, his eyes blazing, and roared across the table. He said many things quickly; in fact he wanted to pull things about and break them. Wells sat aghast, until with restraining arm and tactful words he gradually calmed the troubled waters. Levien growled a lot before he quietened, and then amazed the gathering with a shout of laughter! His proposition was too good and sound to be worth getting angry about. But the serenity around that table had been rudely ruffled; quite squashed, Wells was sure. Lapthorne looked anxious, too.

But it hadn't. They put Levien's wild-man-of-the-woods manner down to the country from which he had come; then considered his proposition fairly. All were impressed by the man and his story and such facts as he had marshalled.

As the result of that meeting, the Guinea Gold No-Liability Company's capital was enlarged.

So was launched the most successful mining company in New Guinea up to date. But its success was not achieved until after the expenditure of £50,000 in cash, a tremendous amount of work, and some bitter disappointments. Levien left for New Guinea like a riotous schoolboy hurrying on a working holiday. Wells and Lapthorne farewelled him with mingled feelings of admiration and relief.

Levien returned to find a hum of activity on the beach at Salamaua. Strings of laden carriers were setting out for the "big climb." With cheery haste he joined them.

Men drifted up more rapidly now. This gold could not be kept quiet— not in the face of the returns from the Big Six, from Darby's "Eldorado" (soon to turn out gold by the dishful), from Williams and Hunt's small claim, and from others. Williams and Hunt's claim was only four hundred by one hundred feet. In a hundred and fifty-two days, sixty-eight of which were engaged in stripping overburden and eighty-four days in boxing, 7088 ounces of gold and 654 ounces of specimens were recovered. A team of sixteen boys was employed. This worked out at an average of £115 per day for the total period. Each actual boxing day returned £209.

Numbers of the latest arrivals, finding all the known ground taken up, had to drift away again. There were very few among them capable of going out into the bush, recruiting their own boys, loading them up, then setting out into the wild lands seeking a new find of their own. One party made a short but rough trip to the head-waters of the Watut and found promising gold that led to a wild rush. But it faded out. There were several rushes to the Watut. It was there in 1931 that Baum (Detzner's old mate) and nine carriers, were killed by the Kukukukus, probably the most elusive and dangerous marauders in all New Guinea.

The Kukukukus who murdered Baum and his carriers, with Native Police.

CHAPTER XVIII

FIFTY POUNDS OF MEAT

It was a boisterously busy Salamaua now after the arrival of a boat. A beginning had already been made at a rough landing-place. The narrow isthmus stacked with goods, strings of kanakas carrying them into Burleigh Gorman's store, now a huge "two-decker" which swayed and uncomfortably creaked in the strong sea-breeze. On occasion, forty men have slept up in the "top deck" or listened there uneasily to the howling wind while their stores and boys lay sheltered below. But, as the kanakas are adept thieves, there was often trouble in the morning. Eventually a depot under lock and key had to be built for the precious stores.

After a boat had come and sailed, and Gorman had packed the carriers and started them on their long trip, he was alone for weeks, sometimes months, at a time. Apportioning each white man's stores, loading up those teams of carriers and getting them away, was a man-size job. In the early days, a white man or two would come down from the field in charge of the combined carriers, but as boss boys were picked out and efficiently trained the carriers were often sent in charge of these alone.

Here individuality came in, for the carriers were from numerous localities; many came from distant rivers and from islands across the sea. Some were truculent or sullen, others were fightable or full of fun; some were steady boys, others plain dodgers; some were "wooden headed," others were cunning. Just like a crowd of men, in gangs of different nationalities, gathered to work for a master they did not care a tinker's cuss about. Every team acknowledged only one master, while each team was mainly antagonistic to other teams: delighting in their misfortunes, hindering them if opportunity occurred and they were game enough, not to mention stealing and brow-beating.

Packing these teams in the heat of work, laughter, scowls, arguments, sometimes vicious quarrels, sullen misunderstandings and plain cussedness, used to drive Gorman nearly frantic. With sweating brow under the heat and vexation he would wave his arms, exclaiming, "Thank heaven! Thank heaven!" when the last loaded team wended its slow way towards the Frisco River.

The Frisco was only a very short afternoon's stage away, but Gorman used to dread the next morning. Yes, here came the malingerers: the sick and the lame, the halt and the leadswinger, some hobbling on sticks for crutches, others with filthy rags wound round their "head belonga me he sore!" an odd one limping on "poisoned" feet, some groaning along expressively rubbing their stomachs. Gorman would roll up his sleeves and snatching a *dee-why* (stick) rush towards them, yelling like a maniac. The lame and the halt would be cured by magic and leaping round speed back for their discarded loads. Once across the Frisco, the harassed storekeeper would feel they were fairly started on their way. On odd occasions, however, the whole of them would come trooping back at dusk all with a chorus of: "Master, tide he too high!" And Gorman would know that the tide then was not waist deep.

On that beach, later, Gorman had the fight of his life. Hundreds of carriers were around him, all talking while they argued and apparently worked, but nearly all hindering one another or Gorman's own sweating boys. That was the annoyance in particular, the carriers from fighting tribes bullying his own boys. This day there was one particularly notorious carrier acting "flash feller," a big sour-faced brute from a fighting Sepik tribe, who was the pride of his own team in that he also dominated every other team along the track. This boy was "roaring" at Gorman's boys; and every carrier present, while watching the Sepik, was watching the white master.

Gorman knew that this particular boy had not long since chased a white man with an axe. Gorman was along: he looked across the bay. Johannsen's cutter was out there, but long before this other white man could row ashore the fight would be over. And Gorman well knew his fate should he be knocked down. He was feeling none too fit either; he was getting on in years and was not himself owing to recurrent fever. He stood it until he was compelled to go to the assistance of his cowed boys.

"These feller boy belonga me," he remonstrated sharply. "You leave him alone, get on with your work."

The Sepik bully turned scornfully on the white man and putting up his fists, exclaimed: "Me fight white feller fashion!" Then he snatched up a dee-why and came at Gorman, who immediately closed, luckily wrenching the stick away and smartly uppercutting his antagonist as he leapt back to dodge those encircling arms. If they closed around him he would be done. As the savage sprang in again Gorman shot out a straight left and thumped harder again as the savage head jerked back. Surprised rage glared from that bleeding face as with lowered head and wildly swinging arms he charged in bellowing fury. Gorman, already feeling short of breath, swung all his chances into one final blow to the temple which smashed his own hand. But the Sepik man crashed down and stayed down, his eyes glassy, blood oozing from his lips. Gorman turned on the silent crowd and waved them back to work. They obeyed without a murmur. Then he walked groggily across to the store and collapsed—where no kanaka could see him.

But Gorman for a long time had been hurt, then seriously annoyed. Again and again Levien had written him:

"Something is wrong. The meat arrives here ten pounds short. You must be packing the boys ten pounds short; their packs always arrive in perfect order, but the boys who carry the meat arrive with forty tins instead of fifty!"

After the first complaint, Gorman had personally packed the cases of Levien's boys. He packed in neat rows of ten within each box, the five layers of one-pound meat tins. Ten fives makes fifty every time, though the stars do fall. Over each nailed-down box he had himself neatly sewn the covering canvas. At last, in desperation, he wrote:

"You are mad. I have packed each case myself; each case contains five rows of ten tins—fifty pounds of tinned meat. And I have supervised the loading myself for these twelve months past. I am neither a thief nor a liar. You are mad!"

Levien received this note late one afternoon from his boss boy as carriers straggled into camp. Ten men were carrying each one case of beef. He marched these ten into the store shed, locked the door and put the key in his pocket. Each man put down his load and stood silently by. Levien examined each case with great care. When it grew quite dark he lit a hurricane lamp. The carriers stood by, all eyes, in that quiet shed. The cases appeared in perfect condition, the canvas neatly sewn around each. Satisfied at last, Levien carefully cut the canvas from the first case. He opened and examined it a long while, staring at the topmost layer of ten tins, level with the top of the box. One by one he took out each tin. Four layers, ten tins each! With his face a brown study under the lamp he unpacked the other cases. Each held four layers, ten tins each.

He compared every case. Finally, he saw by measurement of the boards that a top layer from each case had been removed; then the boards pared down with a carpenter's neatness to the next layer and re-nailed. The canvas had then been recut and sewn together with all a sail-maker's craft.

Out of those ten cases, the carriers had eaten one hundred tins of meat. And they had been doing this for the last ten months. One thousand tins of meat! And Levien was a man who, to black, brown, and white, was notorious for the prodigality with which he fed his carriers and labour teams.

He stood up at last and looked into ten pairs of eyes staring in silent guilt. With grim face he walked to the locked door. Through a crack in the planks he poked the key until it fell with a thud outside. Then he turned, and smashed into the nearest boy.

He thrashed them all, one by one, with his bare fists. Exhausted, he would wait until he got his breath, then smash into another man. Man by man he put them through. Not a man resisted. Exhausted and trembling, with wobbly knees and bleeding knuckles, he put through the tenth man. The men, cowed and bleeding, crouched away from him as he staggered towards the door. The silent labour crew outside opened it to him. He turned and beckoned the cowed carriers. With bent heads, they lurched out past him. He staggered to the cook-boy and ordered him to give the carriers a good meal. Then he felt his way into the shack and collapsed on the bunk.

Ever after that, every carrier who carried meat for Levien brought up to the camp a case containing ten rows of five tins, one pound of meat in each tin.

Frank Pryke's camp at Edie Creek, 1927.

CHAPTER XIX

THE EYE THAT SAW ALL THINGS

Levien was in high delight; the syndicate had accepted Hebbard's report, which recommended his proposition. Guinea Gold had increased its capital; and now Field-superintendent Levien turned the leases into a hive of activity. A chain of carriers was constantly going to and returning from the beach; labour gangs were busily erecting staff buildings, tool store, and laying out gardens. Levien started a small plantation to help feed what he knew must soon be a little army of carriers. All the money paid him for his ground he put back into the company, buying shares.

He hurried away recruiting for labour, grudging every hour absent from the mine. On one trip he brought a hundred and forty boys, and immediately sent them trooping down to the coast to carry up pumps and sawmill, hydraulic sluicing units and equipment. In between times he kept teams of boys working the ground by the old boxing method. These produced three hundred ounces of gold in the first six weeks, which was excellent encouragement for a young company.

Levien slaved. Men wonder now how he did it in the time and under such difficulties. Soon he had the holdings thoroughly established.

Lone prospector and his carriers.

A G31 loading up Austin car, safe, and two tons of rice.

Dead tired at nights he would lie, stretched out, devising ways of expediting the work to the producing stage. He wanted the company to be producing big gold quickly so that they could take up those long dreamed of Bulolo leases.

The company had not even pegged those leases yet. There was plenty of time, for the attention of all men on the field was occupied with thoughts of the far richer ground on the Edie above. Besides, the company needed every shilling of their working capital to develop their own ground. To take up those Bulolo leases would need capital that could ill be spared at present. No one would dream of the potentialities of the Lower Bulolo for a long time to come.

But one night Levien was shocked into wild activity. He was in camp, dead tired, discussing the prospects of the field with several trusted friends. A tall acquaintance from the Upper Edie drifted in and nodded to the salutations.

"How's things?" inquired Levien, as he called to the cook-boy to bring kai-kai.

"Oh, not bad. It'll be a dashed side better when this trouble over the leases is settled. If there's not an all-in fight up there before it's over I'll be surprised. How's things on the Wau?"

"Pretty right. Getting enough gold to pay the coons, anyway."

"H'm. I'm going down to the beach to meet the *Marsina*. Just came down with the — — Group. They're going to peg the Lower Bulolo tomorrow. They've got some mad idea there might be a big dredging proposition down there."

A moment's silence. The next instant Levien shouted for the cook-boy, then carried on his usual lively conversation throughout the evening until his visitor retired. They listened to his footsteps fading down the path.

"Quick!" whispered Levien. "Wake the smartest boys. Get axes, picks, ropes, kai-kai. Come, get a move on!"

Half an hour later a silent party filed away from the camp. That was a hair-raising scramble in pitch darkness down into the great gorge; groping for vines, for a foothold, while climbing ever deeper down into the pit; every man's heart in his mouth as he felt with hands and elbows and feet, yet not daring to say a word for fear of that madly excited leader scrambling away down below. Long after daylight they drove in the first peg, Levien swinging the axe as if a fortune depended on it. He had marked the spot in his mind long ago; a fortune *did* rest on his exact knowledge of the ground now. With shouts of direction, hurried by waving arms, he sent a party across the river to drive a corresponding peg, while he grabbed his tools and hurried miles down-river to drive in the third and fourth. It was only a matter of travelling quickly; he knew exactly where to drive the pegs. George Arnold and young Chapman completed the pegging.

The — — Group stared in stupefaction when they arrived just twenty-four hours too late. Few men, even among the early hands on the field, know by what a narrow margin those big dredging leases were pegged out.

Down at Salamaua they pushed the little wooden-wheeled handcart to the sleeping-place. It was decked with tropic flowers; several mourners wore flamboyant dressing-gowns; all carried bottles of champagne—more or less empty. No one knew the burial service, so they just stood around and sang his favourite song. Then they sprinkled him with his last drink and lowered him in. But one fell in with him.

"Steady, old mate," he said. "I'm not coming with you yet!" He crawled out and had another one.

When Peter Ready died the pub went into mourning with free drinks. Everybody liked old Peter, especially Joe Fanning. He was the chief performer at the "planting." Several men were weeping—with spirit—as Joe declared feelingly that his old mate had gone to a place where the real men go. When Joe died of blackwater five days later, the pub was just recovering, and owing to the relapse, Joe's interment was somewhat delayed and blurred. The kanakas were ordered to make a cross because all others were indisposed. Old Peter's cross was a fine monument of hardwood painted white. But Joe's was a packing-case with one arm of the cross pointing skyward. On it was stencilled: "Keep in a cool place."

There was keen competition, both at Koranga and up on the new Edie field, for teams of labour boys. These irresponsible heathens were very human. In every working team there were generally several good toilers, one "hard case," two or three arrant loafers, and the rest just medium. Every master had to keep an eye on his team if he wanted work done. Easy-going old Joe Darling (brother of prospector Arthur) was much worried in this respect. As he had to feed his boys, it was essential they should work. However, the boys failed to see the connexion between winning gold and eating rice. Each morning after kai-kai old Joe would apportion their tasks then go on up the creek hoping to locate richer ground. When he was out of sight the boss boy would declare: "Master, he go finish!" at which each boy would drop his tools and squat cheerfully on his heels. In late afternoon they would hear Joe's returning footsteps crunching on the gravel. "Master he come!" the boss boy would warn, and all hands would spring to their tools.

The morning that old Joe "fixed 'em" he glared ominously at their bent backs, then sternly calling them to attention put his hand to his face and—pulled out his eye!

They stared in petrified astonishment, changing immediately to the acute fear of a tambaran.

"This feller eye belonga me he strong!" announced old Joe in sepulchral tones. "Now me go. This feller eye he stop, look longa you! Tellim me you no work longa me!"

He walked to a leaning tree and set the eye upon it so that it glared at the boys. Solemnly he walked away up the creek.

"Eye belonga master he lookim!" whispered the boss boy, and they bent to their work, hardly venturing to glance up at the eye that glared back. They worked as they had never worked before, toiling hard for three solid weeks; which set the boss boy thinking. So, one morning after old Joe had gone he revealed his brain-wave thus:

"Now lookim this feller eye belonga master!" he whispered to his team. Thus ordered, all hands stared at the eye to hold its attention while the boss boy carried his shovel off into the bush and, dropping it, sneaked up the creek-bank, warily watching the glass eye as he circled cautiously around the pine-tree. He tiptoed up behind the eye and, reaching over, dropped his old felt hat over it. "Now lookim this eye belonga master," he called triumphantly. "He no can see! Now all boy sit down; stop nothing."

That evening old Joe gloomily examined the results in the sluice-box. He had been doing so well these last three weeks, too! He really thought he was going to get enough gold to send away for a big supply of stores. Next evening the clean-up was just as bitterly disappointing. Old Joe was worried. He glanced at the tiny quantity of ground worked that day and immediately saw that something was wrong. Next morning he set his eye as usual, glared at his toiling boys then went off up the creek. But he doubled back when out of earshot and from behind a tree was just in time to see the boss boy "blind his tambaran."

Next morning old Joe set the eye in the usual place. Then, facing his attentive crew, put his hand to his mouth and-pulled out his teeth! Solemnly placing them above the eye he glared at his boss boy.

"Now these teeth belonga me, he sharp!" he warned and displayed his toothless gums. "S'posem you put hat longa eye, this feller teeth he bite!"

Soon afterwards he was able to send for the stores.

CHAPTER XX
ELDORADO

Burleigh Gorman, the ever genial, while applying for a licence was training as a host. Some white women leaned over the rail of the *Melusia*, anxious for a glimpse of this primitive gold port at the foot of the mountains. Burleigh would invite them ashore for a cup of tea. Naturally, when the civilized met the primitive, complications arose. The ladies were rowed near shore, then in various graceful postures had to be carried to the beach perched on the clasped hands of two kanakas, the while they were objects of interest to every carrier on the beach.

One afternoon Gorman advised his "carry" boys so: "Now you feller boy lift him clothes belonga missus—no let him clothes belonga missus go longa soda-water (sea)!"

"No, master," they promised faithfully. "We carry him strong!"

But Gorman could see that after carrying twenty ladies ashore, his strong men were feeling the strain. And they had left the heftiest girl until last. She was a buxom thirteen stone. Gorman watched anxiously as his sweating boys laboriously neared the beach; he could tell their hands were slipping; their precious burden obviously sagging. With an arm clasped round each desperate man's neck it was plain to see she was sinking astern. Her friends watched silently from the beach; the kanakas not so silently. A fatter wave than its fellows, from a long way back, rolled gently in, gathering weight and momentum, to land on the lady with a resounding smack. Immediately a kanaka roared: "What cheeky fashion this? Lift him seat belonga missus!"

After the jetty and his bungalow store were built Gorman entertained in style. That crude store often held thousands of pounds worth of gold, sent down from the mountains for shipment. Sometimes the miners brought it themselves; often they entrusted it to their head carrier. And, as men sometimes are who deal with the raw metal in plenty, they were often careless. The bags were of any old thing; occasionally of neat, strong canvas, more often of a torn shirt or leg of khaki trousers. (The Sydney office of Burns, Philp and Company were once intrigued by receiving hundreds of pounds worth of gold tied up in the leg of a pair of bloomers. And the clerks knew there were no "gold diggers" up in that primitive spot.)

The bags were quite often torn, sometimes the stitching was undone;

many a bag of gold Gorman has had to rebag and sew up again. The name of the owner and approximately so many ounces, were scribbled in pencil or ink, sometimes, owing to rain, indecipherable. One day Joe Sloane came striding along with a team of carriers and a few little bags of gold—sixteen thousand ounces. With what Gorman already had in the store, the contents of the rough looking shack on this occasion were worth £50,000 in gold.

Gorman found these accumulations of precious metal a weighty responsibility. There was no telling what characters it might lure to this place from distant civilization. However, nothing was ever stolen. When the steamer arrived to take over the gold, Gorman was always very relieved when it was safely aboard.

One extra golden load he had packed in an old portmanteau, and was very anxious lest the bottom drop out. His bowed boys showed the weight of it as they splashed out to the canoe. Alongside the *Montoro* the mate slung over the rope sling.

"Send down the net!" shouted Gorman.

"Aw!" replied the mate disdainfully, "that sling will hold a ton, let alone a portmanteau."

"It won't hold this port!" bawled Gorman. "I don't want to see £50,000 of gold fall to the bottom of the sea! Send down the net."

And the net it was: the most precious cargo this holder of onions and butter and potatoes had ever hauled aboard.

Concurrently with the arrival of several crowds of men, dysentery broke out on the main track. It spread with alarming rapidity right up to the Wau. The government medical officer, Dr Dickson, put the carriers into quarantine, then followed the track up with a medical patrol, burning infected rest-houses in the endeavour to keep the plague localized, while District Officer Skeate directed Police Master Bourke to open up the Bouangs by way of Quasang. The old track for the time being was closed.

Bourke came on tragedy while hacking that track through the jungle. Two elderly men, Erskine and Power, sick and abandoned by their boys, found that track the end of all things for them. It was along this awful track, too, that Ted Bishton was battling, with two hundred carriers, taking the first wireless station to the Wau. Some of the tribesmen declared war on the toiling gangs, which resulted in a skirmish near the Snake River. After a tough six weeks, however, the portable plant arrived and the Wau became vocal, talking now with wireless in place of the kundu drum.

But the epidemic struck the Wau up in the mountains. Hundreds of boys went down like flies. Mrs Booth hurriedly collected her team, built a hospital, and for two months toiled night and day as doctor and nurse to the carriers. She must have saved many lives. She had been doctor and nurse alike to all hands ever since she came on the field, well earning her name as the "Angel of Bulolo."

The epidemic emphasized to the men on the Koranga and Edie how utterly dependent they were on their human beasts of burden. With the carriers ill or terrified, only a few hardy teams dared travel in with the stores. The authorities acted with all speed. Recruiters were asked to go out in all directions. One man, specially commissioned, after a particularly hazardous trip, brought in some six hundred recruits. These with others saved the men up on the field. But months later that recruiter was arrested, and ultimately awarded twelve months' gaol—hardly a fitting reward for a man who, at the risk of his own life, helped the authorities in time of emergency, even if he did punch an unruly recruit on the nose.

The dysentery epidemic would have proved a Black Death but for the foresight of the medical authorities in Rabaul. Dr Cilento, expecting an attack of the plague that years before had devastated the Papuan fields, was prepared and acted quickly.

Word flew around the field that old Ned Coakeley had dug the largest specimen yet found. So he had. He dug it in Midas Creek, a branch of the Edie. The very name thrilled him with a fellow feeling towards that golden king of long ago. "May th' saints rest his bones," he declared fervently.

He showed the nugget to everybody; he couldn't help it. Then he decided to use it for the benefit of his soul instead of his thirst. So he posted it to Archbishop Mannix and hardly growled at the stiff insurance.

Ned was inordinately proud of that nugget and waited anxiously for an acknowledgment. None came. Some weeks later, however, a crowd of miners blew into camp with the mail and ostentatiously handed Ned a large, official looking envelope. With trembling fingers he broke the seal then read a grave acknowledgment for the valuable contribution so kindly presented to—a *Protestant* archbishop.

Ned released a torrent of language. Later on it was found that Ned had not thought it necessary to mail an explanatory letter with the nugget. The Archbishop in good time solved the puzzle and Ned was thanked from the right quarter. But he always wanted to find the knave who faked that letter.

Harry Darby landed on the beach, yawned, then had a stroll round. He was a cheery, happy-go-lucky little chap. A Barnardo boy originally, he had been sailor, soldier, and general adventurer. When gold was discovered in New Guinea he was overseer of the Rabaul Labour Line. Of course, when Edie Creek was found, and returning diggers were "flashing" their gold in Rabaul, Darby did not have a shilling to bless himself with. But a plantation owner named Wylde came to the rescue. He equipped Darby, and did the job well. They were to go fifty-fifty in anything Darby found.

So Darby found himself on the beach. While others were hurrying around vainly searching the bush for carriers or rushing the recruiters to bid over one another's heads, Darby did not hurry at all. Why worry? Let 'em break their necks rushing up to the field. He guessed there might be a little gold left when he arrived. There was, too. Nearly every field has its story of the lazy man who "just came and sat down on it."

But Darby was three months on the beach before he secured carriers. When he arrived at the Edie, "all the ground was pegged out." He accepted the position philosophically. After a spell he decided to put pegs in somewhere, if only for practice. The easiest ground he could see to peg was a terrace a hundred and fifty feet above Edie Creek. Dubiously he pegged, then sat down to think things over. Quite a while afterwards he thought he might as well set the coons to sinking a few pot-holes; it would keep the lazy beggars exercised, anyway.

Time went on. Bill Stower returned to the field still seeking his fortune. He had a few leases pegged out; pegging a few was a habit growing on everyone. Bill had one pegged alongside Darby. He thought he might as well give Darby this one, it was in a better position and poor Harry only had one lease. So he gave Darby the lease-and gave away a fortune. Darby was an optimist; before he won any gold he thought he might as well call his ground "The Eldorado." Darby accepted Stower's lease lackadaisically; he might as well have it; he rarely looked a gift horse in the face. It was a scrubby looking lease, but he accepted it on the understanding that:

"You're on a few quid, anyway, if anything ever comes out of it."

"Right oh!" agreed Stower, as he lit a cigarette. "There might be gold in it; you can never tell."

Darby later bought another lease from Jack Mitchell for £700. That lease also returned many thousands. Thus are fortunes given away—sometimes! The Eldorado was to turn out the richest claim on the field. Gold was won from it in dishfuls, and the ex-Barnardo boy was to tour the world with a famous steamer captain as his aide-de-camp.

But that and many other things were still in the future—the future whose wheel of fortune turns so quickly on a new goldfield.

Meanwhile Darby had to dig his fortune. With a sigh he set to work, or rather, he set the kanakas to work.

Frank Pryke's photograph of the junction of Merri and Edie Creeks, 1927, which he noted as "one of the picked spots."

CHAPTER XXI

THE RACE STARTS

On Koranga Levien wanted an aeroplane. Well, he rushed to Adelaide to get it. Wells called a board meeting, otherwise Levien might have waked the dead. Somewhat pacified, he put the pros and cons before the directors in a forceful manner there was no denying. They promised him the plane and farewelled him with relief. He certainly had put pep into them; his presence was like a breeze that cleared the air and swept them with a storm of enthusiasm. But during the next rapid four years they were jolly glad the storm did not blow in too often.

Quite happy, Levien hurried back to the Territory. He would have to prepare a 'drome. The Administration were discussing a 'drome-site at Lae if ever it were needed. Well, Levien needed that 'drome. To Wells fell the job of finding the plane. A surprisingly hard task: no one had a plane for sale. And events were moving!

In Brisbane there was a certain flying bird called Ray Parer. To him one day came a tall man with the sunburn of the North upon him. He suggested to Parer that they should start a flying company for the New Guinea goldfields. He had a fairish amount of capital and was prepared to give it a go. Parer just rushed for train and car, and soon they were humming through Central Queensland to a station man who had a plane for sale. But fowls were roosting upon it and the plane wouldn't fly.

These plane hunters were an adventurous pair. Parer had flown with Macintosh from England to Australia in a crazy machine. They were just beaten by Sir Ross Smith. Ever since, he had been battling, little knowing that further adventures in New Guinea were to confirm his nickname of "Battling Parer."

Parer is a little man; his North Queensland friend a tall and extraordinarily powerful man. Pioneering a flying enterprise in a new country appealed to him tremendously. They hurried to Sydney, but, finding nothing to fly with, took train to Melbourne and got on the scent of a DH 37—just too late. Several days before, Wilton, a recruiter on holiday, and a friend of Levien, casually walked into the office of Levien's attorney and gossiped:

"There's a chap called Holdgate has an option on a plane in Melbourne. There seems to be some movement in the wind to start flying in New Guinea."

"Know his address?" quietly asked Wells.

"Why, yes, he's staying at — —."

Wells reached for the phone and called up Melbourne. Not many hours later he was in Melbourne and inspecting the plane. It was a DH 37 (375 h.p. Rolls Royce engine), a civil aviation machine, an old servant of Colonel Brinsmead, the Controller, and had won a race across Australia against all comers in its day. At the Essendon Aerodrome a wiry pilot with a keen, quizzical face was messing about the engine. A very large, very good-humoured engineer-mechanic, covered in oil and grease was rasping things at a work bench.

"Want a job," inquired Wells, "flying in New Guinea?"

Pilot Mustar stroked his chin.

"Oh yes," he drawled. "At a figure. It would be a change."

Wells named the figure and Mustar quickly replied:

"I'm on, if Colonel Brinsmead will let me go."

"I'll have a talk with the Colonel," said Wells as he walked over to the big mechanic:

"Want a job?"

"Where?"

"New Guinea."

The big mechanic smiled.

"What screw?" Wells named it, and the big man said:

"I'm on!"

Then things moved. They had to; for Parer immediately got in touch with Larkin and bought an old DH4.

It was going to be a race.

Parer seized on his old war-bird as a good omen. This was the machine De Garis flew when Parer won the first Australian Aerial Derby in the bold old flight days. He wired and booked the available space on the *Marsina,* thus beating Holdgate to the loading. The race had started in earnest. Railway officials were harassed by determined men wanting to rail aeroplanes to Sydney.

But Parer just missed the *Marsina;* he got to the wharf but finances beat him to the ship. With a hard little smile he watched her steam away; then he rushed to book space on the *Melusia* before Holdgate should get it. The *Melusia* would not sail for several weeks. Parer and his mate hurried around seeking further finance while Holdgate besieged the offices of Burns, Philp & Company.

"Every available foot of space is taken up," declared the harassed shipping clerk for the twentieth time. "There's not even space for a crate of fowls, let alone another plane!"

"But you're shipping donks in Townsville!"
"Yes, I know. But their space was booked long ago."
"Well, I want space for this plane!"
"Well, you can't get it!"
"Can't I? We'll see!"

The shipping man gritted his teeth and glared across the desk, then shrugged and hurried away. But the birds of the DH 37 continued to roost in the shipping office.

As sailing day drew near, Parer scoured the city in frantic haste seeking capital to fly with. At the last moment a Sydney company backed him and his friend, and floated the "Bulolo Goldfields Aeroplane Service." So Parer was assured of his capital—

But just too late. In bitter chagrin he had to take his plane off the *Melusia* and see the triumphant Holdgate swing his aboard instead.

The little old *Melusia* sailed on her last voyage (nearly to the bottom of the sea, too) giving the Guinea Gold Company the first lap in the race. This was early in 1927.

Full of enthusiasm Levien bore down on Lae from Wau with two hundred and fifty kanaka labourers. He immediately set to work clearing the ground of trees, filling in holes to make a level landing-ground, building native quarters and, with native materials, a hangar. It was a joyous task, building that 'drome. The visions Levien built into it had wings, while the building of it was the sweeter because of the spirit of fight aroused. Radio had warned him of opposition coming. There is nothing that can put fight into a man so much as a struggle in primitive country; nothing puts spirit into him so much as seeing his dream coming true.

An undercurrent of uneasiness had spread over both fields and down over the many villages to Salamaua on the coast. The primitive passions of a hundred thousand savages were rumbling like an awakening volcano.

The carriers were the menace: the arrogant, overbearing fools who, because of their increased numbers, imagined they could overawe the bush tribes.

Every native village from the Wau to Salamaua had been in a state of sullen unrest for a considerable time. In Lambura Yabbi the luluai crouched, planning with the raiders of Salinkora and Kaisinik, pausing occasionally with cynical leer as carriers padded by.

At night grim ceremonies took place behind the stockades of Kaisinik; the wild women's glee split the silence as terrified men were dragged in over the fighting-pits and slung down under the trees. And now by that subtle "wireless" of the primitive man word sped round:

"The bush kanakas are short of meat!" Ominous words! for white masters as well as carriers.

Here and there with low harsh tone a kundu boomed, and the drummer listened to its vibrating growl, until far away another drum boomed while another drummer listened to yet another drum.

It was the carriers' fault entirely. As they passed through the villages the cheeky ones had taken to throwing down their loads and breaking into the native gardens, trampling underfoot what they did not steal. Emboldened by non-retaliation, the boldest of them began to steal the village pigs. What wild kanaka will stand that? Let alone such men as dwelt in Lambura, Salinkora, and Kaisinik. How the young men were taunted by the village women! Sullen within their quarters they listened to the jeering women passing by. A young girl would whip off her lap-lap and throw it over the fence, shrilly calling:

"Keep it, brave warriors. I have no use for it now!"

How the village laughed! How the children jeered! An odd carrier here and there disappeared. The miners, alarmed before this, had doubled the escort that went down to the coast with the carrier teams. Any carrier caught interfering with the property of the villagers was immediately punished. But what could a dozen overseers do on a seventy-mile track with two thousand (soon to be three thousand) carriers scattered along it?

The presence of more whites with the teams, strangely enough, only emboldened the carriers, for they reasoned that the villagers would not dare to retaliate in view of the white masters' fire-arms. So they stole the wild men's produce the more whenever razor-back ridge or mountain hid them from the nearest white escort. The timid ones among the carriers began to desert, through fear of Yabbi the luluai and his stealthy raiders. But the cheeky ones among them laughed the timid ones to scorn as women, and on occasion thrashed them. Meanwhile, the villagers all along the track tilled their gardens or crouched in sullen brooding, awaiting the coming vengeance. Keen ears listened to the throb of Yabbi's drums:

"Plenty meat is coming—take it!"

Daily and nightly now at sudden intervals the kundus boomed in pulsing throbs throughout the black Bulolo, thrumming in hollow tones that echoed from cliff face to quivering answer on mountain crag miles away. Many carriers now trod closer together as those notes throbbed out; there was no sleeping by the wayside now; they hurried when they came to a village, their eyes rolling to right and left as they slipped quickly by.

Well they sensed the meaning of that drumming.

The whites knew that the carriers who disappeared could not all be deserters, for among them were men from over the sea. These had nowhere to desert to. If they took to the bush they knew their certain fate.

It was not the considerable loss in money and time and the inconvenience that each deserting carrier caused that troubled most the isolated whites; something much more serious was feared. Their supplies from the coast might be cut off at a single blow. So they anxiously watched their carriers; they threatened them; they pointed out to them the danger. Knowing, however, that this would have little effect on the kanaka mind when he thinks his bluff has won the day, they arranged their teams so that they would pass Lambura and other villages in the middle of the day. The night camps were thus a considerable distance from the three notorious villages, and there was less chance of the carriers playing up near these danger-points. But the wild Adzera men and the pugnacious Sepiks among the carriers laughed at warnings—laughed when the white masters could not see. They took to chasing the native women!

No wonder carriers disappeared. Stragglers were picked off; just a crash on the head from behind; the rustle of grass as they flung him clear of the path. A cough as the following team came padding along while the slayers gathered closer over their man and listened to the soft footfalls passing by. Then a quick springing up as they carried their victim away to the bamboo-knife and the cooking-fires.

The brown black bushmen were short of meat! They were taking it after provocation. Theirs was not the white man's law; and it is difficult justly to judge them.

But the innocent suffered. Tovelli was the first boy definitely known to have been eaten; a quiet, industrious New Britain man, the best worker in Burleigh Gorman's team. Herb Wilson had landed at Salamaua, back from the south, with his poisoned hand cured. Gorman was loath to send him, but Tovelli was the most reliable boy he had, the best to get Wilson up to the field as quickly as possible.

Tovelli *knew*. He came to Gorman with presentiment in his quiet brown eyes the night before he started. He helped the white master through, but coming back the Lambura men got him. And Tovelli was the only married man in Gorman's team.

CHAPTER XXII

THE CAGING OF YABBI THE LULUAI

Police Master J. Bourke was quite pleased with the world in general. He was well, and his constabulary were moving with the tread of disciplined men. They were sick, worse luck, but would soon brighten up after a good spell. He was returning from an arduous patrol along the Salamaua track and would be at the Wau, and beginning a well-earned rest, in less than two hours' time.

It was a brilliant morning; insects were humming over the kunai grass; cockatoos were screeching in the open forest country. Bourke envied the police boys their muscular legs, though by no means a weakling himself. Lithe and fit as a fiddle he was a picture of health, a typical police master in a smart and highly efficient service.

At a sharp call from the sergeant he hurried to where the police had grouped on the track. There lay three headless carriers, their bodies quite warm. Quickly the sergeant traced the blood-drips on the green kunai grass. The carriers of the heads had disappeared towards Kaisinik village. They would be furious that the patrol had caused them the loss of a meal.

But when the police master hurried away to report at the Wau the cannibal men came eagerly back and, snatching up their victims, carried them to the hot saltwater springs quite near the track and there cooked them.

Acting Warden Grosse ordered Bourke to proceed at once to Kaisinik and arrest the murderers if possible. But the five police boys were hospital cases, so Bourke conscripted three Aitape mining boys as police and set out towards the headquarters of the notorious villages.

Quickly, but quietly, the patrol climbed down into the Bulolo valley and advanced between the tall pines that grew along the banks of the swiftly running creeks. Bourke got fleeting glimpses of tribesmen in the kunai grass on the razor-backs and saw they were in war-feathers and carried bows and arrows. He ran right into one weird-looking crowd. There is something uncannily repulsive about these savages that instinctively causes the white or brown stranger to keep well away from them. For these are the real cannibals, men who eat human flesh because they love it roasted. They scowled at the police. Their *marl* was a cloth-like bark twisted round the waist, with the long end of it brought up between the legs, then under the "belt" in front to fall over like a disreputable sporran. Their long hair swung over their shoulders in heavy plaits in which bark-strips dyed a deep red were twisted. *Pus-pus* armlets adorned their sinewy arms; dogs' teeth and necklets of cane with inlaid shell, their necks. Their long bows were fitted for five-foot feathered arrows. These were tipped with cassowary-toe and betel-nut.

They were sinewy black and copper-coloured men, their ugly faces strangely prominent, with a round Roman nose made uglier by a long bone, or a circular one through the septum. But their eyes sent shivers down the spines of the newly recruited police. They were strangely dead, fish-like eyes, but with a baleful glare—a remarkable characteristic of the real cannibal's eyes. Tribes who only occasionally eat a man, perhaps from necessity at initiation rites, have quite different eyes.

These savages vanished into the grass. Bourke passed on, uneasy at the throbbing of the kundu drums. Those animal men, too, flitting like giant bats through the tall kunai, gave him the creeps. They did look like bats, with their bark capes flapping on their hunched shoulders as they dived into the undergrowth, and their monstrous beaks of cassowary feathers projecting over their brows to protect their cold eyes from the sun. Only the natives of the deep Bulolo valley wear these eyeshades. They are needed to protect the eyes from the sun that comes burning down between those towering walls. Bourke brushed the sweat from his forehead while pushing through the grass that hemmed the track chest-high. He halted, glowering down. A stick lay by the track, and planted beside it was a broad-bladed bamboo arrow soaked in pig's blood.

War! At last the cannibal men had flung down their gauntlet to the whites! The patrol's situation was desperate. It was getting dangerously late. He turned off down the valley towards where the Gadagadu track came in, selected a strategical position, and camped. But Bourke did not sleep. Next day he worked his way along into the Gadagadu track and for some days patrolled it, conscripting an odd police boy as frightened teams of carriers crept along. There was no dawdling among these fellows now. And how they clung to their lonely police boy escort! With alarm Bourke noted how few these teams were. In demoralized tones they told how other teams had thrown down their bundles and run back to Salamaua. Wild tales of carriers eaten were rife. Greatly exaggerated, of course; but the morale of two thousand carriers was completely broken. The police boys who drove them on were brave men. Although armed and representing the white man, they were fearful themselves; but with impassive face each widely separated man clenched his rifle and marched stolidly on.

A few days later, Bourke was delighted to see Patrol Officer Nichols coming along the track from Salamaua. He had several police boys and a few carriers with him, bringing their combined constabulary to ten.

The officials conferred. To attempt to force entry into heavily stockaded Kaisinik or Salinkora was absurd; to enter Lambura village was equally so. But they might get the murderers of the last three carriers by guile. They were nearly certain to be in Lambura village, where they would be heroes. It was in Lambura that all the trouble was hatched, under the guidance of the notorious Yabbi. Neither Nichols nor Bourke had ever seen this chief; nor had the native police.

It was decided to try and trap the murderers. The combined forces set out on a circular route so as not to disturb until the last moment the hatching of further conspiracies. They came on the village suddenly; but those inside had been warned by the kundu drums. With a sneering disdain they waited for the entry of the party that would not enter. A messenger was sent in to bargain for labour to build a house at Webining village. The price offered for each labourer was a phenomenal one, to be paid on completion of the job.

The tribesmen conferred. They had expected war, not a commercial proposition. While in low-toned council they debated, Yabbi, the luluai, sat aside in crafty thought. Webining village was down towards Salamaua, not back towards the bom-boms up at the Wau. Why not take advantage of these many tomahawks in payment for a house; then, if opportunity occurred, sink the axes into the heads of the payers? With a queer glint in their eyes a hundred naked men strolled out from the village. Bourke lined them up while Nichols with the ten police boys stood casually aside, although ready instantly to fire. Keenly the two officers scrutinized that line of brown-black faces. Knowing that some notorious killers among the natives have happy and saint-like faces, they selected a few of these and then the most murderous they could find— thirty-two all told—and marched them off, unostentatiously but warily marching their police boys among them.

And Yabbi marched with them, although there was nothing to tell who he was.

A young boy, selected at the last moment, was among the crowd. This lad did not look a murderer, but he might be persuaded to tell something. One could never tell! A runaway mission boy was picked for the same reason. As to the luluai, who did not look a luluai, well, he looked a prince of murderers. But the officers never dreamt that the volunteer labourers marched with a leader.

The party camped three nights on the track; the third on a ledge overlooking the Labbibia Gorge, with the torrential river pounding eerily below. Behind them the mountain side rose in a sheer cliff face to a dizzy height, then fell back, densely clothed in scrub. The ledge was long and winding, and of just sufficient width to permit men to sleep side by side with their legs doubled up, otherwise their feet would be over the ledge. The officers, the police boys, and the carriers slept close together; the thirty odd tribesmen a little farther along the ledge.

It was a wild sleeping-place, but strangely safe. If the tribesmen rushed them they could only kill the first two men—but those men did not sleep!

Far above was a bluey blackness without a star, for ghostly clouds were rolling in slow travelling motion up there. Lying side by side in a thickening darkness the officers conferred, their whispers drowned by murmuring waters. Farther along, past the police, the carriers were conspiring too.

To-morrow would be the day. The tribesmen then would realize they were not bound for Webining. What would they do? Nichols and Bourke planned to make an early start and push right on to Salamaua. If the tribesmen objected—?

At 4 a.m. the police boys, with kicks and harsh whispers, woke the carriers. The huddled forms sulkily arose and came shuffling along in the dark.

"We are tired and sore," they growled, low-voiced. "We carried these heavy packs all day yesterday over mountains and across raging torrents while these bush cannibals walked behind and laughed! We are sore this day. The cannibals can chafe their backs instead!"

The carriers were allowed to walk back along the ledge. At long last they did bluff five of the cannibals to carry. In the cold grey of dawn these came peering along the ledge. Instantly they saw that all packs were done up for a long journey. Without a sign of perturbation they bent to the packs, lifted them, then with one accord ran yelling along the ledge. Instant confusion of stampeding men; police snatching at leaping runaways; carriers grabbing; yells, as strong black shadows sped along and down the ledge.

The patrol officer fired, and Yabbi fell. Eleven men only were captured, twenty-one escaped. The luluai lay prone. But he was only stunned; he had tripped on a rattan and struck his head on the rock. His head and one arm were hanging over the ledge as they snapped the handcuffs on. The others were then manacled, and the party pushed on hastily, fearing an attempt at rescue from the rear. The kanakas hastened on sure feet along that precipitous ledge, high above the Labbibia River, but never a man slipped, even those carrying a load. Utterly done in, they arrived at Salamaua late that evening.

Now came the Sherlock Holmes work, to prove which, if any, of the prisoners were guilty of the murder evinced by those headless bodies. Nichols was sure that the black mission boy knew the ringleaders. But it was plain that the man was cowed by his wild tribesmen and afraid to tell the police.

They conversed with this man through an interpreter, having called him and the mission boy aside, well out of hearing of the others. Sternly a patrol officer approached him.

"Rasu! It is all up with you! Laba has just told us how you murdered the carriers!"

As the interpreter translated, the mission boy went chocolate-grey.

"No master," he stuttered. "No—no—killim—finish! He work longa luluai, das all!"

Lason, a big sinister-looking cannibal with enormous feet, was next approached.

"Lason! the mission boy has just confessed you killed the carriers!"

Lason drew his magnificent frame erect as a slow, boyish grin spread over his strong, rugged face:

"No —— fear!" he replied, through the interpreter. "The luluai did it."

The lad who had been selected on the off chance was then approached.

"It is all up with you, boy. We know you killed the carriers!"

The carriers when alive could have eaten him, but he turned grey and stammered:

"No! No! Yabbi did it! He is with us now!"

Only then did the officers know what a capture they had made. Yabbi was then brought before them. A queer smile spread over the interpreter's face as the grim-faced chief strode up. He halted, glaring balefully, and snarled a cynical greeting.

"Yabbi, the mission boy has just told us how you killed the carriers!"

Incredulous astonishment spread over the luluai's deep-lined face; then fury brought a flash to his eyes. "Of all the dogs born of women!" he snarled, and leapt straight up, trying to smash the manacles from his hands. "This —— is a dog of liars," he shouted. "I will slice his liver piece by piece!"

"Yabbi!" said the patrol officer sternly, "Lason also has told us how you murdered the carriers!"

The luluai stood stock still, his forehead a maze of wrinkles, staring as a man dumbfounded. A fleck of foam slowly gathered at the corners of his mouth. Like a mad beast he struggled to smash his handcuffs.

"Yabbi!" called the patrol officer harshly, "the boy also has told us how you murdered the carriers!"

The luluai went mad. He was faced by the three accusers. They were allowed to argue it out themselves. The luluai turned on his accusers like an enraged animal, moaning the terrible things he could not speak. Finally, he turned to the patrol officers standing silently by:

"Yes," he gasped hoarsely, "I killed them. At least I am no woman!"

A game man was the murderous Yabbi. He gave all particulars in careful detail, then slowly turned his head to stare at his three accusers. They cringed before him.

CHAPTER XXIII

THE PUNITIVE EXPEDITION

Shortly after these events, Warden McLean, lent by the Queensland Government, arrived up on the Wau to find it and the Bulolo in desperate plight: the miners starving; the carriers in terror of their lives; only the bravest of them game to venture the track from Salamaua.

In fact, the wild kanakas came dangerously close to driving the whites from the field, temporarily at least. Some men were in despair. Archie Whitbourne and Dover saw their chance of fortune vanishing after two years of heart-breaking struggle. Of all Whitbourne's mining-boys and carriers, but one scared specimen remained. Ernie Banks was almost as badly off; others very soon would be.

Now, a carrier recently killed happened to be a tribesman of the Bouangs. When the kundus boomed the news, the Bouangs promptly resented—not so much the killing, as the fact that he had gone to make meat for the Salinkora-Lambura-Kaisinik men. Moreover, being a crowd used to fighting for their heads, they picked out sixty-four of their best warriors to exact vengeance.

A fortnight later a string of carriers arrived at the Wau under strong police escort. Most carried government stores; the last fourteen were orderlies with medical supplies.

A few days afterwards the carriers left on their return journey to the coast, going light-heartedly, in view of protection. The fourteen medical carriers were the last to leave. Several hours later the remnant of these men came flying back to the Wau, screaming:

"The cannibals! The cannibals! They are eating our friends!" An hysterical boy flung himself down at the warden's office, squeaking:

"Master, master, this feller kanaka he kill him! Alla boy finish!"

Alarmed by their frantic yells, the miners came hurrying to the latest trouble.

At 3 a.m. an organized party under Patrol Officer Bourke left camp and climbed out of the Edie Gorge by the crossing into the Bulolo valley. They travelled fast, but the kundu travelled faster. Later, Bourke enlisted the sixty-four Bouangs as carriers; they were priceless now in this country where carriers were hurrying for their lives back to Salamaua.

Three days later, the Wau track, for some distance, was like a butcher's shop. Freshly gnawed bones were strewn about, lumps of half-roasted meat, scalps and hands; several arms and legs were still hanging to trees where they had been spiked till wanted for the oven. Warden McLean decided something must be done quickly!

"This big field cannot be definitely held up because of a bunch of cannibals," he declared. "Besides, a very little more of this and all the whites will be completely isolated, far from help and the coast. I'm going to put a stop to this before it is too late!"

Bourke's party returned, unable to accomplish anything against the swarms opposed to them. Down in the Bulolo Gorge the kundus were drumming menacingly, savage triumph in their vibrant tones. Lason, the man-eater, had slipped his great feet from the white man's shackles and escaped to Lambura, to become a ringleader in the rising of the tribes. The miners came rolling in to the Wau, looking very nasty. There was purpose in their grim, set faces. Something must be done—and quickly! They asked what the warden was going to do. If he was not acting at once, then they were "going out" themselves.

But the warden intended to act according to law. He and the second in command (Patrol Officer Bourke) laid their plans, and the miners offered their services, their working boys, and all their arms.

Avisia, chief police boy in charge of patrols along the Kaisinik track, was very busy. All the native constabulary within reach were pressed into service; reliable boys from the miners' camps were armed; there was a quick hunting round for carriers, the sixty-four Bouangs saving the situation in this respect. "Dusty" Miller's cook-boy, Anas, eagerly volunteered; he implored to be allowed to go. Miller vigorously refused, but the tears welled to Anas's eyes. Now, Anas was a boy almost worth his weight in gold. He was a highly civilized boy; he was justly considered to be one of the best cooks in New Guinea, perhaps as good a cook as a white woman. Certainly he could "do up" a white suit of clothes better than many a woman. And this wonder, who could cook seven different dishes at a meal, wanted to go and risk his precious life—be cooked for a cannibals' feast maybe. Reluctantly, Miller consented to his being recruited as a special native constable.

Anas smiled like a boy in a tart-shop; while Nasu, Bill Royal's boy, looked on patronizingly, like a big dog pleased that a little puppy should have some play. Nasu was a man who counted: he nursed a shot-gun.

The force set out quietly, keyed up to the challenge of the broad-bladed arrow. There were only a few white miners—the warden would not take more than were needed to stiffen the force.

The first objective was Lambura village. It was proposed to surround the village silently at night. Then, in early morning, send half a dozen carriers up the valley as decoys. When the Lambura men swarmed out for the passing meat, the carriers were to run straight towards the ambush and so lead the pursuers into the trap. The leading pursuers would probably be the ringleaders of the recent massacres. Should the carriers refuse this risky duty, then white men would volunteer. They would strip and blacken themselves; the deception would hardly be noticed in the gloom and excitement of the chase.

However, lik-lik doctor Lambert had patrolled through that country, and he now said that both ends of the gorge could be blocked. The tribesmen would hardly be able to escape up the cliff-like walls on either side. All would be captured; the murderers sorted out and arrested. This plan was agreed upon The force split up and one night, in two stealthy parties, descended into the gorge and blocked it below and above the village. Both parties did their job excellently, landing just ahead and just below the village. Then came the nervy creeping forward—in a gripping fear of crashing into a fighting-pit staked with spears. Each man, too, crept warily clear of village paths, knowing that these were staked with razor-sharp bamboo splinters and with spears whose long-barbed points reached out of the dark grass.

In the silence before dawn, just as the low grass houses began to take shape in the chilly light, they encircled the village. Two very early cockatoos screeched overhead, their wing-beats heard distinctly by those crouching below.

At dawn they rushed the village. It was deserted! A derisive howl made the breathless attackers look up to see the tribesmen, like monkeys, scaling the cliffs on either side of the gorge. The growing light showed the plan of the force down below. The tribesmen hooted derisively, while dancing on the rocky ledges above, flourishing their bows and arrows and shooting far out into space in an attempt at dropping fire.

Deeply chagrined, the force sat down to breakfast. The whites laughed woefully. They had been through some nervy days and nights, and now were laughed at by those men monkeys upon the cliffs. Even the piccaninnies shrilled their derision. As they watched, the monkeys bent themselves into licentious attitudes and howled:

"Come on bom-boms! Come and be eaten, pigs of women!"

These and coarser invitations annoyed the native constabulary excessively.

The force dined hungrily, then wrecked the village. But to teach these people a lesson without being brutally severe was going to prove extraordinarily difficult. It is hard to reason with a cannibal. However, they had already split the Lambura tribesmen in two, driving the larger portion to the opposite side of the Bulolo valley. The force spread out with the object of driving the whole crowd still farther away. The tribesmen enjoyed it. They spread out, too, hilarious mobs of them, on every height dancing and howling:

"Come on! Come on!"

The rugged country compelled the attacking force to split into groups. One of these, under Patrol Officer Bourke, presently found themselves opposed by a fightable body of tribesmen who faced them determinedly, bending their long bows from partial cover, eager ones loosing their arrows to enthusiastic howls as the feathered shafts sped far out over the gorge to turn in mid air and hiss swiftly down.

These bowmen commanded a precipitous razor-back up which there was only one narrow approach. Wishing to avoid bloodshed and yet apprehensive for his own tiny force, Bourke halted just out of bow-shot and reported to Warden McLean. The reply came:

"Use your own discretion."

The party moved cautiously forward to the tune of a welcoming howl from above. Arrows came zipping down. Bourke eyed a small patch of jungle growing at the foot of the razor-back. He halted the party.

"Miller!"

"Yes?"

"Very soon I am going to disappear in the kunai grass. Take your boys on ahead, but when at the foot of the razor-back, dive into that scrub and wait among the undergrowth just five minutes. Then come straight back!"

"Right! What's the game?"

"I'm going to see whether those coons really mean business."

Bourke's party disappeared into the long grass, like quail in a patch of wheat. Through his glasses Bourke watched the manoeuvres on the razor-back. The tribesmen, as Miller's few men advanced, shouted for fight, then, apparently losing heart, faded away. But immediately Miller's party entered the scrub the tribesmen crept back, to run along the razor-back, then plunge down on either side and vanish in the grass, leaving the steep narrow track open and bare. It was an ambush from which not a man could have escaped.

As Miller's party returned from the jungle the tribesmen leaped back up on to the razor-back, howling in chagrin, shooting their arrows high in an attempt to pierce the retreating figures. Bourke's crowd then fired over their heads, only to be greeted with a roar of war-yells and leaping, insulting gestures. The next shots whipped the ground below them, cracking sharply, to echo and re-echo down the valley, chorused by shriller howls of "Come on!" The next shots were at them and the tribesmen disappeared like scalded cats.

Late that afternoon the expedition, from vantage-points, saw winding in the distance a long line of kanakas going towards the Upper Bulolo, while another big crowd trailed up the gorge towards the Kaisinik side. The constabulary gazed in disappointment. But the white leaders said:

"Good riddance! That's the last of them. If they will only keep in that district they can eat one another to their heart's content."

Those turbulent savages would have a cold and hungry camp tonight, unless they turned in towards Kaisinik. If they did that, the warfires would be blazing and the kundus booming within the big stockade.

Excitement blazed up again, however, as yet another body of tribesmen threateningly appeared on a height right near the Bulolo. As the main body of the force faced towards them, the warriors howled for fight and really wanted it. They were arrogantly confident because they had just defied several parties to drive them by peaceable means after their comrades. From the vantage-points held by the expedition, the leaders could look down at these tribesmen, and, over them along the valley, get just a glimpse of the goldfield track. As they looked they were horrified to see a line of carriers emerge from the trees and come winding slowly along the track. The carriers could not see the tribesmen, nor could the tribesmen see the carriers; and the expedition dare not open fire lest the tribesmen leap behind their ridge and see the oncoming carriers.

Ten native police were detailed to run down the gorge and try to intercept the carriers. The expedition waited breathlessly. The carriers toiled peacefully on. They were almost on top of the tribesmen when a carrier dropped his bundle with a terrified yell. The tribesmen leapt round, then with one glad, impassioned cry swarmed down towards the carriers who, dropping their bundles, fled with wails of horror.

Down along their line was one police-boy escort armed with a shotgun. He hesitated. Startled by the screams, with the fear of death in his heart, yet clothed in the constabulary's uniform, he stood motionless while men raced past. A moment later the ten police boys panted into view. The constable instantly rushed forward, levelled his gun, and fired at the howling pursuers. With the report the constabulary's rifles rang out in the nick of time to avert a general massacre. The scrap was lively but short, with brave men among the cannibals twisting round, to loose their arrows at unexpected enemies firing from they knew not where. Caught between two fires of unknown strength they leapt to cover, fought a few moments, then fled.

With the dispersal of this crowd all the tribesmen were driven well away across the valley, all fast disappearing towards the darkening mountains.

In the chill air at sundown a little party of patrol officers and miners wearily stripped for a swim in a quiet pool. Sentinels were posted, Nasu with his beloved shot-gun being placed behind a bush. It was a formal precaution, for the tribesmen were miles away.

The cool, refreshing bath was rudely interrupted by the roar of a gun. Nasu had shot a tribesman right between the eyes! A party of them had crept through the long grass to within twenty yards of the pool, and were just bending their long bows when—Bang! Which explains why, as night drew on, bringing all details marching into camp, a very arrogant man strode among the police and carriers. Stiffly he ordered two kanakas to cook him food; roughly he ordered two others to prepare him a warm soft bed of kunai grass. He glanced around at the awed looks, spat betel-nut, then hoarsely commanded a kanaka to cut him tobacco, fill his pipe, light it, and to use his own tobacco too!

For Nasu had killed a man.

Strong guards were posted that night. Eerily in the silence a wind came moaning up the gorge bringing a burst of distant song, harsh with menace. Then the Kaisinik drums began to rumble.

Next day the force rested, while the leaders planned. Kaisinik, built on top of a razor-back, surrounded by a mighty *banus* (stockade) and of remarkable tactical strength, was the red-hot stronghold of the cannibals. Its stockade had grown in many places to be living trees. The natives plant the stockade green, in a gigantic circle, and much of the green timber takes root and grows. The queer-looking houses inside were shrewdly high walled, built by primitive engineers, with the floor of each important house a deep pit, a dug-out primarily for defence. When enemies surrounded Kaisinik by night, and loosed showers of arrows over the stockade, the sleepers inside were down in the pits under the roofs, with ladders ready set for the rush up to the counter-attack. He sleeps soundly who sleeps protected in New Guinea.

Outside the banus itself were deep fighting-pits filled with embedded spears, points upwards. The tangled kunai grass on the edges of these pits was trained to grow out over them, while riotous creepers completely covered the death-traps from view. Pointed bamboo-splinters were planted along every path, the points protruding to tear through naked feet. A thin layer of leaves hid these splinters in daylight. Inside that stockade were now perhaps more than a thousand fighting men boiling with fighting lust. Kaisinik was going to be a hard nut to crack—if the warriors stood at the last moment.

The warden wished to take Kaisinik without blood-shed, if that were possible. The only way was to quietly surround it. Then, when daylight came, the tribesmen, seeing themselves completely hedged in, might lose heart (particularly after a few volleys had been poured into the banus) and hand over the actual murderers without bloodshed.

So it was planned. After a cautious night march, twenty-five trusted native constabulary were to creep round the rear of the village while the whites with the carriers linked up the surrounding circle and advanced at daylight.

Late that afternoon they tied white bandages round the heads of the carriers to distinguish friend from foe, then marched when evening shadowed the great valley. It was an eerie march. The men were treading with every sense alert as they crept from the trees, through tall grasses that rustled and clung to whisper unwillingly aside as the shadow forms pushed by. Well before dawn they neared the silent village. Noiselessly the force divided into parties that pressed on to take up the positions allotted them. With an instinct inherited through centuries of primitive war- fare, the native constabulary unerringly passed round to the rear, where each man separated until all had formed a long invisible line which crept stealthily up towards the village. The whites and carriers manoeuvred almost as craftily until just before dawn the village was completely surrounded. Each man then waited, listening, in a silence that could be felt. Dimly the trees around the banus took shape in the chill light before the dawn.

Then Nasu must get a tickling in his throat. He was squatting with his treasured gun between his knees. Though all had been expressly warned that "the night has ears!" Nasu wanted to cough. He did cough, and immediately received an arrow in his chest, for he had coughed behind a Kaisinik outpost.

Then Nasu coughed in earnest and let off his gun. From the line of keyed-up constabulary broke a rifle-shot, then two, then a spluttering as the whole line broke out in stabbing flashes and sharp reports that spread with the roar from Kaisinik.

A terrible roar that, and the ground trembled under the war-stamp of frenzied feet. That human volcano set shadowy figures rushing forward. The whites called them back in vain. Those in rear and on the flanks thought the firing was a signal to attack and the rush started in earnest, man calling to man in fierce excitement. The whites had to race forward too, lest they for all time lose prestige with friend and foe. They shouted to the Kaisinik men to surrender, to hand over the murderers, and no harm would be done them, but the derisive roar just swept their voices away.

The Kaisinik outposts ran for the stockade, yelling their war-cry, then halting to crouch and send arrows hissing towards the oncoming figures. Gamely they bent their great bows, delaying their leap to the stockade until the very last. Anas bowled over a foeman and gripping him by the hair sunk the blade of his tomahawk into the warrior's neck. Anas was not now kneading bread or cooking cakes, neither was he pressing out a white suit.

The Kaisinik men found that stockades will not stop bullets, nor fighting frenzy a disciplined rush. They stampeded to the rear and leaping the stockade were away in one frantic mob.

Kaisinik was burnt. A red history was blotted out when that ill-famed village went up in smoke.

After Kaisinik, the force marched back to the Wau, leaving a patrol officer and native constabulary to patrol the goldfield track. This party experienced a very lively four days until District Officer Appleby came hurrying up from Salamaua with constabulary. In three months he had the long track well under control.

Mrs Pryke on the verandah, Koranga 1927.

CHAPTER XXIV

THE CYCLONE

Meanwhile, the little *Melusia* was ploughing north through lively Australian seas: Those aboard were mostly bound for Salamaua. Of the women, Mrs Pryke was going to join her husband. There are pioneering women to-day, despite the great attraction of the cities.

Mustar and Mullins, with their aeroplane crew, were happy as the day is long. They were sailing to pioneer a new enterprise in a new country; to introduce the most modern machine to the most primitive land. And against competitors they had won the first lap in the race. Passengers and crew alike gazed ever and anon at that mighty case lashed securely 'thwart-ships, the ends projecting over the *Melusia's* sides. A veteran slumbered in that case; a monster of wood and steel that had roared above shell-torn fields. There was something ominous about it. What if bad weather came and that inert monster broke loose!

Captain "Taffy" Williams eyed it distastefully. During a long island service he had shipped just about everything that could be shipped, but he'd never yet commanded an ark that carried an aeroplane. From the bridge he frowned down on the thing. A rollicking comber, as if feeding his misgivings, lifted the bow high in the air. Phew! Now, if that case should break loose and come crashing back into the saloon!

Grimly he watched the aeroplane crew as, in proud ownership, they climbed all over that prized case; examining for the hundredth time the tautened cables that lashed it to the stanchions of the ship. The captain scowled at the mate: the mate scowled at the case.

Mustar was a keen-faced, slimly built fellow who had been observer to Ross Smith in Palestine and had won a breast of flying decorations. Mullins was a cheery giant recommended by Colonel Brinsmead as one of the best engineer-mechanics of the day. They mightn't be able to ride a horse but they could make an aeroplane do almost anything except eat oats. They winked amiably, with a side glance towards the bridge, and a cheery laugh for the bright blue sea.

At Townsville the *Melusia* took aboard her last passengers, thirty-three donkeys and mules with three donkey foals at foot, thirty-three packsaddles, and half a dozen horses. To a rattling of winches, exasperated shouts of men, kicks, and shuffling hoofs, the trembling things were somehow packed in the narrow reserved space forward.

These last passengers were welcomed aboard with curiosity and laughter intermixed with good wishes. For the donkeys, like the aeroplane, represented an attempt to solve the transport problem on the distant goldfield. Some enterprising miner had put his faith and money on them. They reciprocated with brayings and lashed out at their big mechanical rival immediately they were slung on to the deck.

"Planes an' donks," growled the skipper. "Why don't they send me white mice! It's enough to make the sea sick."

"Gives me a headache," said the mate.

"We'll have bad weather!" prophesied the cook.

"You don't know your onions," growled the skipper. "Get out of my sight!"

The *Melusia* sailed from Townsville out into the Barrier Sea. From the Pacific, swelling rollers came in to crash on the Great Barrier Reef and, surging on, form an oily swell that rose sullenly against the small steamer.

"Dirty weather!" growled the skipper at the rapidly falling glass.

"And the donks will know it!" echoed the mate glumly.

The skipper glowered at that huge case. The mate sniffed and spat over the side.

She got it. It came with a growing wave that lifted the *Melusia*, to hold her, trembling, with that great case menacing the saloon. As she quivered down again chains creaked to the forward lurch of the case. A blast of wind whistled overhead; then a chilly breath sped a frightening feeling through the air. The sky turned leaden as if to the flick of a movie camera; the vessel responded to growing waves in longer, deepening plunges; she began to roll; wind came whistling from a blackening sky, and icy spray whipped the faces of passengers and crew. Miserably the donks turned their rumps. A wave burst right on the bow and came aft to surge upon the case and roll men and donkeys on the deck. The case groaned to the trembling of the ship. Waves rose up to a peak-point that, when about to break, was sucked off by the wind in whistling clouds of spray.

A low moaning came from far away. Suddenly across the sky—men held their breath and clutched anything, turning bowed shoulders to the wind.

"Cyclone!" roared the skipper. "All passengers below!"

Massed waves thundered upon the bow and came leaping aft in torrents of whirling foam.

"Overboard with those broken-legged donks!" yelled the mate. "Put that horse over too. Move now. Move!"

The vessel lay over, to tremble in seas that tumbled all around. In a ceaseless shriek the wind slapped salt-stung faces as men fought their way across the deck, dodging the sliding bodies of animals that struggled in helpless misery. Some floundered pathetically; others kicked frantically, unable to regain foothold as wave upon wave smashed upon those thin iron plates and rolled in hissing tons towards the case, swirling the men aside or sucking them under among rolling bodies of drowning animals.

Poor donks! And hard luck for the owner; his hopes of solving the New Guinea transport problem were smashed by a furious sea. Night came to the accompaniment of a terrifying howl. Phantom clouds tore across the sky. The skipper clung to the bridge as he altered the course to run for Willis Island; he felt he was steering into a roaring pit with its walls in convulsions.

Below deck all was a heaving and a rolling in a smell of sour sea, with crash following crash, dreadfully muffled by tremulous iron plates. Weak electric lights shone on eyes fear bright and sickly lips that said nothing or made some groaning joke.

"Oh, Bill," wailed Mrs Pryke, "let us women sleep in the saloon. We'll smother down here!"

Bill the barman looked his perplexity from a good-humoured face, rough shadowed in the light. He was swaying in the cabin doorway thinking what pictures of misery those women were.

"Go on, Bill!" they implored in looks and stuttered words. "If we've got to drown it will be better up there than here like rats in a trap!"

Bill swayed backwards and forwards, side on and side in, smiling in perplexed sympathy.

"If I could get you there," he said dubiously. "But even then I'd have to lock you in. Orders!"

"That will do us!" exclaimed Mrs Pryke, staggering from her bunk to get her arm round a sick friend. "We'll get there—Oh! That was a big one! —somehow."

Bill got them up there somehow—the few women who were able to move. They breathed more easily in the tiny saloon, although it smelt of stale bread and onions.

"This will give you air," comforted Bill as he opened a couple of portholes a little and secured each by a chain. "But don't open them any more, and the others not at all, else you'll have to swim out. By-bye." He seized his chance and dived out of the door. Above the howl of the cyclone they heard the bolt clang home. A woman sighed.

A thunderous crash outside shuddered through the *Melusia,* but she rose up high, hesitated, then, tilting, sank down again.

"Doesn't feel too cheerful," chattered Mrs Pryke.

"Hang on to the legs of this settee. I never knew I could grip so hard before."

The women clung to anything within reach, but they couldn't talk. The ship changed course until the port side dipped and a raging sea crashed against it, breaking the saloon port-hole chains and pouring in to lift the women bodily, carry them over the four little tables, and stand them in a group on their feet. A second later the back roll dragged them to their knees. A sideboard was torn away and crockery clattered in fragments to the floor. Then a sister sideboard came down, followed by a blended smell of sea-water, sauce, and chutney. The women clung in misery all through that heaving night.

Down below among the iron bars and the coal-heaps, swaying devils heaved coal into the furnaces. The stokehold was a rolling hell. As the firemen swayed they hunched their backs clear of the hot pipes, knowing that, should she take the plunge, they would dive straight into a hell of red-hot iron and steam.

Up on the wind-swept bridge the eyes of the captain were salt sore; his mind a pain from thought of coral reefs; his ears ringing as he listened for the crunching lurch that would tell him the case had broken loose. He screwed his eyes towards the east, praying for a gleam of light. When at last it came he looked on a scene of desolation.

With grey dawn the aeroplane crew were down on the deck, dodging the seas as, with feverish haste, they strengthened the tortured lashings.

Bill the barman was the most popular man at sea when he unlocked the saloon door.

"Oh, Bill," sighed a little lady with a wan smile, "I thought I was never going to see a man again."

"While there's life there's hope," comforted Bill.

"In between throwing compliments," declared Mrs Pryke, "we just must have a wash. Can you help us to the bathroom?"

"You're not short of water," said Bill with a grin and nodding at the floor.

"I want the bathroom!" wailed a girl with splashes of tomato-sauce draping her sopping dress.

Bill piloted each in turn, holding her arm while she held on to the steep rail. He managed the first to the bathroom, only to listen apprehensively as the ship's lurch sat her with a thump on the floor.

"Are you all right?" he shouted.

"Yes," she wailed. "Go away!"

Bill was a hero. The last lady was heavy and they slid down the steps, to bump hard, Bill underneath. But he helped her up and apologized with his humorous old smile. Bill was a much sought after man during the cyclone; and, though that was in 1927, the women passengers still remember the kindness of the stewards.

On the bridge the chief steward was harassing the skipper.

"Can't get below hatches for tucker!" he yelled. "Galley's flooded too! What'll I give 'em for breakfast?"

"What's in the pantry?" roared the skipper.

"Two eggs!"

"Well, scramble 'em. Mix plenty flour. An' if there's any complaints tell 'em to come up here to me!"

There were only six men and one woman, Mrs McPherson, wanting breakfast, however. There were no complaints.

Mrs Pryke crawled along the alleyway to visit a little mother, very sick. It was her first sea-voyage and the baby had been sick too—until the cyclone came. Now it was sitting up clapping its chubby hands in glee as it gurgled "Mum! Mum!" Mrs Pryke hung on to the door as she gazed at the agonized mother. The baby pointed to "Mum! Mum!" and gurgled, with delight in its eyes of corn-flower blue. Mrs Pryke laughed until she felt ill.

The *Melusia* rode out the cyclone behind Willis Island. All but five of the mules and an old grey horse went overboard.

As the cyclone subsided Mustar and Mullins were in an agony of doubt as to the extent of the damage done inside.

The race had developed into a hurdle race, and the sea had given the first jump to Parer.

1. Dancing masks.
2. Young woman of Talasea.
3. Sacred stool, Parumpai village.

CHAPTER XXV

THE MOUNTAIN FLIGHT

Parer and his North Queensland mate shipped their plane from Sydney by the *Marsina,* mentally handicapped by the knowledge that their rivals had a three weeks' start. "There's many a slip…" consoled a returning miner.

"Not in a cup like this," answered Parer as he gloomily leaned over the rail.

"Isn't there! I've seen many a slip made at sea."

There were a number of parties aboard, all bound for New Guinea. When, six weeks later, they steamed into pretty Rabaul harbour Farer's spirits rose, for Mustar and Mullins were ashore, still busily repairing their plane. The race was not won yet!

With a feverish energy the late arrivals began assembling their machine. Dr Cilento had cleared a landing-ground on the race-course; the Rabaulites were keenly interested in the mechanized race. Mustar and Mullins were wrestling with a deeply seated trouble in the cylinders and carburettor. As the days sped by the odds favoured Parer on assembling his machine first. He did. Then a tyre punctured, and it looked an even chance to the start. Parer hurried around Rabaul seeking a spare aeroplane tyre. No one had any; "never had any use for 'em." In desperation he fixed it as best he could, uneasily aware that the odds were heavily against this old plane and this lightning assembling; that leaky radiator and those worn cylinders and—the whole box of tricks in fact.

Mustar and Mullins were almost ready to start! Parer and his mate climbed into the cockpit: all Rabaul crowded round as the plane took off with a roar.

He circled a few times just to make sure, and surely found that the radiator was overheating. He glanced at the air-speed indicator. It was not registering—nor was the thermometer! He circled, hoping against hope that the god of luck would right the odds in a moment.

A menacing roar from the engine was followed by a puff of steam that whisked over his face as he peered over the cockpit.. With his head bent against the wind he thought how like a postage-stamp the landing-ground looked. And he must land quickly. Luckily the wind was light, for, as the air-speed indicator was not registering, he was very concerned about "overshooting." The stalling speed of a DH4 is fifty-five miles an hour. If he came in under that speed he would drop before reaching the ground; if over, he would overshoot and crash into the trees. Anxiously he peered down at that stamp, calculating how he could take advantage of the full length of landing-ground so as to drop nicely on his wheels—blinding steam swept hotly on his face.

He pulled the stick back slowly and came in, skimming the ground edge, seeking his stalling speed as he glided low over the trees, then pulled the stick right back—she stalled unexpectedly, to land with a bump, but ran along nicely until a wheel caught in a hole and over she went.

Parer slid out of his seat with a thump but his mate struck heavily. "You're a bit late," observed Parer with a dazed smile.

"Ough!" replied his mate.

People came rushing up. A kanaka sped to Burlington, his eyes almost popping from his head as he pointed towards the 'drome:

"Master! Master! Big feller pinnace alla same pigeon belonga white man 'e die finish! Long feller master me tink 'e broke 'im bone belonga him—lik-lik master friend belonga you he break him skin that's all!"

Parer spent one day in hospital, but his mate was more seriously hurt. He returned to Sydney by the following boat. The plane was a wreck. Parer was to come another second in the second great race of his life.

Mustar and Mullins radioed Levien "Coming," then flew away *en route* to Lae, four hundred and thirty miles across sea and islands.

The great day had dawned for Levien. He had not slept a wink. How could he when he had dreamed of this for four years? Expectant miners down from the Wau and hopeful men who had ferried across from Salamaua, sat smoking and chatting round the palm-leaf 'drome, alternately encouraging the antics of a bull-terrier pup and restlessly glancing skyward.

"If these birds arrive," drawled one, "it means the world to us!"

"Means certain money—made in comfort."

"I'll never climb the Gadagadu track again," declared another half unbelievingly. "Nor the Bouangs!"

"It ends the carriers. White men will run the country so far as the goldfields are concerned anyway."

"It's going to bring the place twenty years ahead at a leap—or a fly."

"Do you think they can fly over those mountains when they do arrive? It seems too much like a dream. Look at old C. J.—Like a hen with chicks expecting a hawk!"

Restless Levien with waving arms was hurrying up and down that cleared runway, alternately shouting chattily to the miners and haranguing the excited boys who, at his heels, snatched up wisps of grass, matchboxes, anything they could lay their fingers on while chasing the cackling hens away.

If the white man's monstrous "pigeon" did really come it was assured of cleared ground to land on anyway.

It was a glorious day. The blue waters of the Huon Gulf lapped the beach, to a crinkly music of coral, shell, and sands; the sky was bluer than the gulf; the hills encircling the flat Lae country stood out sharply; and beyond them the white cloud-capped mountains towered almost black. And little insects made a humming noise.

All the natives from Butibum village were clustered round the 'drome. Kanakas from the hills were constantly arriving in gala dress of paint and grease, or marl of bark, or girdle of cane, as taste and necessity dictated. A few came in full dress—a lap-lap. Among them were brave men who, venturing from mountain fastnesses that had not yet seen a white man, were doubtful of what might befall them.

"Tame" kanakas had spread the news far and wide. Though they did not believe in this "big feller *balus*" (big pigeon) that could carry a man, still Master Levien had said it would come and he always "spoke true." Around the landing-ground the air now fairly hummed with tribal dialects, interspersed with the scornful "pidgin" of the boys who knew. Heatedly they debated as to whether the coming balus would be as large as their famous *puk-puk* (crocodile).

The length of this reptile, the pride of Lae, has been marked on a tree to confound posterity. A monster it was, speared many years ago. They dumped its snout at a young tree butt while a boy climbed up and held the tail high, cutting a notch in the bark so that the measurement would be plain for coming generations to see for themselves.

The tree has grown with the years. But the natives still take the unbeliever to the tree and vindicate their honour by pointing to the notch now away up in the branches!

With expectation growing every moment hundreds of eyes gazed skywards, hundreds of ears listened.

Levien glanced up again and again. But it was only his heart he heard.

In late afternoon the big pigeon came with a fast increasing hum that drew all eyes, then excited shouts and pointing arms. As the hum grew to a roar the bush kanakas, men, women, and children, stared in astonishment; petrified until the plane roared overhead; then they took to the bush. Uncertainly the tame boys stood their ground; uncertainly too the plane circled; the aviators peering down like gnomes who, waving greetings, ascended again and circled, to glide low and come speeding down.

She landed to an astounded sigh from the labourers, many trembling with fright. Levien ran forward to shake hands with Mustar, the miners crowding below the good-humoured face of Mullins.

"I knew you'd make it," cried Levien. His hands were fondling the plane while he kept up a patter of jokes and banter, in relief from the anxiety that had gnawed at his heart for hours.

"I wasn't so sure," said Mustar as he climbed from the cockpit. "There's only about six gallons of petrol left in the tank. If we hadn't picked up the 'drome when we did—"

When greetings were all over the reassured kanakas timidly crowded round the plane, and stared at the leather-coated gods who had stepped from the belly of the balus. The braver boys touched the wing-tips first. Incapable of speech, they expressed amazement in deep-drawn breaths and grunts. The Lae village people from the outskirts of the crowd then began to creep forward, while farther back among the trees that lined Lae timid heads were peeping, ready to dive back among the timber at the flutter of an eyelash. Farther back still, among the tall timber, their legs going like cassowaries, were certain tribes-men making for the immemorial hills.

The labour boys stared as at a phantom. At last one remarked:

"Me no savvy this feller fashion belong white master! Strong feller too much!"

Uncomprehendingly they adored the pilot and mechanic, so fascinating in their weird head-gear. These mysterious beings could not have caused greater astonishment had they been men from the moon. The pilot stands 5ft 6in. in his socks; the mechanic is a huge man over 6 feet. The kanakas could not understand why the smaller man was "number one longa pigeon!" Size comes first in kanaka mentality.

The whites stood watching with laughing interest the kanakas measuring the plane with strips of lawyer-cane, taking full and careful measurements of the wings, the tail, the under-carriage, the propellers, everything. There were exclamations of amazement as they proved that this "pigeon" outmeasured the giant puk-puk. Unbelievable! Carefully each man wound up his measuring string preparatory to hurrying back to his village to convince his tribesmen. "Big talk" stirred the villages for nights, while for days afterwards, kanakas with long strips of cane came hurrying down from the mountains to convince themselves by taking independent measurements.

So, very happily, ended the first flight made by aeroplane in the Mandated Territory of New Guinea: Route, Rabaul to Lae, four hundred and thirty miles, and no emergency grounds. Failure would have meant "No trace."

Well into the small hours of the next morning Levien fell asleep, with the engines of many planes roaring in his head. He was up at dawn, gazing at the machine, he and it in the shed alone.

Now to prepare for the maiden flight to the goldfields with its problem of "How to find an uncharted landing-ground at an uncertain distance in a sea of mountain tops!"

"You'll do it on your head!" declared Levien energetically as he made rapid plans to walk in as a vanguard.

"I hope not," replied Mustar with a quizzical glance away across at the peaks. Whistling cheerily he climbed in over the cockpit to begin to overhaul.

A week or so of preparation passed, then for the last time Levien set out on foot to the Wau, his thirteenth trip! But he battled on with a song in his heart and fine thoughts in his head. On the eighth day he reached the familiar Wau, collected his labour team, and toiled to clear the kunai grass ready for the coming of the big pigeon. Would this flight prove more hazardous than the long hop from Rabaul over the sea and the serrated peaks of New Britain? Anxiety crept into his heart again.

It was a Sunday morning. On the coast at Lae all the pilot had as guide was the advice and rough sketch-maps made by those who had trudged down among the mountains but had never seen them from above. How differently they looked to Mustar, soaring up there while staring down like an uneasy god at a strange world. Low clouds settled round him, joined by misty wraiths and pierced ahead by ghostly peaks that melted in the clouds. So the birdman droned his way along looking for a goldfield camp, smaller than a pock mark in this upturned face of Nature. He had no idea what a goldfield looked like on the ground, and now must guess its appearance from the air. How wonderful, how unbelievably different, the earth looked when gazing down on it like this! What a titanic handiwork it all was!

Something in the engine's throaty roar warned him it would not thus fly on for ever. In two hours he had more than realized the magnitude of his task. He flew back to the coast. As a surer guide, they advised him then to follow the biggest river to its source.

But there were other rivers. The one he followed only led him farther out into abysmal depths where the clouds settled down and smothered the peaks while enveloping the plane. The ghostliness of it chilled his heart, perhaps with premonition of what was to happen to poor Les Trist three years afterwards—a terrific headlong plunge out of a cloud into a mountain side at a hundred miles an hour.

On the third attempt a miner accompanied him as guide. They flew on over ridges dense with forest until the broad Markham gleamed below as it flowed to its fertile delta. They gazed down on alternate forest and swamp speeding by until at twelve miles they turned and followed a tributary stream. Then veering almost south they flew above the Wampit and climbed up the valley where mountains towered ten thousand feet to the left, eight thousand to the right.

Frighteningly beautiful they are seen so: massive, cold, and solid! But not one flat spot that the smallest plane could land on. At the source of the Wampit he espied a gap between the mountain tops, but the great cumulus clouds were sliding down into it. He pulled the throttle full open and thrilled to the roaring machine as it raced to forestall those clouds. Icy air flicked over the cockpit. Ravines and cliff walls to right and left sped up and vanished in quick succession. From a stockaded village below, wild men gazed spell-bound. The clouds slid down into the gap too late, for the plane coughed through with its wing-tips whirling the mist-wreaths aside as it shot out over the steeply falling second valley of the Wampit. Mustar sighed in intense relief as the trees slid from under and the great gorge opened below with an almost clear sky above, and revealed mountains walling the valley whose grassy slopes rose to the six-thousand-foot level. After another fifteen miles the kunai grass of the valley changed to a carpet of timber which clothed the craggy heights like black mittens.

The miner leaned over, tapped the pilot, and pointed. Miles ahead, down among all that tangle, Mustar distinguished a postage-stamp of green—the Wau incline!

A unique 'drome, that tiny patch of cleared grass hedged with jungle, upon a mountain top. He circled dubiously over it; it was triangular in shape. He guessed it at seven hundred yards long, seventy-five yards at the top end, four hundred yards at the bottom, with a landing slope of ten degrees! He must land on the slope too and disregard the wind while praying he would not "fall back off the top." He swooped down, his hands grasping the controls, his eyes staring at the edge of the uneven slope that rushed up to meet him—if he landed too low he would fall back down the mountain!

In the last few seconds he manoeuvred to land so that the machine would stop on a flat portion of the slope; he handled the controls with a thrill in every nerve. He bumped alarmingly as he opened up full with a roar and at a terrific run turned the machine at a right angle to the slope.

He did it—safely—and stopped the engine—a wry smile upon his lips. It had been a near thing.

Frantic cheers rolled over the Wau as Levien led the miners with a

lips. It had been a near thing.

Frantic cheers rolled over the Wau as Levien led the miners with a rush. Mrs Mellor cooked a duck. Somebody tried to make a speech but was howled down good-humouredly. That night there was high carnival at the lonely Wau.

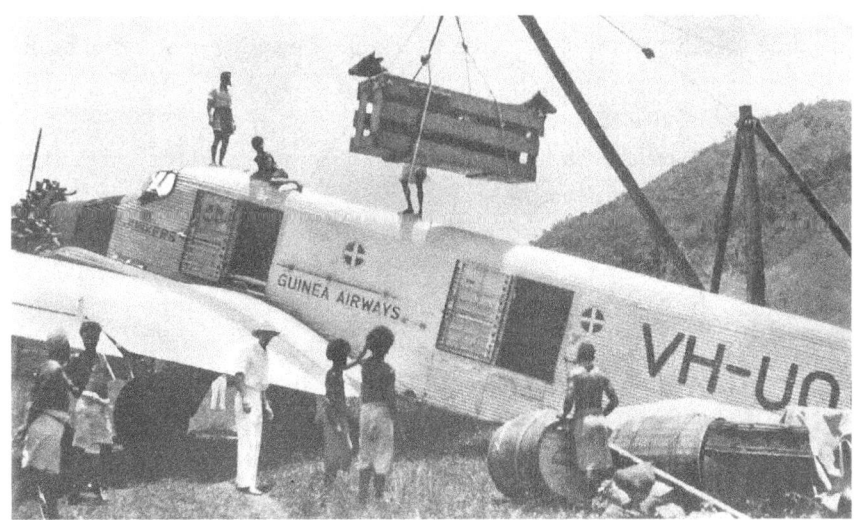

CHAPTER XXVI

THE OPPOSITION ARRIVES

Back at Lae again Levien stood gazing as his first loaded plane took the air after the trial trip. He was happy.

That DH37 had a "useful" load of eleven hundred pounds including pilot and petrol; which means that it carried six hundred pounds of cargo, thus doing the work of two hundred and fifty carriers who would have cost at least £10 each to procure and £1 per week to maintain. The machine would accomplish the return trip in one and three-quarter hours; the carriers in three weeks. The plane would do two trips in one day; the carriers, at the fastest, two trips in six weeks. Each pound of freight the plane carried would return the Guinea Gold Company 1s., or £30 per trip! Each passenger carried represented £25. High prices these; but many times worth while to the prospectors. The benefit to the field was past calculation as yet. "Two hundred and fifty carriers immediately dispensed with," thought Levien as the plane disappeared towards the mists. "But there will soon be three thousand on the track. Right! More aeroplanes. Then the carriers can be converted into labour boys to work the diggings."

The day of the flying prospector had dawned.

He glanced around at the rough-built sheds piled high with stores, at the congregated miners who were almost fighting in their anxiety to get quickly to the field. The demand, inevitably, would become greater. Then, after the human and the stores freight, would come the call for machinery freight—machinery to work the ground with twentieth-century speed. And such freight would not be wanted in pounds weight but in tons—bulky stuff too!

Could machinery be carried by plane over those mountains? A road was on every man's lips; but a road would take years to build. One hopeful wanderer even suggested elephants as roadmakers!

Levien stared after the disappearing plane. Larger planes, giant planes, might do it. The world had not built them yet. Levien wheeled round and shouted to his labour teams to get knives and mattocks and axes. He was going to build another 'drome, a larger one.

Those giant planes *were* built—in his mind. He had built the plane that had just flown away, built it mentally long ago up there on Koranga Creek. Now, it was flying loaded where men had sworn a plane would never fly.

Eagerly he worked, while never interfering with any other man's work; improving the landing-ground, building larger barracks as well as a larger 'drome. He chatted cheerily beside Mullins who was planning an engine repair shop. Yet all the time he was thinking. The faster he could prove to the company that there was money in planes, the faster they would send him others—larger ones. The quicker he built up a fleet, the sooner would his giant planes arrive—from somewhere.

At night while the camp was sleeping his mind was clank-clanking with a phantom dredge deep down in the Bulolo valley. How many times had he carried that dredge, in his head!

At the end of the first week the plane had made fourteen trips, carried 2850 pounds of stores, and fifteen passengers.

Levien wrote to the directors for a second plane, using voluble but logical arguments, infectiously enthusiastic. They sent him a Gypsy Moth with slatted wings. He thought it the most beautiful thing in the world. They also sent him a motor pinnace, to transfer stores quickly from Salamaua port across the Huon Gulf to Lae.

But he wasn't satisfied. He gazed at the wave-washed shore near the 'drome. He wanted to convert that shore into an anchorage so that steamers could call at Lae direct and land more planes, machinery, stores, petrol drums, so that he could dispense with the tedious eighteen-mile water trip across from Salamaua.

The workshop was beginning to hum. A little motor-driven engine daily singing, lathes revolving, wheels spinning, sparks flying when metal bit into metal. Spare parts of planes began to appear on rough-hewn benches, propeller blades came and wings. Each day at "eat-up" time he hammered the great gong for kai-kai. How all the staff downed tools and trooped out laughing and whistling and joking to the resonant call of that gong!

On his first flight Levien realized physically what that first plane meant to the field. He gazed down at the moving panorama and vividly recalled the troubles of the track hidden in those gorges—the track he and others had climbed so often with such pains. In half an hour he had reached Lae, somewhat dazed as he realized that the flight was over and he was at his destination.

Meanwhile for Parer in Rabaul, time just drifted by. One day when down in the dumps he ran into Burlington, a tall young Englishman with plenty of laugh and energy. Possessed of aviation experience, some bright ideas, and the gold-fever was Charles Lexius-Burlington.

"How about fixing the plane?" suggested Burlington.

"How can I? No money—no machine shop—no nothing!"

"I don't know. There's always some way of doing things."

They talked it over. Burlington is a man who, when he comes to town, soon gets to know everyone and learns what's going on and who's who. Hence Parer was soon hopefully walking to the store of Aloysius Akun, to which enterprising merchant he sold two hundred shares in the flying company at £1 a share. Burlington looked up George Robertson, Arnold's old mate who was spelling in Rabaul from the Edie. "Robby" pulled out £100 and refused the proffered shares.

"No," he declined firmly. "This is in appreciation of Farer's flight from England to Australia. Take it!" The joyous couple hurried to interview Captain Komini and readily obtained permission to rebuild the plane in his dockyard. Then they radioed Larkin for dope and lacquer, wing-fabric and engine spares. While waiting they stripped the machine and got to work. For sheet metal to repair the wings they cut up an old boiler of Komini's, and made the petrol tank out of galvanized sheet iron; a worry, because the sheet iron was three times heavier than the original tank. In six weeks they had rebuilt the plane. During that time the Royal Commission sat at Rabaul in an attempt to settle the grievance of the Edie leases.

One bright day Burlington came striding gleefully to Parer. "I've booked our first passengers—two Frenchmen. They've chartered the plane for £100. They want to fly to the goldfields."

"Let 'em all come!" replied Parer with a smile. "You're certainly a lively bird."

"I believe in feathers to fly with," agreed Burlington.

"Well, I hope these two birds enjoy their flight," said Parer dubiously. "They might need feathers. This radiator has got me troubled."

On their first test flight the radiator burst; so they came more or less gracefully to earth and repaired it. They went aloft where it promptly burst again. For the third time they rose aloft; only to swoop down in a cloud of steam. Their two would-be passengers left for Kokopo.

"We prefer to lose our money to our life," was their good-bye.

The diehards eventually traced the main trouble to the aircraft meter. So they installed a motor meter, tinkered up a few more gadgets here and there, and declared the job a "go."

"Well, Lex," said Parer with a sigh, "it's now or never. To-morrow morning we're off! As you're my moral support what do you suggest next?"

"Get rid of this fever!" replied Burlington, uneasily. "Right. We will. We'll thump the quinine in thick and heavy. We've got to get over there and make some cash."

They took thirty grains each, a tremendous dose which gave them a buzzing head but an appetite.

The Bulolo Dredging Company's workshops and machinery yard, 1931 and the Dredge No. 4.

(Top) Explorer Mick Leahy meeting natives 1930.
(Bottom) The Lae aerodrome.

They satisfied it in a Chinese restaurant with the finest turtle soup ever made. Next morning the rain did not prevent Rabaul seeing them off. Parer shook hands all round then smiled at Burlington.
"Well, Lex, got the tucker—water-jar?"

"Yes, everything's aboard, except our insurance!"

"Oh, we won't need that if we crash."

"Right. Then we're off."

They climbed aboard while willing but somewhat awkward hands turned the propeller. It behaved in stiff and sulky fashion and insisted on fifteen turns before condescending to suck mixture into the cylinders.

"Stand all clear!"

Parer switched on; then turned the starting magneto. The engine started first pop. Parer smiled. With the engine warmed to 75°F. he opened the throttle and tested the revolutions up to 16-15 per minute. She ran sweetly and smoothly—a purring music to his anxious ears. He waved the chocks away. The crowd roared adieux as he taxied out and, turning her into the wind, opened her out. She took off with a roar.

It was an eventful flight in a crazy machine over sea, island, and mountain. Space does not permit to tell the romance of the flight. But they got there, although, when humming over the silvery Markham, Burlington was staring down and praying for Lae village and an aerodrome. As they flew towards a little hill Burlington stared at a prominent tree adorning its crown, a heavily foliaged tree of many branches, overshadowing the smaller trees around. He stared as if remembering a dream.

"I've never been here before but I've seen that tree! Where have I seen it?" Suddenly he called aloud:

"'While I live I'll grow.' That's Anthony Hordern's tree! From now on that motto will do me."

Suddenly they espied the 'drome like a wee tennis-court among scrubby hills. Parer circled low. From a quaint native-built structure someone came running out into the centre of the clearing, another little figure appeared running, natives came running and waving and yelling from all directions. A Very light shot up into the rainy mist, Parer circled while watching the ground, until, feeling his landing measurements, he glided down to the final landing.

Mullins, Mustar, and Blandon helped swing her round towards the 'drome. And all hands offered congratulations. Native labourers crowded round to view this new white master "pigeon."

Parer had arrived.

"Where's Levien?" inquired Burlington. "Perce" Blandon pointed across to a shack near the hangar. "Fever!" he said. "He's been expecting you chaps—wireless from Salamaua."

Burlington entered the rude shack and smiled down on the sick man.

"Hey! What ho, Burlington Bertie!" called Levien instantly. "So you've come along to give us some competition have you? Well, we're going to give you a run for it. Anyway, you'd better go and get a good feed before you get fed up with us."

"That will do me!" said Burlington with a laugh. "I was a bit doubtful whether I was going to dine again."

"You can consider yourself lucky you got through," replied Levien. "I didn't think you would ever again see Piccadilly."

It was a fine meal. Burlington felt himself privileged to enjoy it. Parer was delighted to find the 'drome stacked with freight. Miners crowded around him offering staggering premiums for the transport of themselves and their stuff. Mustar was flying as hard as he could go up to and back from the Wau. Parer had lost the race, but here was a big second prize he never expected. He went for it for all he was worth.

"The man who never sleeps" was busy. While pioneering a new aviation enterprise, on the coast at Lae, he had his company's gold leases to attend to sixty miles over the mountains at Koranga, and the immeasurably larger proposition on the Lower Bulolo flats. He fairly threw himself into these tremendous tasks. As superintendent he was in his element, being here at Lae, sixty miles up at the Wau, and twenty miles down the Bulolo in quick succession. Always up to the collar. He set men to work cutting a three-mile water-race through dense jungle (in places the fluming boxes had to be suspended from precipices) from the Kulolo into the Bulolo at Kaili. This was to provide water-power.

To get those great lower leases properly working meant yet another chain of carriers, ceaselessly moving over miles of mountains between Wau and Bulolo, to keep the examining engineers supplied.

The bulk of the gold won from the Koranga leases was sunk in prospecting the lower Bulolo flats, to prove the dredging proposition. The Guinea Gold shareholders in Adelaide were wonderfully patient for two years. During that time the directors of the company had many anxious hours, for it looked as though even plucky Adelaide—the cradle of many famous mining ventures of the past—had met a proposition too big for it to handle.

But the transport problem was Levien's favourite. He realized that all else must follow if transport were solved, not only his own dreams but the undertakings of other men. At Lae, another big shed, rough built of palm, was erected for the growing staff; a house-cook too, with a smiling Malay cook and huge gong all complete.

That first DH37 was Levien's baby. He would have thumped any man who called it "little." He used to help wheel it out of the hangar; watch it humming away. His were the first ears that caught its returning drone; his the first hand to grasp a wing-tip to get it again under shelter.

How carefully he would examine it at every weekend overhaul! He never interfered with the mechanic; but he would be the first to detect a defect in the fabric, or the ominous signs where the insidious damp heat was beginning to rot the struts, or to loosen bolts and glue, or to warp the woodwork. The weather, with its alternate rain and heat, caused great deterioration within that wood and canvas framework.

One night a terrific storm crashed down upon the palm-leaf hangar, flattened the sheds, and ripped the fabric off the wings of the plane. Levien could have cried. But as that was futile, he swore in an anxious crescendo. That proving equally ineffectual, he listened when Mustar quietly mentioned all-metal planes.

"They are making them overseas, trying to beat the weather," he explained.

Immediately, Levien wanted an all-metal plane, a large one. He wrote the Guinea Gold directors about it. They had already planned, however, for in the first six months the two small planes had proved themselves not merely helpful but vital links with the coast for the struggling mining population.

Meanwhile Ray Parer was doing well—carrying almost night and day. In a very short time he had made enough to go south and return with a DH9 and an old Bristol Fighter, bringing Charlie Pratt of Geelong with him. They flew from Port Moresby to Lae, the first flight made from Papua into the Mandated Territory. They arrived just at a time when misfortunes had temporarily put the Guinea Gold planes out of commission. The miners up in the field were in dismay. Levien—well, if you knew Levien you could imagine it. The miners were panic-stricken at the possibility of the old carrier days coming again. Parer saved the situation like an angel from the sky. Levien immediately chartered those planes until his own big new ones arrived.

After that Parer did well until the gods of chance took a hand, and he was again "Battling Parer." He passed through many vicissitudes before he finally became established.

As a qualified engineering staff now began to appear on the field Levien devoted all his time to the development of the aviation scheme. Engineers J.C. Coldham and Tom Horton arrived to test the Lower Bulolo. Levien knew it was he that was being put to the test. If giant Kaindi had not shed that gold—!

As Guinea Gold No-Liability could not legally trade as a "common carrier" company, Wells and his colleagues formed a second company in Adelaide, Guinea Airways Limited, to satisfy the growing clamour for air transport. New capital was asked for and quickly subscribed. Levien mobilized all his savings and himself underwrote the whole issue.

Thus was floated what was to be the most successful commercial aviation company in the world; quite unsubsidized; and which was to accomplish a feat now acclaimed by the aviation world as unprecedented.

Pilot Allan Cross was hurried from Melbourne to Lae to relieve Pilot Mustar who sailed overseas intent on the purchase of a large metal plane suitable for tropical conditions, capable of a big lift over mountains, and of carrying a pay load of eighteen hundred pounds.

Many technical details, quite a number of engineering and scientific problems, had to be thought out before that order could be filled. New Guinea is too far away from civilization and the work too important to forgive errors of judgment.

Up on the field the Wau was now growing into a town—in the very rough stage. There was even a pub there; a shack as yet; but beer could be bought in the case at 7s. per bottle, and as the planes were soon bringing in the refreshment in tons, you can guess money was flying. There was Burns Philp's store, the warden's office and house, the little wireless station, the house-sick (hospital), the shacks of miners, and the big hangars built of partly European, partly native material. Planes were busily "coming in" and "going out." A sawmill was fast laying low the pines and cedars of the Wau. Giant nozzles for hydraulic sluicing had made their appearance and would soon oust the little sluice-box with the chattering kanaka labourers "forking" out the stones by hand. Koranga Creek had changed indeed from the day when Shark-eye first stared down on his gold. The bird of paradise had gone, but another bird had come.

Down on Darby's Flat was Darby's house, a pretentious building indeed. He could afford it: the Eldorado was producing gold in dishfuls. Darby was boyishly enthusiastic about it. What man would not be when, on an occasional day, the glittering clean-up represented £1000. But Darby's sleeping partner had stiff luck. Before Darby struck gold, the partner had sold his share of the ground for the money he originally put into it. That is the luck of the game. A number of men had "come in" with their little capital and "gone out broke." Gold favours only the few.

Old Ned Coakeley, by judicious working of a little rich ground here and there, was fast getting his "flour-tin full" of gold. But it was bad cess to his luck when the Wau pub ran out of firewater, just when Ned was right in the middle of a holiday too. As a consolation prize they sent him the last precious bottle they had.

"Open it!" growled Neel to his celebrating partner. But as the man took the bottle from the grinning boy Ned saw the label.

"You can't drink that!" he roared, and snatched the bottle. "That's the Pope's drink!"

It was a bottle of Benedictine.

The stiff climb from the Wau to the Edie was soon to be a well-trodden mule-track. There is tragedy in the story of the first mules to negotiate that awful climb. They were landed at Salamaua and Mellor and his wife drove them up the mountains, losing numbers on the way. There were grades there that even a mule could not make. But the woman did it; she was the first woman to climb to the Edie. Her husband was killed in an accident shortly afterwards. Levien found Mrs Mellor a job as cook at the Guinea Gold camp. Later, when she flew out, the plane circled over her husband's grave and there came floating down flakes of paper-fragments of old love letters.

CHAPTER XXVII

FACING DISASTER

Mustar wasted no time overseas. He first tried the British plane manufacturers, but unfortunately found the machines unsuitable. He found what he wanted at Junkers factory in Dessau, Germany.

Germany had outpaced her rivals in plane construction for commercial use. The restrictions on plane building for military purposes, imposed upon her at the Peace Conference, caused her to concentrate on commercial planes. She was ready to go to unbounded trouble to satisfy a customer, placing the aerial construction brains of Germany at his service.

Mustar's keen eye soon spotted the ideal type of "bus" for New Guinea flying; art all-metal, low-winged monoplane, fitted with a Bristol Jupiter air-cooled engine of 420 horse-power. Useful load of 2860 pounds (about a ton of cargo). Travelling speed of 120 miles per hour, and a rise of 16,000 feet in thirty minutes; which meant a big and quick "lift" in flying over mountains. She was designed for cargo-carrying, with three seats for passengers. Neither heat, cold, nor rain could affect this all-metal machine. Such was the first Junker bought for the New Guinea service: gracefully lined, a model of steadiness, no vibration, and of general utility as a freighter.

With his Junker snugly packed in a gigantic case, Mustar shipped back to Rabaul, smiling at the thought of Levien's face when he should first see this lovely grey bird on the wing.

At Rabaul he assembled the Junker, and flew it to Lae. Levien, his face twitching with emotion, gazed up at the big metal beauty tearing through the air. He had heard the roar of that engine before—in his dreams. Immediately, he was wondering what was the bulkiest article she could carry. Could she take a boiler? a fly-wheel? a long steel girder? the frame-work of a stamper battery? What was the largest single portion of a dredge she could carry?

As the grey metal thing skimmed to the ground he ran forward all smiles and congratulations. He would keep his own planning and surmising for the night. He jumped up to the cockpit and hammered the pilot, between the shoulders.

Exactly one year after his first New Guinea flight Mustar roared up into the air with the first metal plane. He was carrying two passengers, a ton of rice, luggage, petrol, and oil. Levien watched him soar away. In an hour's flight, that plane did what it would have taken a hundred human carriers three weeks to do.

He sized up the 'drome. An amazing improvement in twelve months. Labour barracks, staff barracks, houses, a large hangar, a longer and wider landing-ground, a workshop humming busily, labour gangs of three hundred kanakas methodically working, the white staff increased, pinnaces, large vegetable gardens. The old native-material shelters were being replaced by large wooden buildings—soon to be steel! He glanced across the flat country where there was plenty more space for hangars, then hurried into the repair shops where "Mull" the mechanical wizard and his mechanics were busy. Levien swelled with secret pride at the efficiency that had evolved so marvellously in this lonely spot. Even he began to wonder a little. He saw that in the near future Lae aerodrome would find it almost possible to build its own aircraft. With a shrug of impatience he wheeled round and hurried away. He had forgotten to see whether that wretched kanaka had fed the chickens!

There was no 'drome up at the Edie. From the Wau to that field was a twelve-hour climb of four thousand feet. Up there, the Big Six had cleaned up a fortune. Their show (now the Edie Creek Proprietary Company) they were selling to the Ellyou. A new era had dawned on the field, the era of get rich quick by selling leases. Companies were eager buyers;. the majority were get rich quick companies. Just a few, however, were solidly in earnest. Men rushed to peg leases until the country for miles square was pegged. Some companies bought their ground with cash, generally buying an option first; but the majority bought with a few thousands in cash and many thousands in shares. For instance, a lease that might be bought at £25,000 was paid for at £5000 cash and twenty thousand £1 shares. Those shares, of course, would only be worth £1 each if speculators on the Australian Stock Exchanges gave that much for them. In several cases they wouldn't. In that event Sydney would soon have quite a number of men walking about the streets worth a fortune—on paper.

Some men "over there" pegged a number of leases and cleaned up thousands in cash. A few were leases with big values in them; others weren't. Pegging and selling leases became all the rage. Companies soon had bought up almost all the proved available ground—and much that wasn't proved. It was then that dredging on a gigantic scale began to be talked of in earnest. But men shook their heads, believing it impossible to build a road into that country. How could the weighty machinery be transported? Aeroplanes would never carry it; planes could only carry a ton weight.

But busy Levien listened to all that was said for and against and quietly smiled to himself.

He kept on thinking far ahead while watching practical developments. Transport was on his brain. He had climbed those mountains. Then he had seen the kanaka beast of burden climb them with fifty pounds on his back. He had seen his first plane do the trip in a few minutes carrying six hundred pounds. His latest planes were each carrying over two thousand pounds, as well as passengers. He knew planes were being built in the world capable of carrying tons. It simply meant getting still more improved machines here at the right time to do the job. A dredge weighing a thousand tons could be made like a child's meccano set, to be transported in sections to the field and there assembled. He was sure the weightiest parts of this machinery could be made not to exceed a tonnage that giant planes could carry.

Just then Fate sent him the chance to put dreams into practice. Day Dawn, a promising reefing show, wanted to erect a battery—there was a hundred tons total weight in it. Mining-engineer V. L. Newberry had planned the machinery in sections; the heaviest sections weighed one ton each. Could Guinea Airways transport this machinery up to the Wau? Levien replied that Airways could transport anything. Then he entered into earnest consultation with Mustar as to *how* it could be transported.

They did the job: it was a great triumph. A triumph for Australian mining engineering too, and for the Australian firms that so successfully built that machinery to exact and unusual design.

That small plant created the first machinery transport record; travelling by rail, sea, plane, and carrier, and up over heights undreamed of. Then, when once up at the Wau, Newberry had to get it carried to the Edie, a twelve-mile, precipitous jungle track rising four thousand feet, running along the sides of precipices, past places where the rains constantly caused landslides that blotted out portions of the track. The carrying part of the job took three months, during which seventy-eight inches of rain fell. Added to this, "war" interfered with transport.

The braves of Lambura were engaged in their age-old war with the warriors of Winima. Normy Neale walked into the cluster of fighting villages and persuaded them to make peace for the time being. The price of peace being very high the tribesmen accepted on the understanding that the "war" be resumed immediately the last boiler pipe was carried to the white men's ground and the warriors were paid off.

This gentleman's understanding worked out quite smoothly for all concerned.

Women had begun to appear, and every old miner knows what *that* means.—It is time for him to push farther out! District Officer Macdonald's wife was the first white woman to reside at Salamaua. Then came plucky Mrs Hendry to start the first boarding-house in Coonland. After her came a little hostess, a favourite now, who brought with her merry chatter an indomitable spirit that has cheered many a man, and helped her husband build up a fine modern business there. Mrs Wisdom was the first woman to fly up to the Wau; Mrs Pryke the second.

Mrs Booth, earliest woman of all; and the early women of the Bulolo and Koranga, Salamaua and the Edie have proved that the pioneer spirit is as indomitable as ever in the breasts of Australian women.

"Plenty grass belonga him!" said the kanakas admiringly of Mrs Pryke's hair. "Whizz-bang" adopted her, gazing disdainfully at her dress:

"Lap-lap no good longa this feller place, missus," he advised with lordly air. "You wearim trosers alla same master." Practical advice, during the pioneering stage, in a country made for trousers and heavy boots. Mrs Pryke "turned to" straight away, mastered the country lingo and "fashion belonga me feller" and signed on her own team of recruits; set them to work, and bossed them on leases she pegged herself. She won gold too. Naturally, it took a lot of battling and determination before a woman was an accepted master, and had learned "fashion belonga me feller."

A boy was very ill one day, so she detailed four others to carry him to the hospital down on the Wau. Next day late she saw her henchmen sauntering back. "You put him boy longa house-sick?" she inquired.

"No got," they replied stolidly.

"What you make long him?"

"He finish!"

"You run!" she called to Whizz-bang. "Go look out long this feller boy he sick. Quick time!"

In the course of plenty of time Whizz-bang returned with a grin.

"Where this boy he stop?" called the white missus.

"Long creek," answered Whizz-bang unconcernedly.

"What name he stop long creek?"

"He die finish!"

The stretcher-bearers had decided among themselves that the man would probably die. He was heavy to carry so they left him.

Such is "Fashion belonga me feller."

Suddenly, in 1928, a bomb-shell fell upon the directors of Guinea Gold, N.L., for the Sydney company holding the option withdrew after testing the Lower Bulolo. Could not raise the capital, they said.

The directors were nonplussed. All their hopes had been centred on those leases; £45,000 of the company's privately subscribed funds and even the gold won from the Koranga ground had gone in development work and testing. How could they tell the shareholders that after two years' patience, hard work, and glowing expectations, their leases had been turned down? The company had barely £1000 in the treasury. Utterly impossible to hold those great areas with that! What was to be done?

The directors did not know. Time was pressing. Funds were running out. The world depression was gathering on the horizon. Was there no way to save the leases from forfeiture?

Then Levien arrived. *He* knew that the directors dare not let his great scheme die out. He threw his arms about and talked loud and long, while his flashing eyes expressed all his tongue could not say quickly enough. He threw his heart and soul into the fight; and he made threats too. He said furious things about mining engineers in particular and in general; then warned the directors that if they threw up the sponge he would buy up every share in the company and let the world know it.

He bucked up the directors so, that they got angrily cheerful. Then, just because they did not know what else in the world to do, they decided to spend the last £1000 on one forlorn hope.

They would send Director W. P. A. Lapthorne to London to see if he could raise money there. Lapthorne agreed to go and his passage was booked at a week's notice.

He went to Sydney on final business. There Director George Jeffrey joined him and threw himself into the fight. After a visit to a city office Jeffrey felt gloomy and depressed. The future was full of doubt in spite of Levien's terrific confidence. In Martin Place a hand reached out and stopped him.

"I hear that Sydney Investments turned your property down," said W. A. Freeman.

"Well, no. They had to withdraw."

"What option do you want on it?"

Jeffrey looked his surprise.

"Lapthorne's going to London for the money," he said stoutly, wondering at his own assurance.

"I know. But what do your people want for an option of the property?"

"I'm not sure offhand; but I know it's worth a whole lot," replied Jeffrey.

"I'll take it!" said Freeman.

"What? Well, you'll have to go to Adelaide."

"I'm going now, by to-night's train."

And he did.

W. A. Freeman was president of Placer Development, a group of technical experts quietly looking about the world for likely alluvial mines. Freeman already knew a good deal about that far-away Bulolo proposition. How he knew is a secret known only to the great mining groups from overseas. They have their own system of finding out things.

Like an angel from heaven he dropped in on the directors in Adelaide. He took a twelve months' option before they got their breath, and for which he paid £2000, a thing he had never done before.

They were very relieved directors. The depression was just setting in on Australia then and they knew they had little hope of raising much money there.

Les Trist and Frank Drayton. Trist died in an air-crash near Wampit Gap in May 1931. Drayton died at Wau aerodrome in 1932.

CHAPTER XXVIII

THE DEAD MAN "SHOUTS"

Meanwhile Mustar, while flying, instructed a pilot in the handling of the metal W34 which in five weeks had done sixty-seven trips, carried 115,081 pounds of cargo, and twenty-six passengers. It would have taken a thousand carriers nearly as many months to do this.

The immediate success of this machine induced Guinea Airways to radio for another which duly arrived in Melbourne, where Mustar hurried to assemble it. It was a slightly more powerful machine with certain added "gadgets" which made the pilot eagerness itself to assemble it. His hand trembled to get a clutch on the controls; he wanted to feel that machine rising up under him and roaring far away along the seaboard of the northern Australian coast; for he was going to fly this one, with floats, all the way from Melbourne to Lae, a distance of over three thousand miles.

There was not a pound of wood in the new machine. Duralumin took its place. It gave a high degree of visibility, and had an efficient self-starting device; even a fire extinguisher. Its dual controls side by side enabled one pilot to rest if necessary. Behind the pilot's seat was a spacious cabin for passengers and space for cargo, with little windows sliding horizontally by manipulation of a revolving knob. Passengers could sit in it and imagine they were in a sitting-room at home, and feel as safe. It took four days for mechanics to attach wings to a comparatively similar craft in Australia, but it only took four minutes to complete the job for the W34.

The machine's weight when empty was 3050 pounds, with a useful cargo load of 2450 pounds. The total-lifting weight was thus 5500 pounds. This meant it could lift the useful load of one hundred carriers and land it in forty minutes instead of ten days. Its dimensions were: wing span, 62 feet, length, 31 feet 10 inches; wing area, 505 square feet. Power loading, 10 pounds per horse-power; wing loading, 9261 pounds per square foot. It was quite safe to climb all over these broad, strong wings.

The useful load of 2450 pounds was therefore nearly as great as the empty weight. When fully loaded its cruising speed was 100 miles per hour, maximum speed 127. Petrol consumption, 16 gallons per hour, tankage range, 350 miles, easily increased by carrying extra petrol in the cabin. Its ceiling height was 20,000 feet. It was a seaplane, convertible into an ordinary land plane simply by removal of the floats.

The powerful engine which lifted this machine and kept it on its job was British: Bristol Jupiter Mark VI of 450 horse-power; a remarkable engine, and a tribute to British aerial engineering. No wonder the born pilot itched to put her at the mountain hurdles.

At Point Cook, with Mrs Levien aboard, this W34 took off on the trial flight in an almost vertical climb above the lowlying clouds. The Australian test flight was a complete success.

Later, Mustar, with floats fixed, left for Lae via Eden, Sydney, Bowen, Cooktown, and Thursday Island; 3300 miles in easy stages in six days. His experience in charting the Great Barrier Reef from the air stood him in good stead on this trip.

Levien was so proud of the great plane that he could hardly speak at first. Then he could hardly stop speaking.

Good-humoured "Vic" Horsley, while medical assistant at the Wau, looked serious when one evening old Davey was carried into the "house-sick" with fever. Davey's clothes were sopping wet, so the orderly hung them in front of the roaring fire all night. Next morning he noticed a pocket bulging, so, inquisitively, he put in his hand and pulled out—a packet of dynamite!

In due time an Australian Naval vessel anchored off Salamaua. A kanaka with terrified eyes rushed to his master crying:

"Master, master, sun he finish (die) altogether! He fall down longa Salamaua!"

Rather dazed at this catastrophe, the white man hurried out into the night. The dazzling rays of a searchlight were over sleeping Salamaua.

The little hostess of Salamaua was superintending the house-boys installing the brightly-flowered linoleum and carpets that had just arrived from Sydney. Next morning she heard the bedroom boy discussing the linoleum with the kitchen boy. They agreed that "the pigs belong Siteni (Sydney) all had skins with big flowers painted on them and no bristles." But for the life of them they could not tell what wallaby-skins the carpets were made of. The little lady smiled to herself and called out to the second cook-boy: "How many eggs are left, Magwa?"

"Ten he stop!" came back the cheerful answer. "One he no got!"

The busy housekeeper knew the cook had nine eggs. She entered the pantry just in time to catch the pantry boy stealing the sugar. "Sombula! How dare you steal that cup of sugar!"

"Me no seteal 'im, missus!"

"You no makim gammon talk long me. Me been lookim you catchim one cup sugar long store!"

"No got, missus! Me no seteal 'im! Me like catchim give 'em long brother belong me, das all. 'E present, missus! Me no seteal 'im!"

It all went to show how fast the district was becoming civilized. Six years ago it was a head-hunter's land, now a man hardly dared walk down the main "street" without wearing a collar and tie. And the thoroughness of the "civilizing" was surprising. Dusty Miller one day, after a few hands at poker, ran out of cash, so playfully shouted to his boy:

"Bring me a fiver quick, Watch."

Old Watch ran in with a five-pound note to the amazement of his master and his own delight.

"Now where's dat you catch him?" demanded Miller suspiciously.

"Me got 'im plenty money, master."

As the boy earned ten shillings per month, and had drawn no money except his "mark belong moon" (shilling per month) for the last year, Dusty and his friends were certain he had stolen it. The police master questioned him.

"Oh me catch 'im one moon mark. Me no buy 'im (spend); me give 'im long 'nother feller boy. Now behind (after) one feller moon (month) this fella boy pay me back *two* fella mark!" And the dusky Shylock produced a wad of notes and traced every shilling of it.

Of course, there was occasional trouble over the tardy delivery of stores. "The Irish Blight," a brusque fossicker of the old type, wrote to a storekeeper and, after a page of righteous abuse, expressed himself thus:

"Youse blokes in Salamaua gets too damn sleepy in yer jobs. The bloke who had the store on the Yodda used to walk seventy miles around the field and gather his orders, put them up and deliver them, keep all his books, cash our cheques, make up our gold returns, cook a bonza feed, then census all the young gins in his spare time."

An old miner was found dead of exhaustion outside his tent, which necessitated a hurried burial. They carried him to the only level patch near the river and saw there a sluice-box with the ripples neatly set ready for gold-saving. Now sluice-boxes were scarce but so were coffins. They had just finished planting him when the man who owned the claim hurried along:

"Hi! where is my sluice-box?"

"Had to make a coffin, old man."

"What! And left the ripples in! Struth, do you think the angels are going to get any gold out of old Roger?"

There was Blister's grave too. They had planted him in golden ground and now they wanted the gold. "I doubt if it's a decent thing to move a grave," protested a digger.

"Too right it is," answered old Ned vigorously. "The old cow never bought a drink for man or dog in his life. Can't see why he wants to hang on to good thirst-quenching ounces now. Put your pick in, Grady me boy; Let old Blister shout for the crowd for once."

"Blister's" area yielded seven ounces.

And there was tragedy. Chris Holleris had battled up on to the field and started a little business. He got it going famously; the future of the field pointed every week towards bigger things; he wrote his sweetheart in Sydney. He flew down to Salamaua to meet the Montoro and the bride-to-be. He enjoyed afternoon tea at Mrs Hendry's; was in little Salamaua hospital by evening with blackwater fever, and died several hours later.

The girl arrived in time to place the cross on the grave.

There was high delight in Adelaide when word was radioed through that Guinea Gold's mining-engineer, J. C. Coldham, after six months' testing of the Lower Bulolo areas declared them highly suitable for a dredging proposition. The gold was there, as Levien had imagined it long ago. It now remained to exploit the mine, to put it on the market. At this point Freeman and his Canadian friends sent up their overseas experts as Levien had foreseen. They reported a huge mass of easily dug wash, no boulders, no clay, plenty of water and timber; no malaria.

"Except for the transport problem," said Mining-engineer Frank Griffin, "you have shown us a Placer man's dream!"

CHAPTER XXIX

SIDE SHOWS AND GOLDEN LININGS

A twelve months' period of feverish activity began along the banks of the Lower Bulolo. Some of the world's great financiers and engineers were busy there—Charles A. Banks of Vancouver, Frank Griffin of San Francisco, L. V. Waterhouse of Sydney, F. R. Short of San Francisco, and others—with a staff of assistant engineers and overseers superintending huge gangs of kanaka labourers. Jungle was cleared for miles along both sides of the river; shafts were sunk; hundreds of bores put down; costeans and trenches were dug, criss-crossing the great flats; all to test if there really was payable gold in those forty million cubic yards of stuff washed down from the ranges above.

The Placer Development Company were making no mistake. They were spending thousands of pounds in order to save many scores of thousands. They were scientifically testing the gold contents of every acre of those forty million cubic yards before they spent a million dollars on dredges to recover it. The valley now rang to the blows of picks, the song of the hammer on drill, the shouts of men, the labour songs of the gangs, the thud and stamp of the big boring machines the clutter of the motor engine. Daily the gorges thundered to explosives where only nature's land tremors had rumbled before. Axes rang sharply, to cease in a waiting silence as great trees leaned slowly over in trembling hesitation before creaking down in a crash that thrashed away up the valley. Pit-saws chorused in a harsh, biting swish-swish, swish-swish; and a sawmill sang in strident whining. Houses, barracks, workshops, sprang up like mushrooms. Tractors hauled fine cedar logs to the mill where the saws ripped them into planks for beds and sideboards and kitchen tables.

Up at the waterfalls, engineers were busy at survey and excavation, preparing for hydro-electric power. Seven thousand feet of deep races were dug along the mountain sides, past George Arnold's well-known leases, down from Cliffside Gorge. Through these races would rush the water that was to drive turbines generating three thousand horse-power electric energy to work the dredges. Tunnels were driven through mountain sides.

All this brought the kanakas into a new world—a much better world for them. Rid of their ever-present fear of sorcery, they grew fat and strong under the white man's care. When first recruited, many kanakas were nervous, thin and ulcer stricken, others had frightful skin diseases. The miner often took a despairing chance in risking money upon such a diseased crowd. But after six months of the white man's care, what a change! Clean skins, vigorous frames, a laughing personality, mentality fifty per cent improved, the majority of them two-stone heavier men. Some who worked at the mines began to take an interest in the "yellow stone gold" and would come hurrying to the master when their pick unearthed a specimen. Exceptional boys among them grew expert at cleaning up the sluice-boxes, and in their own way were quite pleased at a rich clean-up, not being bashful at taking the credit to themselves.

Occasional boys even complained of the lack of gold. When the visiting *kiap* (district officer) asked Bill Abbie's boss boy:

"Any complaints?"

"Yessir!"

"What is the trouble?"

"'E no got gold," replied the boss boy and gazed disconsolately at the ground. "All time me feller me work long bokis now 'e got lik-lik gold das all."

There were other complaints made to Kiap Eric Feldt. He visited one of the New Guinea Goldfields workings and at the end of a drive saw a boy toying with a hammer. The kiap looked at the hard rock bar the boy was working at, then, after the usual inquiries, asked:

"Any complaints?"

"Yessir!"

"What is it?"

"This feller stone he strong (hard) too much!" growled the boy as he viciously jabbed a drill at the rock.

Throughout the history of the field, there has been an extraordinary lack of crime, especially considering the large quantities of gold left lying about in any old receptacle, and the fact that the carriers coming down the long lonely track carrying gold, sometimes entirely unescorted, found in their burden something "'e heavy too much!" Modern bushrangers missed wonderful opportunities of rich "clean-ups" over there. Feldt, on one trip, travelled in a leaky pinnace from Lae with ten thousand ounces aboard (now worth £60,000) lying "any old how" on the bottom of the boat. Hector Wales once, escorted by his diminutive "monkey," Mamoote (whose job it was to look after the gold), came down from the Edie with £4000 worth and called at the Wau pub where sixty men were enjoying a few quick ones. Someone shouted to Hector that a plane was just leaving. So he rushed off, forgetting his gold.

Landed at Lae, Hector ordered Mamoote to—

"Catchim gold belong you-me, put him long place—sleep!"

"What name this gold?" demanded Mamoote.

"This gold belong you-me!" answered Hector irritably. "What you think?"

"Gold belong you he stop long house-drink long Wau!" answered Mamoote.

"Why!" demanded Hector. "What name this something you lose him?"

"Baloose 'im 'e no nuff long you-me threefeller gold!" was Mamoote's explanation. He considered the plane was not safe enough to carry three men and a heavy £4000 parcel of gold.

"Arright," threatened Hector. "S'pose we losim gold finish behind-me throw him out you belong baloose."

To this threat of being thrown out of the plane Mamoote shrugged and replied resignedly:

"Maski" (never mind).

"It's worth £100 to fly me back to the Wau!" said Hector to the pilot.

The pilot looked at the sky. "Too many clouds. We won't fly again until to-morrow! This is the last plane coming in now," he said, pointing skyward.

Out of that plane stepped Awasa, Hector's young house-boy. He was staggering under the gold. After seeing his master safely off, he had realized that the gold should have gone too; so grabbing it up he went to the 'drome and caught the next plane to Lae; then took the gold down to the pinnace and sat on it all the way to Salamaua. Wales was talking to Feldt on the wharf when the big-eyed youngster approached and drew his attention to the gold. "Oh, take it to B.P.'s,"[2] ordered Hector, and the youngster staggered with the gold away into the dusk.

As the "company men" arrived on the field, many more labourers were recruited for the coming big operations. But the miners began to dwindle, numbers of them selling out to the companies. Planes, faster and larger, were coming and going in increasing numbers. Sawn-timber houses with corrugated-iron roofs were supplanting the shacks. The old hangars were being greatly enlarged and built of sawn timber and iron. Women and dresses and shoes appeared with greater frequency here and there. Ambitious ones were talking of a tennis-court. Mrs Pryke's daughter was the bride at the first white wedding on the field. The Bulolo and the Edie had become civilized.

Simpson and Lumb were the first to bring cattle in. They drove them

---

[2] Burns, Philp & Company.

up the Bouang track. People said it couldn't be done. There were patches of good grass here and there among the scrub and jungle, and when the cattle arrived they were fat and contented, although immediately turned into beef which brought 4s. per lb.: ox-tail, 10s. It was New Guinea's first droving trip, and panned out well. W. G. Shorter pioneered the sheep. He took them up by plane; he was, probably, the world's first plane drover. That mutton promptly brought 4s. per lb., including bone. Not even the knuckles were knocked off.

The planes had lowered the cost of living enormously: it was to be still further reduced. Several of the mining-companies introduced freezers. Then came the sparkle of electric lights. One morning a plane landed on the Wau with a piano aboard! A wonderful change in a few years; from the boom of a kundu drum and the harsh voices of head-hunters, while a white man listened all alone—to a piano and women's voices singing!

At Salamaua the strip of palm-clad beach was transformed. Burleigh Gorman had made good; he had floated his hotel-store into the "Salamaua Trading Co." and had toured the world as a guest of the "Waratahs." An hotel-store was erected that was soon to be one of the most up-to-date hotels in the South Pacific, complete with electric light and refrigerators, lounge-rooms, library, wireless, and easy chairs. Very different to the days of old—the recent old days—when Will Money built his palm-thatched shed. Since then, a million of gold had come down past that pub. What tales the old place and the beginning of the new could tell! There was "Lilley's Death Mask" (with the legend—"born 1820 died 19—") nailed to the bar, and toasted many a time, before and after. That once white, but indescribably battered helmet was to be his epitaph; and he declared the numbers would soon be filled in. Lilley used to practically sleep in that helmet; he made a football of it many a time, but could never break it. He died of blackwater up the Markham, and his friends completed the second date—1928.

When the tiny cemetery began to fill, it was the natives that were washed out; never a white man. The waves went over the top in the nor'-west season. A new God's acre had to be found across the Huon Gulf.

Salamaua was an unhealthy spot in the early days, before the Administration drained the mosquito-infested swamp. Sickness was not nearly so bad as it might have been. But it was expected, and Salamauaites knew they were far from help. In the spirit of the day, with the thrills of the times and the glamour of gold over all, men lived fast and sometimes died that way. Perhaps their going was not noticed as it would have been in civilized places. Those who could, left the wherewithal for friends and acquaintances to drink their health in plenty.

And the mourners did as expected. At one time, a depressing series of deaths occurred, so bad that the chief actors did not dare to take it seriously. Salamaua got so used to funerals that men acted as if drilling (the kiap then represented the parson) and all had their places. At one "planting" a comparative stranger took a rope from a "regular." It almost started a fight; the dead man was the only one not interested. At another "planting" when rain was pouring down, a mourner glumly asked:

"Can't we put him in the freezer until it's cleared up?"

Ernie Bowden was very game. Friends were carrying the stretcher past the pub; Ernie had blackwater; he weakly waved to the crowd and croaked out wanting to know the odds on his recovery.

"Thirty-three to one against!" they shouted back.

He took the odds to three fivers—and collected!

Levien was justly proud of Lae aerodrome; he himself had swung the axe that cleared away the first tree. The large landing-ground was now flanked by neat rows of barracks of wood and iron, a huge hangar built of steel, the most up-to-date aviation engineering shop in the southern hemisphere, and a big iron cargo shed. There was a large staff of skilled pilots, engineers, and mechanics, and a native labour pay-list of four hundred boys.

"And the longest tram-line in New Guinea," he chuckled; "from the beach to the aerodrome, three-quarters of a mile!"

The wharf, too, was built, and other big improvements made. Steamers could come now where only native canoes had beached before. There was a big steam-lighter of a hundred tons dead weight capacity lying off shore, and a ten-ton locomotive crane on the wharf to pick up the machinery and stores.

The growing fleet of planes, busily coming and going all day, now comprised four W34 Junkers, with auxiliary Moths. As far back as June 1928 Guinea Airways had carried a world's record cargo. Now they were breaking their own records, in quick succession. Merrily the pilots flew, carrying houses in sections, poultry, eggs; the Wau hotel in sections; live bullocks, pigs, and sheep; billiard-tables, pianolas; bags of potatoes, rice, and onions; quinine and needles and dog-chains and a baby's pram. Even a Ford flies in New Guinea! To the Wau, planes carried each month now, among many other things, two tons of frozen meat, fifty cases of beer, sixty of whisky, and goodness knows what else of whatnots. Even a bride was carried to the Wau. Transport grew so fast that soon the planes were carrying six hundred tons of freight per month, another world's record, made in Australia's wild colonial empire—that monument to the statesmanship of the Right Hon. W. M. Hughes and the driving force of

Cecil John Levien.

As an indication of future happenings, they were now carrying material in solid bulk too. One piece was a four-hundred-pound cast-iron bed for a wireless station which Placer Development was erecting at Bulolo; another was a Babcock and Wilcox one-ton boiler for the Day Dawn mine. Levien saw with delight those solid pieces lifted, for they proved that larger planes could lift still larger machinery—Dredges?

With a humour that was bright and cheery even when he felt sick, he speeded up the 'drome to the limit of his mental capacity. They were a long way yet from solving the problem of heavy transportation over the mountain heights, and Placer Development might soon want those dredges. If they could not be transported—well, a hundred years ago the world had laughed at the idea of steel ships.

After nine months, Mullins gave the first Junker a complete overhaul.

"She's earned it," he said. "And she'll be flying again in no time."

"You can't keep a good plane down," answered Levien adoringly.

"She's made four hundred trips," said Mullins as he grabbed a screw wrench, "carried three hundred tons of cargo and five hundred passengers. I'll give her a new dress too."

"I've radioed for the best paint in Australia," replied Levien as he gave a hand to lift off the propeller. "Make her tail shine! I like that glint of the sun just as she disappears into a cloud."

"Like a woman," said Mullins, "she responds to good treatment." Admiringly he laid a grimy paw upon the cylinders.

The maximum transport capacity of the fleet was now twenty-four thousand pounds. the basis being short tons and assuming three trips daily. It would have taken a thousand carriers ten years to transport that quantity by the methods used in the early days of the field.

But as yet, numerous single parts of a dredge were heavier than one plane could lift at a load.

Mustar's biggest human load in the Junker was fourteen men (two whites and twelve kanakas). He packed four kanakas on the cabin floor with their backs to the bulkhead, four more sitting on their knees, and four others sitting in front. Then, before closing them in he pulled an awful face and said hoarsely:

"S'pose you move, you die finish quick time!"

They didn't move.

Often now the miners transported their boys. It only cost £1 a head, whereas if they walked it would cost as much to feed them. Some of these flying kanakas crowded round the machine like youngsters about to ride a merry-go-round—to the envy of their mates. Some tribesmen, however, were stolidly indifferent. Others crept into the machine and, crouching down, pulled a rag over their faces in a cold sweat of fear, never moving throughout the trip. Yet others were full of the liveliest curiosity; all on tiptoe, and peeping into the cabin to gain a glimpse of the pilot. When he gripped the controls they thought he was lifting the machine up into the air and exclaimed:

"Strong feller too much!"

Passenger fares were now £25 to the field, £10 return. Luggage and cargo, 1s. per pound, carefully weighed on scales too, as the miners weighed their gold. The largest parcel of gold brought down from the field on one flight was ten thousand ounces, then worth only £30,000. If that plane had crashed in the forest gorge, someone, years later, might have found a compact gold-mine. It took three months to find poor Pilot Trist and his big plane; then the discovery was only by chance.

The freight on gold was 3d. per ounce. Shark-eye Park never dreamed of that.

The loading for the planes now included everything that a mining-township needs; from picks to petrol engines and from goats to gramophones.

The Wau, now, was a town with electric light and a freezer; wireless, and a tennis-court. Besides, after a leisurely business morning, a man could fly down to Salamaua; transact his business; have a yarn with friends; see the *Montoro* come in; step aboard for a chat; then fly back to the Wau, nicely hungry for the evening meal.

Emergency landing-grounds were made at Watut, Sangan, and Zenag, for the planes flying both to Bulolo and the Wau, so that while flying at five thousand feet a plane always maintained a gliding distance to one of these grounds in case of trouble. A favourable peculiarity of the atmospheric conditions was the absence of air-pockets. Had sudden drops of a thousand feet been known over such country, as they are in Europe, few pilots or machines would now have been in service.

CHAPTER XXX

THE FLYING MEN

And so the day of the Flying Men came; a splendid crowd, fast building up an efficiency and morale which has placed Australia among the world's best in civil aviation. Guinea Airways quickly built up to a staff of seventy-five whites and several hundred kanaka labourers, with huge planes, big steel hangars, and modern engineering works.

"Battling Parer," after numerous vicissitudes, built up the Pacific Air Transport Ltd with a fleet of one W34 Junker (one ton, single engine), two Fokkers, a DH9, and a Moth.

A few companies commenced operations and experienced more or less success, while adventurous freelances hopped across, bringing their own machine. Les Holden built up with the *Canberra,* a Waco, and a Moth. Captain "Jerry" Pentland came smiling with a Moth, and got another. Shoppee brought a Moth, too; as did Pratt. Shaw pinned his faith to a Bristol, as Ross and Taylor did to a DH9. But few of these aerial ventures survived. Some crashed, and some were absorbed by Guinea Airways, which from 1 May 1927 to 31 May 1931 carried 5490 passengers, 5,783,278 pounds of general cargo, and 377,423 pounds of machinery for Bulolo Gold Dredging Ltd. Since then, huge tonnages of machinery have been carried in with only one life lost. Australia has easily gained the world's record for tonnage-carrying and aerial transport. Recent tonnage carried for the Bulolo Gold Dredging Ltd alone, is four thousand tons. The giant triple-engined G31's did this and similar jobs, after the 'dromes had been still further enlarged and reinforced. The huge quantities of dredging material, hydro-electric and other power-plants, and sundry mining-machinery successfully carried, has caused world-wide attention.

Truly, Levien's thoughts were weight-carriers when he watched that sleeping carrier hardly four years ago. It is a lively house kai-kai at Lae aerodrome now when the big bell rings for meals. Hungry pilots, mechanics, and passengers soon crowd the tables. Some lively Aussie airmen have "stretched their legs" under the big staff table, with the Malay cook and his wife glorying in the praise from hungry men.

There were great fliers among those New Guinea climbers; Mustar and Cross, Matheson, MacGilvery, Shaw, the irrepressible Captain Jerry Pentland, "Skip" Moody, the late Frank Drayton and Les Trist, Bert Heath, Bob Gurney, Bill Wiltshire, Captain Ross, and others whose names slip one's memory.

Their ups and downs, their hairbreadth escapes in the clouds and down in the mists of the gorges, their very occasional crashes, they accepted in a spirit of great adventure. Crashes were remarkably few even though, at the start, they flew handicapped by makeshifts in a primitive country under unknown flying conditions. When a crash did come the pilot was chaffed about it, as if a dizzy fall upon a forest of tree-tops with cannibal villages below was an amusing experience.

In 1928 Pilot Cross took the *City of Brisbane* on her maiden flight; Mullins was the mechanic, and Pilot Gardiner went aloft with them. The plane behaved as if tail heavy, but eventually took the air, to soar with an angry buzz and then come roaring down on her back. No one was hurt despite the thump and jarring of teeth. They recovered their breath, felt for broken bones, laughed, then pushed her over on to her wheels and flew away again. That plane made thirteen trips: the last was on a Sunday. Jerry Pentland's search-party found Cross the next morning down in the Bulolo Gorge. The *City of Brisbane* is still there. When "up above," her engine had cut out. The silvery Bulolo looked softer than mountains so Cross "pan-caked" her into an island—and thanked his lucky stars when he thundered into mud!

When he regained nerve he clawed up out of the mess, feeling worse than, and looking like, a mud tortoise. Then he felt he'd like something to eat. Now, a rule of Guinea Airways is that every pilot must carry five days' emergency rations. On this day Cross had decided to change the ration. As he walked across to the store for fresh rations someone spoke to him; he put the rations on the ground, and went away without them. He stared at the mud—when he had got it out of his eyes and nose and ears—and felt very hungry. Since then they know him as "Mudlark."

Matheson, when up ten thousand feet in a Moth, thrilled to some hair-raising minutes. Below him sped a pimpled greenness with black valleys through which ran silver streaks. The engine stalled—so did his heart as he turned the machine seawards and volplaned. Like a fluttering dove he just reached the mouth of the Markham River.

Pilot Moody had a similar sensation while hurtling through the air in an uncontrollable Ryan monoplane, to crash in the sea near Lae. His dive for "soda-water" was the subject of humorous remarks for some time afterwards.

Captain Les Shaw did great work in a little Moth for the Morobe Trading Co. before setting-out in a Bristol Fighter (once Kingsford Smith's) on a "rush" trip to the Wau and back. He judged he could just do it. But it was dark before he left to return to the coast. Tearing through the air at a hundred miles an hour he stared over the cockpit, seeking the landing-ground. You have no idea how hazy the speeding earth appears when evening is rapidly falling. He came in too low; the undercarriage struck a bank and he was thrown out with great force. He was walking around the next day quite all right, except for a kink in his neck.

That kink was the subject of many a joke until some weeks later he decided to visit Sydney for a spell. He didn't feel too bright. He was in Usher's Hotel, having a refresher with a crowd of New Guinea identities. Of course they were talking "gold" and "flying;" and there was a general laugh when Shaw told them how he got his "sprained" neck.

"By the way, *is* it sprained?" asked a listening doctor curiously. "Better let me have a look at it!"

Shaw submitted while the crowd collected round.

"My heavens, man!" exclaimed the doctor. "You've a broken neck! Boy, you might snap that vertebrae at any moment."

He immediately engaged a taxi and took Shaw off to the Sydney Hospital where that neck went straight into plaster of Paris.

Few men, indeed, have walked Sydney streets with a broken neck. But Shaw is as lively as a cricket and flying again. It takes a hard knock to kill a New Guinea pilot.

Jerry Pentland, one fine morning, felt all his old wartime instincts revived. While flying up to the Wau he swooped low over a range where a large stockaded village showed like a brown box among the timber below. Away from the timber belt was a broad patch of kunai grass, like a bright green blanket. Jerry thought he saw two lines of excited ants rushing at one another across that blanket so he dived, the urge of the observer tingling within him. How often he had swooped down low over the battlefields of France! He shut off his engine as the grass rose rapidly to meet him. Yes! There they were, going at it hammer and tongs, two ranks of befeathered warriors shouting and screaming as they charged forward, arrows and spears flying, clubs waving.

Pentland was over them, then up with an ascending roar, laughing in delight as he "left 'em at it!" his fingers tingling with memories of pulling the bomb lever. But this was a good old-fashioned fight. Those battlers knew nothing about bombs.

MacGilvery had a nasty thrill in the old original DH37. He was in mid air above the Wau when something happened to the works; the gears stripped with a startling whirr as the propeller blades shattered off! In a hurtling half-mile swoop he made a miraculous though bumpy landing on a kunai grass patch, awfully close to some nasty boulders. He didn't even burst a tyre or crinkle the old MacGilvery smile.

The kunai grass saved Bobby Selk too. It is like a dense cushion, sometimes six feet thick. Bobby's machine whirred down in a snorting hurry and tore into the grass, which ripped the undercarriage off while Bobby tobogganed ahead in the cockpit of the machine. Neither skin nor hair flew, but plenty of grass did.

Rex Boyden was coming in one morning, on the early trip over the top, with a precious cargo of beer, when the engine cut out. There wasn't a moment to do a thing—the plane crashed straight down into a bog, right up to the cockpit. There was just sufficient moving room unsubmerged for Boyden to crawl out. He had not received a scratch but the mud and water filled him right up.

The boys cheered lustily when they found not a bottle of beer was broken. Not even a meat case, or a tin of biscuits, or a petrol tin, was burst. All hands had a burst on the strength of it.

Pilot Frank Drayton "broke in" a number of new 'dromes, making his landings by the oral descriptions of the man who had laid them out.

When thus "trying out" the big Bulolo 'drome, Mrs Bayliss was a passenger, with Tom Yeomans who pointed out the "lay" of the 'drome. As they hummed down low over the timber, the crowd assembled to witness the landing held its breath, for the plane appeared to be diving straight down into a gully that edged the 'drome.

Mrs Bayliss cried "Up Frank! Up Frank!" frantically beating with her hands as though to lift both pilot and plane which just skimmed the gully and landed nicely. The lady passenger gazed around and sighed.

But Drayton's name will be remembered in history in a more interesting way than as the breaker-in of New Guinea aerodromes, for Peter John was the first son "born to Guinea Airways." There was excitement when Peter John arrived. Guinea Airways staff immediately celebrated with a case of champagne, while an opposition crowd pledged the healths with lager. The Lae godfathers claimed the youngster's name should begin with "Lae," but every other camp demanded he should be labelled their way. The young mother was worried over a cradle; there was nothing for the elect of Lae to sleep in. So word was hurried to District Officer Eric Feldt, who picked up the first case handy, nailed a tarpaulin where the lid had been, and sat upon it. When the tarpaulin sagged enough, the cot was made, and a proud crowd escorted it to the anxious mother. So Peter John slept his first night in style with the side of his bed labelled "V.P. Bitter."

Drayton was gifted with judgment and steady nerves, eye, and hand. One bright morning when eight thousand feet up, flying to the Wau in one of the W34's, he turned to Yeomans and asked:

"Have you seen the Handley-Page Tom?"

"No."

"We'll have a look at her then."

So he sailed over Mount Lofty and Tom gazed at the big wreck lying below on the slope of a hill. In the brilliant sunlight her crumpled tail looked as if she had flown straight into the trees.

"It's a miracle that Thompson and McMurtie weren't killed!" said Yeomans incredulously.

"Blessed if I know how they got out alive," admitted Drayton. "I wouldn't care to crash like that. Well, this is no place for us—we'd better fly down to the Wau."

Those big W34's are built with a dual control, and Yeomans was sitting in the pilot's cabin with Drayton. "I shouldn't like to go spinning right down there!" he observed thoughtfully.

Drayton smiled and turned the plane for the Wau, then—the engine cut out! In that sudden silence Yeomans heard his heart beating. Drayton, pedalling rapidly at the foot controls swiftly ran his hand along various gadgets; bent down and worked quickly on the little hand pressure pump.

"What's wrong Frank? Run out of petrol?"

"Can't be," answered Drayton puzzled. "But she's not getting the juice."

Already they were losing height. Only the force of the wind was turning the propeller. They could speak now without shouting in each other's ear, but—it was a chilling silence!

"You give her a go Tom while I handle the plane." ordered Drayton crisply. "Pump for your life!"

Tom bent to the petrol pump and worked as he had never worked before, while Drayton handled the plane on a magnificent six-mile glide. The wretched pump wouldn't give even a gasp. To reach the nearest available landing-ground he dare not lose one foot of height, otherwise the machine would lose speed and drop; yet if he sped down too steeply he would never reach a landing-ground.

"How's she going Frank?" inquired Tom. His eyes were blinking from the sweat.

"I don't think we'll get there," replied Drayton. "But keep going, we're not dead yet."

The gorges were speeding past down below, their jungle-clad sides swiftly growing plainer. Yeomans, with his head deep down in the cockpit, pumped and pumped and pumped.

"Well, how's she going now Frank?"

"Not too good; but we may get there."

Swiftly the plane sped down in that long, perfect glide.

"I don't think we can make it," said Drayton as he stared steadily ahead. "I've got a moment yet to decide definitely. If we can't reach the Wau, we'll make for the kunai patch instead and chance it; but I won't turn until I'm sure I can't get the Wau."

He was trying to land on a mountain top, a pimple in a sea of ranges. And if the machine was only one foot too low when they arrived there— well, it meant crash.

The propeller spun idly round, the little hand-pump wheezed to Yeomans's long-drawn gasps.

"She's going pretty well," remarked Drayton brightly. "I think I'll go for the Wau."

The die was cast. From this decision there could be no turning back.

"Go for your life Frank," encouraged Yeomans. "I've got the whip out too," he added grimly, feeling the ache of his muscles. But not one drop of petrol flowed into the dead heart of the engine. When gliding in over the Bulolo the tree-tops rose perilously close.

"We're not going to get there," said Drayton casually. "We'll hit the trees. Buckle yourself in as tightly as you can—she'll most likely stand on her nose."

"I'm all right Frank," gasped Yeomans. "You look after the plane. Don't mind me!"

"Buckle yourself in! —we're going to hit the trees. No we won't! My heavens we won't! We'll miss them! Oh never mind any more Tom, you can't do anything now. Hold tight!!"

The clearing at the Wau rushed straight up at them as they sped, dizzily skimming the tree-tops. There was an instant in which to hold breath as she thumped straight down into the grass.

Drayton jumped out with a boyish laugh. Yeomans stretched his tortured arms. Death had been so very close.

As these lines were being written, poor Drayton was killed, with L. H. Harper, 26 December 1932. Another fine airman has gone west.

Parer flew his old DH4 until it almost ended like the one-hoss shay. He is the world's genius at coaxing a "flying crate" right to her very last gasp.

When he brought across a new DH9 he shocked himself: worse, he shocked Sir Hubert Murray's niece! She went up on a flight at Port Moresby. Neither was scratched, but the plane was. Parer was all apologies—when he got his breath.

He was not so with Joe Bourke. But he vowed he would never do it again. It was at Lae 'drome and there was another passenger besides Bourke, a big old boar weighing a hundred and eighty pounds, heavier than either of the men. The kanakas had tied its legs, then rolled it up in bags. It grunted and kicked in muffled fury as three struggling kanakas flung it into the back seat.

"You're not taking *that* aboard?" questioned Bourke in alarm.

"Oh yes. His passage is paid. He belongs to Normy Neale."

Doubtfully Bourke climbed into the front seat; Parer into his; the pig squealed in violent protest behind. The DH9 snorted and rose with a protesting roar, and they were away, to the diminishing laughter of the kanakas. All went well until they hummed up over the Gap, then a strange vibration sent an icy chill down Bourke's spine. The plane fairly trembled, Bourke could feel it shaking. He glanced over his shoulder. Parer smiled and nodded apprehensively backward. The machine wobbled as the rear passenger freed himself of the bags and tried to jump overboard. Bourke wished it would commit suicide quickly. It didn't. With savage grunts and pressure of powerful shoulders it used its weight to ram the plane to earth. The fuselage was only three-ply thick and Bourke could hear those hooves crunching into it. A series of pronounced wobblings proved the boar's energetic labours. Anxiously Bourke looked ahead for the Wau; he wished he had a parachute. That was the longest flight of his life. When they landed, the boar had one hoof through the bottom of the plane.

"I'll never ride with a pig again!" declared Bourke as he climbed out.

"Neither will I" answered Parer fervently. "Never again!"

On the very next trip he brought a sow and two suckers in the front seat and a big fat old sow in the seat behind.

Ray, on another trip, flew alone from Port Moresby, quickly climbing to get up over the range. More than one range, for the Papuan Alps tower in majestic grandeur above sierras of lesser height. These must be crossed before one can drop down into the Mandated Territory.

It was a beautiful day and Parer enjoyed the rush above that titanic beauty below. He climbed again to pass over a yet greater range and glimpsed the bulk of Mount Albert Edward towering far ahead. Just then he flew into a cloud, but sped on, expecting momentarily to burst out into the open sunlight. He did not. He sped deeper into an eerie opaque nothingness that closed around him, yet allowed him to speed blindly on. This formless opacity smothered the plane; water-mist crept into his nostrils and dissolved itself around him and all over the ghostly wings. The homely, humming drone of the engine dimmed as if it was being choked. The lone pilot realized that the clouds had come down and were massing tightly, yet yieldingly, around him.

In growing anxiety he climbed higher, knowing that the Albert Edward Range somewhere in front rose to over thirteen thousand feet, and his plane could climb but very little higher! He peered at the compass—and stared horror-stricken. The needle was spinning round and round and round! He was lost, lost in the clouds of the Papuan Alps! With horror at his heart he clutched the joystick and began flying in a repeated figure eight, clinging to the figure only by mental guidance. If he could continue flying so, he would keep in the one position until the clouds, broke and he could see where he was. Otherwise he must crash into a mountain peak or fly out into savage New Guinea and crash far from white people and hope. With a new dread he glanced at the petrol tank. How much fuel remained? How long had he been flying? Suddenly a glistening black wall loomed beside him. He frantically swerved as the wing-tip almost grazed the cliff face. With thumping heart he sped far out into space; space that he prayed *was* space. Oh, where was the sea? He peered for the faintest sign of a break in this world of silent clamminess.

He was losing height—the fuel supply was failing! For the first time in his life Battling Parer gave up hope. Had he done all the things he could do? He knew he had! There was nothing left to do but trust in the Power that rules all things. He sat there clutching the joystick, with the throb of the dying engine echoing in his heart.

Straight through the clouds there pierced a shaft of light that spread in golden radiance. Instantly Parer pulled the stick and hurtled down like a silver thunderbolt, with the light that opened a jewelled port-hole showing a circle of trees far below. He roared straight down before that vision splendid should vanish.

Captain Moody turned his Ryan monoplane into a submarine and experienced thrilling moments getting out of it, all alone there, down under the sea. He was on the return flight from the Wau when the petrol gave out. He was only ten miles from Lae and, being aloft at a goodly height, he glided down nicely, to find that the 'drome was far too small for manoeuvring a plane without engine power. By landing as usual he would run into the sea, so instantly decided to land *from* the sea.

He stalled and fell straight into it.

Imprisoned within the closed cabin, he ripped it open with his knife, then battled through the rush of water and up to the surface. His friends were more than surprised at his escape. But that did not prevent them passing remarks about submarines and lobsters and things.

That monoplane had flown just two months for Airgold Ltd, and had paid for itself in that time. It was a sister machine, by the way, to the one in which Lindbergh flew from New York to Paris. Ronald Nott was then chairman of directors of Airgold and he immediately cabled Los Angeles for another. It arrived within six weeks. British plane manufacturers should watch the New Guinea flying market more sharply. It is worth it!

Captain Ross, with Taylor, while testing a machine, flew away up the Markham; the engine cut out, and down she shrieked—to wrap herself around a tree. The occupants, amazed but unhurt, crawled out and straddled a lower limb, where Guinea Airways' manager and his search-party found them.

"How many gooseberries did you find in that bush, Rossie?" they yelled.

"Hang it all, old chap," called back Ross, "can't a fellow go bird-nesting without all this fuss?"

All the same, it was no easy job getting them out of that big tree.

Most of the accidents have happened while pilots have been testing new or reconditioned machines. Occasionally the unavoidable has occurred with a passenger aboard. Several of these have picked themselves up out of the smashed plane, swearing outrageously. It is the reaction, I suppose. When a man comes hurtling through the air, with the earth rushing up to meet him with a crash, he lies quiet a moment; then claws himself clear of the wreckage in a fearful glee that he is still alive; glares up at the sky; feels his limbs without looking at them; gets his breath and—swears.

Customs Collector Nettleship, though, was really annoyed. It was in a DH9. When she came down, the pilot most cleverly averted a fatal accident by "feathering" the water, that is, he tipped it with a wing, thus retarding speed. When they dragged Nettleship from the sea he was full of it. While he was blowing for breath, they noticed, by his eyes, he had something to say. He said it:

"Dash it all! Every time someone gives me a buckshee box of matches something happens to them!"

The boys talk about those few accidents far more than they do about their thousands of successful flights. No doubt a man lives those seconds when he comes hurtling to earth in an aeroplane. If he jokes about it—well, all the better for him.

CHAPTER XXXI

TRIUMPHS OF THE AIR

It was a triumph for all concerned when Placer Development announced their intention of exercising the Guinea Gold option. Their engineers had finally reported that the Lower Bulolo areas were a payable dredging proposition.

The Company would start operations immediately it was shown that the necessary dredges could be transported to the areas where they were to work. Could they be transported?

Besides the hydro-electric power plant, the two first dredges would weigh twenty-five hundred tons. Some steamships weigh less! Air transport on such a scale appeared fantastic. However, if the dredges could be transported by any means, then, in order not to delay construction, about two hundred tons of machinery per month would have to be carried.

Could the weights and the dimensions of the equipment be sectionalized to aeroplane requirements? If so, would the cost of that sectionalizing and the extra cost of field erection be excessive? And, if not, was the capital cost of suitable aeroplanes and the cost of operating them to stop the scheme? Was the risk too great? Further, the smash of an aeroplane, involving the loss of a critical dredge part, would delay the enterprise for months; while a run of bad luck might, at tremendous cost, easily kill the whole enterprise.

The directors and engineers of Placer Development and Bulolo Gold Dredging had many conferences over the problem. Specifications were minutely drawn for the construction of the dredges. They were to be in handy parts; each part numbered to ensure correct and speedy reassembling when landed on the Bulolo.

The decision on the transportation was a romance in pioneering aviation, engineering, and commerce. On 22 December 1929 the directors of Guinea Airways Ltd and Placer Development Ltd, with Captain Mustar, met in conference at Menzies Hotel, Melbourne, to decide on Road versus Air. The responsibility was enormous.

As for a road (the only apparent solution of the problem) perhaps £300,000 might build it in two years. The Commonwealth Government, despite the overshadowing financial crisis, was ready with a subsidy of £50,000 if it meant large gold production. The maintenance of that road, under heavy rains and landslides, would be enormous. Worse still would be the freezing of much capital for two years or more. On the other hand, could the dredges possibly be transported by aircraft?

Trained engineering opinion was against the air. Safety first. But the Airways' directors were grimly optimistic. They had a talisman: two in fact! Mustar and Levien.

The scheme was to build each dredge in sections, to transport them by plane that way, and then reassemble them in position on the ground. But the engineers had unfortunately proved that even by making a dredge so, a number of single heavy parts of it would still be weightier than any plane yet made could transport.

Mustar had been called into conference as the technical expert of the air, together with Major Berryman, who represented the Junkers Aircraft people in Melbourne.

Then circumstance helped the airmen. Berryman had received that very morning a blue-print from Junkers in Germany illustrating how an enormous passenger Junker could be converted to a cargo carrier. Here was a great point for the air protagonists! It was to prove decisive.

Mustar was supremely confident. The flying man in him, that had leaped to those successful jobs on the Barrier Reef of Queensland, now jumped at this vastly greater project. The major, with the blue-print of this huge machine from overseas, was positive, too. These were two experts talking; keen on their job; sure they could do things!

Banks and Wells weighed the pros and cons, going over and over again the case for the road; its paralysing loss of two years' time; the uncertainty, even in building, let alone in maintenance; the cost in interest. And the big planes: if they decided these could be built to carry the heaviest sections of a dredge, and if they failed, the companies would lose £30,000 on each plane alone; lose twelve months' time before the failure was proved; lose the Government road subsidy of £50,000; and then after all would have to build the road, and lose three more years.

"Which proposition would work out right?" murmured Banks.

"Plane," cried Mustar. "We'll prove it! It *can* be done!"

"We'll show you how!" exclaimed Berryman eagerly. "We'll show you down to the very last rivet!" He took his hat and left the room. Mustar laughed, his eyes eagerly taking in the blue-print of the plane, while his finger emphasized his remarks.

Griffin, of Placer Development, produced his plan representing a dredge in sections, each section neatly numbered with its weight. But the heaviest single piece weighed about seven tons!

The heaviest single piece the W34's were capable of carrying was one ton. But the blue-print of the proposed Junker showed it could be made to carry considerably more—on paper, anyway.

Berryman returned with a carpenter and pointed to the blue-prints:

"Make an exact model of this Junker," he said: "then an exact model of these heavy dredge parts. Get to it; nothing else matters."

The carpenter did. He worked all that afternoon, all through the night. Next day (23 December) the directors were still in conference; the sleepless carpenter was working at fever heat over his little models; Berryman and Mustar were staring across the table; the engineers were poring over figures and weights and lifts and time and loss and speed, and the other complicated problems that engineers are trained to solve. Griffin thought long and deeply. Could he reduce those seven-ton pieces by half? Yes, yes. It *must* be done. While the hours ticked by he concentrated on the problem.

At last, with a tired sigh of triumph, the carpenter handed over the neat little Junker model. Expectant silence gripped the room. Men bent over the table; others waited erect as Griffin thoughtfully reached for the small model of the tumbler shaft, a model that represented three and a quarter tons of solid steel.

With steady fingers he lifted it into the hold of the model Junker. The shaft fitted exactly into place! Those models were to exact scale. The directors, like schoolboys with model toys, played in earnest confirmation with this box model of a giant air-liner cabin and little wooden pieces, each of which meant portion of a dredge, each piece representing a metal mass that in reality and in motion could smash its way through a town hall!

According to engineering blue-prints and models, and the guarantee of some of the world's best aeroplane designers, the proposed Junker could carry a dredge!

The directors smacked their hands together, the austere room ringing with excited chaff. The planes had won the day. The directors of all the companies concerned hurried into committee and in barely an hour had drafted a skeleton agreement for this colossal undertaking. Then all dashed off to pack bags and catch trains back to Adelaide and Sydney for Christmas.

A. S. Cross, now chief pilot of Guinea Airways, left immediately for Germany, *en route* to the Junkers Factory to superintend the trials of the first G31.

Placer Development created a subsidiary company, Bulolo Gold Dredging Ltd, to work the ground. Within six months finance was arranged and construction on the first two dredges was begun—the pontoons in Sydney; the machinery in San Francisco. The Bulolo Company would buy two G31's, and Guinea Airways, which would operate all the planes, would buy a third. Ninety thousand pounds' worth of aircraft at one stroke! England, where are your business men?

Mustar now became technical aviation adviser to Bulolo Gold Dredging Ltd, to collaborate with Cross for Guinea Airways Ltd. The engineers estimated that the first dredge would be built, transported, put together, and be operating by 11 March 1932, twenty-one months from the date when financial plans had been completed. That estimate was to prove uncannily accurate.

It was actually only twelve days out, a feat without parallel in the long record of dredging enterprise.

Two dredges, it was estimated, would treat 3,400,000 cubic yards of ground per year. Levien thought of those first two little sluice-boxes of his up there on Koranga Creek. How pleased he had been that they had treated 3650 yards per year.

Dredges must put through enormous tonnages to pay their way. His ground had contained sometimes ounces of gold to the yard, whereas the dredging areas would only average grains. His ground had often yielded more than £4 to the yard; the dredging ground would probably return only a couple of shillings. But the quantity—millions of yards—millions of grains—probably tons of gold!

Shark-eye had washed his first gold in a dish. Every single bucket on the huge chain of buckets on each dredge would dig up more than one hundred dishes at a dip! Shark-eye could wash fifty dishes a day. The dredge would do the same in a few seconds, and work on all through the night, too.

Six months after the order was given, the test flight of the first G31, carried out in an icy European winter, was an unqualified success. On two engines only it climbed 7900 feet in twelve minutes, carrying three and a quarter tons, the load being an exact replica of the heaviest portion of the future dredge. This promised well for the quick upward bound necessary should a mountain suddenly loom out of a cloud like a ship's bow in a fog.

Not long ago, in Britain, a war pilot, testing a bombing plane at 6000 feet, emerged from a cloud to see a sheep on a crag fifty feet away. His plane's lightning lift alone saved him.

The useful "ceiling" of the G31 was 12,000 feet (meaning that it could not climb much higher). Each engine was a 525 horse-power direct drive, 9 cylinder, radial, air-cooled, American Hornet, the total power being 1575 horse-power. Nearly £40,000 worth of engines in one order. Once more, where were England's engine salesmen? These are battling days and the nations of the Empire should work together in trade as they fought together in war.

After the severest of tests Cross was ready to swear that "she" would lift any dredge in the world, bit by bit.

Away back on the Bulolo an aerodrome (the site found by Tom Yeomans, one of Placer Development's pioneers) was levelled for the aeroplanes that were to keep this industrious beehive quickly supplied with the thousands of things needed. This was a big pioneering job in itself. (All aviation over there has been pioneering from the word go.) A sandy-gravel site was chosen for the 'drome; the jungle cleared, the tree-stumps burnt out, and the hollows filled in. The area eventually cleared was 4000 feet by 1500 feet. And all timber was topped off for a further 500 yards from the boundaries to make landing and getting off easier. Then the ground was graded and levelled by tractors, for if a root or hole were left exposed an aeroplane wheel would eventually strike it and the machine capsize.

This long white level patch, deep down in the gorge, surrounded by dense green, so reflected the sunlight that it dazzled the eyes of the pilots and made it difficult to keep their machines at the correct gliding altitude when landing. So the whole area was planted with couch grass which quickly spread into a dull green carpet twelve inches thick.

The huge planes that land there at the rate of seventy-five miles per hour have no cutting effect on the surface of the 'drome, for their landing wheels bounce with the impact of half-inflated balloon tyres on matted grass.

The airmen experienced thrilling times in cloudy weather, uncertain whether they were speeding into a storm or out of it. Three different squalls might be rumbling through the sky at once, and the electricity would so disturb the instruments that the pilot flew almost blindly on. But when progress built a little wireless station at each 'drome, then Lae was warned if it was not safe to send out her birds.

On New Year's Eve 1930—a year after the great conference in Melbourne—Levien watched the *Temeraire* anchor at Lae. Eight huge cases were lowered into lighters, then tugged by pinnace to the wharf.

At the shore, the ten-ton locomotive crane landed them on to the tram-line and puffed along to the spacious air base. The first G31 had arrived!

When the monster was assembled, Levien gazed in rapture at its size: its wing-spread, its height, its air of giant power. As the W34's had dwarfed the Moths, so this giant dwarfed the W34's. Yet he loved the little

Moths. They could be tucked into their hangars like real moths into a cocoon. Beside the G31 even the steel hangar looked small. Luckily this colossal albatross could defy all weathers: there was no necessity for a hangar to house it. It reminded him of a big man, scorning to use an umbrella. On each trip that bird would do the work of twenty-five hundred carriers, and do it better.

A few days later the *Montoro* anchored at Lae with the first shipment of dredge parts from Sydney. Work began in earnest. Soon twenty-five hundred tons of machinery would be humming over the clouds in the race for gold.

The second G31 for the Bulolo Gold Dredging Ltd would soon be due, to be followed by a similar giant for Guinea Airways' own squadron.

The mining machinery, each part complete in itself, was loaded by crane down through a large hatch cut in the cabin roof of the fuselage. The inside looked like the hold of a ship. The crane-driver was above all things a "key-man." If he made a slip and allowed even a minor part to fall on the fuselage, it would crumple it, destroy the streamlines, interfere with the balance and strain, and necessitate major repairs impossible, perhaps, to accomplish locally. But the key-man never dropped his lifts too soon.

The more delicate pieces were packed in crates or casing. Awkwardly shaped ones were bolted to wooden frames upon a flat bottom so that they could sit snug. Narrow steel girders and plates were laid flat, while wide plates were carried standing on end and leaning against an inverted V-shaped frame built down the centre of the cargo cabin. Rubber pads were placed between the heavy solid pieces and the wooden cradles. The pads absorbed the shock when the plane landed and taxied. Smaller pieces were carried upon a layer of bags of rice, which proved good shock absorbers. The heavy pieces were lashed fore and aft to the floor and along the sides of the cabin. It would have been uncomfortably thrilling for pilot and passengers, soaring thousands of feet up in the air, if any of those pieces had come unfastened and begun to roll!

Experience and ingenuity quickly taught the loading crews. But on the 27 November 1931 came the flight of flights, when the upper tumbler shaft had to be carried. This was the key load. This shaft was twelve feet long and weighed three and a quarter tons. If it could be safely transported, then any number of dredges could be carried over the mountains of New Guinea or any other mountains on earth where a thousand yards of plateau could be found for a landing-ground.

It was carried without difficulty or mishap under the sure hand of Pilot Cross at the controls. The most critical loads proved to be the three tumbler shafts, twenty-two-foot steel girders, the steel hull plates, and a steel latticed mast (103 feet long.) carried in five sections. A light motor car, complete with wheels, tyres, hood and all, was an easy load. Seventy-five tons of rivets were carried, and not one single rivet was lost.

The pilots handled with delight these monstrous birds. They had such a reserve of engine power and could climb so fast that the pilot didn't care how high the mountains were so long as they were not over 12,000 feet! The flying distance from Lae to Bulolo and return was only a hundred miles—they were hardly there when they were off back again. There was a nervy interest in it, too. The safe landing of a ten-ton eagle at seventy-five miles per hour, even against the wind, necessitated unerring judgment and perfect eyesight with hands and nerves under instant control—even with compressed air-brakes to check the run on landing.

A day came when Levien saw spread out before him an aeroplane fleet worth £180,000. That fleet had carried, in three and a half years, more than 12,000,000 pounds of cargo with 6776 passengers, and had made 5987 trips with only one casualty. In *one* month in 1931 no less than 581 tons were flown in over the mountains, a far greater quantity of cargo than the combined air fleets of the world had transported during the previous *twelve* months!

A world's record, both in aviation and in engineer-mining. That is not a boast: it is a simple fact. For long we have admired the accomplishments of other nations. Let us still admire them. But let us, too, admire the achievements of our own men.

CHAPTER XXXII

GOLD-DUST AND ASHES

Salamaua had its trim, nicely painted little hospital. The house-kiap was now a fine bungalow: Burns, Philp and Company and W. R. Carpenter each had built a fine store; Allen-Innes managed the most up-to-date hotel-store in the South Pacific; a wharf had been built and steamers were calling regularly.

Billy Cameron had long since introduced music to the kanakas. He started the "Salamaua Tramway Band" and at the opening concert craftily concealed a gramophone among a heap of instruments arrayed in "luluai hats," sashes, and streamers. He sat among the instruments and, when the curtain rose, surreptitiously started the gramophone on a blaring band record while he blew a dummy instrument with might and main. Enthusiastically the coloured audience congratulated him afterwards:

"Master Bill, you savvy blow too much!"

Here they couldn't carry on until they'd had another little drink. But the life of the field and the joy of the kanakas was Bill Stower. They'd follow him for miles when he was giving a show. He was "Master loose 'em catch 'em," the most famous conjuror New Guinea had ever known. There was, however, a strong dash of fear in the kanakas' attitude towards him. "Loose 'em catch 'em," could perform miracles that flabbergasted their own sorcerers. Bill's magic brought forth yells of delight and adoration as he made passes with his handkerchief and pulled coins out of kanaka noses. His star act was swallowing an egg and then finding it in the ear of one, under his armpit, or in his hair. On one big show night he was about to do this favourite trick, little knowing the history of the eggs. Now eggs were scarcer than gold on the field, and one canny wife had had a setting carried up by plane and placed under an ambitious hen. Those eggs mysteriously disappeared. Master "loose 'em catch 'em," after tossing his eggs, swallowed one, then with bulging eyes stalked amongst the thrilled natives seeking his victim. He found him in the person of a frightened-eyed monkey (young boy) in whose hair he located the egg. The terrified monkey yelled and grabbed the egg—it broke, and an immature chicken made a magical appearance. The monkey screamed, "Me no steal 'em fowl Master!" and bolted.

A wealthy American tourist called in at Salamaua for ten minutes and spent eight trying hard to pierce the density of one of the mining boys.

"Your master's yacht?" he asked a boy, pointing to a little schooner, belonging to a recruiter.

"No got master! 'E no ot! Too much!!"

"Here! Can't you see? That little YACHT!!"

"'E no ot master! Him canoe belong Siteni (Sydney). 'Im got sail, 'im no OT!!!"

Then there was that cunning boy, Tomatore, recently a head-hunter, more recently civilized. His specialty was taking silver from his master's trouser-pocket. One morning, after the night before, the master got up with sleepy head and felt for his silver. Gone! "What for you stealim money?" he accused.

Tomatore looked his disgust.

"An' that feller boy last night he tellim me you drunk!!" he cried.

But old Ned Coakeley's horror when the first two women and goats arrived on the Bulolo!

"Onest it was God's own country," he groused. "Now it's a blessed suburb!"

Old Ned came down to Salamaua, in agony with a poisoned arm. He almost fought the woman who lanced and poulticed it. But there were tears in his eyes as he tried to present her with a rich nugget when his arm was cured.

"Tiny Tim" too, that good-natured giant, so quiet that you would never guess it until his failing makes him talk. His beautiful daughters are acclaimed as world-renowned musicians.

There's the young chap, too, the "Embryo Woman Hater," who is so tremblingly anxious for the scented envelopes that arrive every six-weekly mail. And the quiet chap with greying hair who staggered in from the Upper Waria:

"Been out two years! Struck a patch!" he murmured, in the delirium of fever, "the old mother will finish her days in comfort, thank God!"

Another who added interest to the little community was the young Dane with the wonderful blue eyes. To anyone who would listen he could only talk of his Queensland sweetheart. They were to be married—after he struck it rich. When he proudly showed a treasured photo, and one looked at the winsome face, one found it easy to congratulate and sympathize.

The Dane was lucky—he struck it rich! A week later the crude little handcart was pushed along the beach at Salamaua. It was covered with flowers, as they wheeled it down among the palms. The Dane slept under the flowers. They always gave them flowers when they died of blackwater at Salamaua.

In happy contrast was the send-off to the kiap and his pretty wife, so laughingly bashful as the hilarious crowd wheeled them down the croton-covered palm-way.

These and numerous other little sidelights show the wonderful transformation that has happened to a lonely New Guinea beach in a few years. Salamaua is now a port, with a very colourful community, definitely put on the Australian national map by a little three-pound prospecting pick.

Mrs Hendry sleeps in the little plot across the Huon Gulf. Old Ned Coakeley flew down from the field, somewhat quietened by the knowledge that he was a rich man. He could hardly realize it. A lifetime of battling, kept alive by dreams; and now he was sailing home to "ould Oireland," a Midas indeed.

He died at St Vincent's Hospital, Sydney.

Darby, flushed with gold from his Eldorado, arrived at Rabaul in a blaze of glory, intent on a trip round the world. He intended to paint it red. He did it very well, too, with his skipper aide-de-camp. Poor Darby died suddenly in India. Life is the most uncertain thing in the world.

The mountains and the Bulolo were ringing as the riveters hammered together the plates of the great dredge. Its framework was rapidly taking shape, and looking like a clumsy battleship stranded at low tide. The forecast of the engineers was working up correctly. She would be in full action almost to schedule. Christmas was near.

Levien took a long look over the monstrous robot of his dreams as it squatted down there, ready to engulf in its maw the golden sacrifice from Kaindi. He strolled along beside it, nodding up at the men, smiling a greeting among the clanging of the riveters. He must sail for Melbourne to be home for the New Year. He was feeling a little tired; somehow he felt he had come to his limit. He would just have a holiday; look up the Adelaide men; then return in March to see the dredge start on its twelve-year task.

After that he believed he would retire—before the country "got him."

He was fifty-eight! He had accomplished a lot in these last few years. All he had dreamed had come to pass. Others would carry on beyond his dreams. He supposed he was worth £100,000 now. But he found little interest in thinking of money; nothing like the satisfaction he felt in having done all these big things. He would give all his money for the priceless pleasure of doing some other big work again.

He was tired. He had often felt tired, physically tired before, but never tired in this way. Yes, it was time he had a spell.

He walked slowly towards the waiting plane. A little group of men stared after him; none had ever seen him move slowly before.

Arrived in Melbourne, Levien caught a chill and died within three days. His last words were: "Placer shares will go to £10." Events have justified that prophecy.

Levien died from meningitis on 20 January 1932. Two months later a crowd of people, strange beyond the head-hunters' wildest dreams, had congregated near the great dredge in the old Bulolo valley. It was a wonderful day, sweet sunlight bathed the majestic slopes; the smell of old New Guinea was in the air; far up a bird of paradise called in strange, harsh song. Around the walls of the dredge, the white women's dresses gave a pretty touch of colour. They were a chattering crowd that gazed up at the massive machine. It seemed almost miraculous. Across there on the lovely Bulolo 'drome rested a fleet of ten planes; the giant eagles among them spreading protecting wings over the sturdy W34's and the cheeky, fledgling Moths. The great G31's had that day transported these hundreds of people in lots of forty: men in snowy white, women in coloured fabrics, brown-skinned natives in gaudy lap-laps.

Interesting people were there to-day. Pioneers, prospectors, directors, a governor and his suite of high officials, some mining engineers of renown, pilots, magistrates, wardens.

In a brief but eloquent speech, the Administrator of the Mandated Territory, Brigadier-General Wisdom, recalled the thoughts, the struggles, the aspirations of all those responsible for the successful accomplishment of this stupendous task. In conclusion, he voiced the general regret that Mr Levien was not there that day.

(But Wells was there, gently holding a little package under his arm.)

When the speeches were over, Mrs Charles Banks named the dredge, calling out in a clear ringing voice: "Long life and success. Good feller Dredge, Bulolo No. 1."

The Administrator touched a switch, and instantly the machinery turned in ponderous motion; dynamos hummed, wheels revolved, huge buckets rose and clanked down, to dig deep into the spongy earth. The monster groaned and wallowed like a mammoth lumbering from the midday mud. The dredge had started!

Wells turned away. He walked slowly to a G31. Pilot MacGilvery climbed into the cockpit and Cross followed into the big cabin. The pilot wondered what Wells was carrying in the package. MacGilvery, too, had been much attached to old C. J.

With a roar the plane took off, and rising, skimmed on its way up the gorge: and up, till the river looked a silver thread below. The cabin porthole was opened. Gently the little package was unfastened and a slit made in the canvas covering within. Two arms were thrust out into the gusty air and the ashes of Levien floated away over the Bulolo valley.

Gold-dust and ashes, each to each, down in the gorge below.

Unloading a G31 at Bulwa.

GLOSSARY

Adzera. A numerous and upstanding Markham River tribe.

Bêche-de-mer. Edible sea-slug; regarded as a delicacy by Chinese.

Bom-bom. A term, in certain districts, meaning white man. First applied to the report of guns. The term, in both senses, is rapidly fading out of native speech; it has only been used in a few districts. Elsewhere it refers to the leaf of the coconut palm.

Box washdirt. To put washdirt through a sluice-box, thus separating the gold from the dirt.

Boys. The common term for native carriers or labourers.

Bubu. Bubu tribes and river in Mandated Territory.

Carriers. Kanakas who carry loads.

Copra. The dried kernel of the coconut.

Curse of Kaindi. The native belief that a great sorcerer of olden days cursed certain slopes of Kaindi Mountain.

Diorite. A rock often associated with "gold country."

Dish washdirt. To put washdirt through a dish, thus separating the gold from the dirt.

Forbidden land. Was then, German New Guinea. Is now the Mandated Territory of New Guinea, administered by Australia under Mandate from the League of Nations.

House-kiap. The house of the District Officer. House kong-kong. Chinaman's store.

House-money. Bank.

Ikori. Warriors from the Ikori River, Papua.

Ironstone. A rock often associated with "gold country."

Kai-kai. Food; meal-time.

Kanakas. Natives of the Mandated Territory. Applied also to natives of South Sea Islands generally.

Kukukuku. A nomadic troublesome tribe with branches ex- tending right across the Mandated Territory into Papua.

Kunai. Tall, coarse, thickly growing grass.

Kundu. Bamboo; and lawyer-cane.

Lap-lap. Loin cloth.

Lik-lik. Little.

Lik-lik doctor. Medical orderly.

Living kanaka. To live with the natives. or to live in the bush on native foods.

Luluai. Hereditary chief.

Luluai hat. Generally the term given to the government cap presented to the man who was made a chief or headman by a government officer.

Madang. The Administrative centre for the Madang district. A beautiful harbour, pretty little township, and prosperous plantation district, on the north-east coast of the Mainland.

Make paper. To sign on for employment.

Mana. Prestige.

Marl A native loin cloth.

Mary. Common term for woman.

Mitre Rock. An historic rock near the boundary of the Mandated Territory and Papua.

Nakanai. A village in New Britain, where the natives murdered four white prospectors.

New Guinea Company. A German Company, with a strong influence on the colonization of German New Guinea.

Osmiridium. A rare and very valuable mineral.

Outrigger. A buoyant log fitted to booms jutting out from a canoe. The outrigger prevents the canoe from capsizing.

Pegging. To peg a claim or lease.

Place-sleep. A sleeping abode or camp.

Puk-puk. Crocodile.

Queen Emma. A Samoan girl, daughter of an American Consul, who made history in the South Pacific.

Razor-backs. A term applied to peculiarly steep hills typical of New Guinea.

Ripples, or riffles. Contrivances for saving gold in a sluice- box or race.

Sandalwood. A small, valuable tree containing sandalwood oil.

Schistose. A rock sometimes associated with "gold country."

Sluice forks. Somewhat resembling hay forks. Used to "fork" the stones out of a sluice-box.

Stripping overburden. To strip the surplus earth off washdirt.

Tamata. A Papuan gold post.

Tambaran. Devil; evil spirit; something not understood and supposed to possess malignant powers.

Tambaran houses, "Devil-houses." On the Sepik River they are of enormous size. Known in "pidgin" as house-tambaran.

Tambu. A sign of ill omen.

Tappa-cloth bark. A bark which, when treated, yields a rough cloth.

Taubada. The Papuan name for "master."

Tul-tul. The village interpreter, appointed by a government officer.

Uncontrolled country. Country not officially under control. Dangerous country.

PROSPECTING FOR GOLD

ION IDRIESS

From the Dish to the Hydraulic Plant, and from the Dolly to the Stamper Battery. With chapters on Prospecting for Opal, Tin, and other Minerals; and a chapter on Prospecting for Oil, by Dr W. G. Woolnough, F.G.S., Geologist to the Commonwealth of Australia. Illustrated.

This book, written by a prospector with a lifetime's experience, will save the new chum gold-seeker much labour and time and disappointment, and will teach the old hand many a payable wrinkle.

Dr W. G. Woolnough (Geologist to the Commonwealth of Australia) :-"Your hints should be invaluable to all, beginners and experienced men alike."
Canadian Mining and Metallurgical Bulletin:-"The volume will arouse the reader's interest at the outset and hold it to the end."
Queensland Government Mining Journal :-"It tersely sums up a lifetime's knowledge gained at first hand acquired by a man well equipped to pass his experience on to others."
Engineering and Mining Journal (New York) :-"This book is replete with good methods, described simply. Lack of space forbids quoting the terse directions."
Rabaul Times (New Guinea) :-"Invaluable. Each bit of advice and information is practical, as it comes from an old-time miner himself."

Now in its 20th edition, 190 pages, available from ETT Imprint.

THE YELLOW JOSS

ION IDRIESS

With Foreword by Tony Grey. Illustrated.

Sydney Morning Herald :-"The Booya is a masterpiece of the weird and terrible. But of all the tales "The Castaway" has most power and surely merits a place with similar episodes in Conrad. Mr Idriess is adept in working up the feelings of his readers to a pitch of expectancy .... Here the excitement is terrific."

The Herald (Melbourne) :-"Every one of these tales bears the impress of truth. Anybody who lets unreasoned prejudice against short stories deter them from reading this book is missing a treat."

The Sun (Sydney) :-"Idriess tells a good story. These come from another world, a primitive and violent world, where things that seem fantastic and incredible to dwellers in the Australian cities are commonplaces of life."

Queensland Times :-"He has the happy knack of being able to blend truth and fiction in such a way that even commonplace things assume an important role and have definite and impelling force."

Woman's Budget (Sydney) :-"They give a clearer insight into his varied and adventurous life than anything he has previously written."

Honi Soit (University of Sydney) :-"Rich humour enlivens the book, particularly where the exploits of one 'Scandalous' Graham are concerned."

Producers' Review (Brisbane) :-"The name of Ion Idriess has become a household word ... as a maker of short stories he has lost none of his flair for tale-telling. Indeed we prefer this style."

Now in its 10th edition, 210 pages, available from ETT Imprint.

LASSETER'S DIARY

Transcribed with Mud-Maps

Harold Bell Lasseter had always claimed he had found an immense reef of gold hundreds of miles west of Alice Springs. In 1930, with Australia in the grip of Depression, a privately funded expedition led by Fred Blakeley, accompanied Lasseter in an attempt to relocate the reef.

Blakeley left Lasseter at Ililba, and Lasseter continued his trek towards the Olgas with a dingo shooter and their camels. Lasseter continued to be introspective and brood, prompting Lasseter to go off alone.

In March 1931 an expedition led by bushman Bob Buck found Lasseter's body at Winter's Glen, and his diary at Hull's Creek, wherein it describes how after his camels bolted, he was alone in the desert, encountering a group of nomadic Aboriginals who offered offer him food and shelter. Blind, exhausted and dying, Lasseter made one last attempt to walk from Hull's Creek to Uluru.

The diary was purchased by Ion Idriess from Lasseter's widow in 1931, and from it he wrote the best-seller Lasseter's Last Ride. Tom Thompson has transcribed the diary with its original mud-maps, including those not in the diary itself and Lasseter's drawings.

First edition, 90 pages, available from ETT Imprint.

LASSETER'S LAST RIDE

An epic in Central Australian Gold Discovery

ION IDRIESS

The 45th edition now out from ETT Imprint, Exile Bay, illustrated with photographs, extracts from Lasseter's Diary and letters.

Morning Post (London):-"Perhaps the greatest of Australia's real life epics."

Daily News (Perth) :-"No grimmer tragedy than Lasseter's Last Ride has been recorded in the annals of our exploratory history .... Yet Idriess manages to keep his reader wavering between laughter and tears."

Otago Daily Times (N.Z.) :-"One almost finds it difficult to believe that the story is modern and true."

Sydney Mail:-"One of the most graphic, most poignant, and most absorbingly interesting tales that the chronicles of Australian exploration - those treasure stores of dramatic adventure - have ever revealed."

The Herald (Melbourne) :-"A true story that for sheer excitement, thrills, and sustained suspense, cannot be surpassed by even the most imaginative novelist."

The Telegraph (Brisbane) :-"This thrilling book reveals in convincing colour, the details of a story that is history and that has all the elements of stark tragedy."